Brand Islam

Brand Islam

The Marketing and Commodification of Piety

FAEGHEH SHIRAZI

University of Texas Press ◆ *Austin*

The University of Texas Press and the author gratefully acknowledge financial assistance for the publication of this book from the President's Office at the University of Texas at Austin.

First edition, 2016

Requests for permission to reproduce material from this work should be sent to:
    Permissions
    University of Texas Press
    P.O. Box 7819
    Austin, TX 78713-7819
    http://utpress.utexas.edu/index.php/rp-form

⊗ The paper used in this book meets the minimum requirements of
ANSI/NISO Z39.48-1992 (R1997) (Permanence of Paper).

Library of Congress Cataloging-in-Publication Data
Shirazi, Faegheh, 1952–, author.
    Brand Islam : the marketing and commodification of piety / Faegheh Shirazi. —
First edition.
        pages   cm
    Includes bibliographical references and index.
    ISBN 978-1-4773-0925-4 (cloth : alk. paper) — ISBN 978-1-4773-0946-9
(pbk. : alk. paper) — ISBN 978-1-4773-0926-1 (library e-book) —
ISBN 978-1-4773-0927-8 (nonlibrary e-book)
    1. Consumption (Economics)—Religious aspects—Islam.   2. Brand name
products—Religious aspects—Islam.   3. Islam and culture.   4. Branding
(Marketing)   5. Consumers—Attitudes.   6. Consumer behavior.   I. Title.
    BP173.75.S524   2016
    381.088′297—dc23
                                                                          2015033122

doi:10.7560/309254

I dedicate this book to the memory of my parents, Dr. Mahmood Shirazi and Aghdas Simafar, and also to my loving children, Ramin Shirazi Mahajan and Geeti Shirazi Mahajan, and to my husband and friend, Ken T. Barnett.

Contents

Acknowledgments

I would like to acknowledge the College Research Fellowship (CRF) of David Bruton Jr., Regents Chair in Liberal Arts (Spring 2013), the University of Texas at Austin, which allowed me one semester off to complete the first draft of this book.

I would also like to acknowledge the superb editorial skill of my dear friend Anya Grossman. I appreciate her professional dedication and interest toward my project.

I am also thankful to many friends and family members who helped me by providing information and taking images from many corners of the world.

Most of all I am thankful to be surrounded by good people and showered by *barakat*, Al-ḥamdu lillāh.

Brand Islam

Introduction

The purpose of this book is to provide an original intervention in the field of Muslim cultural studies, specifically to demonstrate how and why a wide range of commodities from food products to children's toys are being marketed as "halal" or "Islamic" to Muslim consumers—in the West as well as in Muslim-majority nations. Many of these products may or may not be authentically Islamic or halal. *Halal* is an Arabic word meaning permissible; it also refers to any object or action that is permissible according to Islamic law, or Sharia. Most production of these commodities is profit-driven, exploiting the rise of a new Islamic economic paradigm, and not necessarily created with the objective of honoring religious practice and sentiment. The entrepreneurs and corporations that develop and market these commodities to twenty-first-century Muslim consumers often use "Brand Islam" as a clever tool.[1] In this book not only do I define and analyze Brand Islam as a highly successful marketing strategy, but I also demonstrate a growing trend toward consumer loyalty that is exclusively linked to Islam. This exclusivity has allowed for a new type of global networking, joining product and service sectors together in a huge conglomerate that some are referring to as the Interland.[2] With the exception of chapter 1, in which I offer insight into Western xenophobic responses to all things Islamic, each chapter in this book presents a wide spectrum of products that have been developed in alignment with Brand Islam. Some products actually are halal; others are fraudulently labeled.

Having said that, I must make the following distinction: halal products and services are usually considered Islamically sanctioned, yet not every "Islamic"-labeled product is considered halal. This phenomenon is explained in detail in chapters 2 and 3. For example, all ingredients in a packaged foodstuff such as wheat crackers may be halal, but the processing facility or area in which the crackers are stored before distribution may be non-halal, or haram. Therefore, the crackers may not be sold as halal. Furthermore, in the conclusion, readers will encounter a product for Islamic ablution introduced in 2009 and marketed as the Auto Wudu Washer—which sells for $3,000 to $4,000. This is a good example of an Islamically sanctioned product that is not considered halal. To qualify as halal, generally speaking, the product or service must be certified by a religious authority with power to interpret and issue religious rulings according to Sharia (Islamic law).

Although the behavior of seeking out like-minded individuals and creating strong community ties is not limited to Muslims, my focus in this book is necessarily narrowed to Muslim identity and experience. Still, it is noteworthy that goods and services are being packaged today to appeal exclusively to Muslims—and particularly to devout practitioners of Islam for whom conspicuous piety is important. Multiple phenomena are involved in the huge success of Brand Islam at this specific time in history. Particularly relevant, in my opinion, is the concept of shared identity among Muslims living in non-Muslim-majority communities as diverse as Brussels, Toronto, and Sydney. Not all Muslims are seeking this sense of connectedness; however, those who are intentional about strengthening their ties to the global *umma* (Muslim community) are making conscious decisions to select and purchase from the halal marketplace.

Younger diaspora Muslims especially tend to cope with "Islamophobia, racism, and peer pressure to conform to dominant lifestyles by committing themselves to maintaining Islamic identities."[3] Indeed the simple act of purchasing hamburgers from fast-food chains that have been halal-certified or buying cosmetics with a halal logo on the packaging can be psychologically reassuring. One might assume that such purchasing patterns signal alignment with and connection to the greater Islamic community.

In 2009 the Russian writer Elena Tchoudinova published a work of fiction titled *La Mosquée Notre-Dame de Paris: Année 2048*. This political thriller describes a future in which France has been Islamicized and the French government, dominated by radical Islamists, has failed to prevent Notre Dame Cathedral from being transformed into a mosque. The same year the novel was published, the Italian newspaper *Il Foglio* launched a raft of media coverage when it "crowned Rotterdam the future capital of Eurabia."[4] After all, in 2008 Rotterdam had elected a

Muslim mayor, the son of an imam. The city's growing Muslim presence is seen in entire neighborhoods comprised of "immigrants of Islamic faith" and huge mosques imposed upon the urban scene.[5] Rotterdam has been called "the most Islamized city in Europe."[6] These two examples, of fictional and news media predictions of a more Islamic Europe, reflect an increasing concern on the part of Western Europeans that their nations are inexorably succumbing to Muslim domination.

Bat Ye'or, a specialist "in the history of the Christian and Jewish minorities in Muslim countries—called the *dhimmi*"[7]—coined the term "Eurabia" to describe the fate toward which Europe is moving. It is a fate of submission to Islam, of "dhimmitude."[8] This Egyptian-born British author represents a conservative backlash to the shifting Muslim demographics in the West. Her politics are Islamophobic, and her use of the term "Eurabia" reflects a fear-based adherence to what the far right alludes to as a "Muslim conspiracy."

The terms "Eurabia" and "Islamophobia" reflect a growing concern that Muslims/Arabs/Middle Easterners will once again—like the Ottomans occupying southern Italy in 1480 or the Moors reigning for seven hundred years in Spain and Portugal—subjugate Europe and replace the Western way of life with a dreadful tyranny. In short, some would argue that Muslims are fast becoming the new scapegoats for Europe's multiple economic and identity crises. The notion that Islam is a strange, threatening entity to be dealt with harshly will continue until the West embraces diversity as a positive and rich evolutionary pattern. However, according to a current assessment by Walid Saleh, associate professor at the University of Toronto, "Muslims now engender disgust, a visceral revulsion, an emotional response, in many non-Muslims in Europe and [North America]. This is something that is beyond rationality and reason . . . [, and] it will take either a miracle or a generation to reconfigure this situation."[9]

In response to disparaging media reporting and xenophobic portrayals of Muslims in the West, halal marketers and manufacturers are more than happy to step in and offer products that reinforce Islamic identity—for a price. Some would argue that this market penetration is being fueled by Islamophobic trends sweeping the globe.

Vali Nasr, a Middle Eastern scholar, author, and influential adviser to the Obama administration, has asserted that "the great battle for the soul of the Muslim world will be fought not over religion but over market capitalism."[10] Brand Islam and capitalism go hand in hand. Shrewd marketers recognize that a consumer's purchasing decisions, when intentional and linked to religious identity, are unusually predictable; therefore, these consumers are highly subject to manipulation. Not all Muslim consumers, of course, buy halal products to strengthen their sense of religious identity and connection to the larger Islamic community. Numerous economic and sociopolitical factors play a part in the evolution and growing popularity of halal commerce. These complex factors cannot be explained entirely within the limited confines of this single volume. My hope is that scholars from other academic disciplines will step forward to address these theoretical complexities in the future. No matter what theoretical positions are emphasized, few would argue that the popularity of halal and the resurgence of Islam are grounded in the relation of imperialism between the West and Islamic nations, as Sen Gautam has observed: "The US in particular and western countries in general have . . . been cynically sponsoring and cultivating perverted brands of official Islamic religious sanction[s] to deny democracy in Islamic countries and ensure rule by unpopular monarchies [tyrants]."[11] Beginning in 1926 with the League of Nations, the French received mandates over Syria and Lebanon while Great Britain took control of Palestine and Mesopotamia (present-day Iraq). Thus the Ottoman Empire was partitioned, an historical moment that signaled the beginning of Western dependence on Middle Eastern oil. The eventual decline of British influence led to a new wave of colonialism, this time initiated by growing American interests in the region.

This history, in which the West has acted upon indigenous people while ignoring the agency of those people themselves, has produced an arrogance of ignorance. Multiple factors, therefore, must be taken into account when debating the relationship between Islam and capitalism. What one can assert with confidence when speaking about postcolonial globalization is that the contemporary market for halal goods and services is indeed mushrooming. Beyond halal food and beverages, one finds a wide range of offerings and services, from halal banking and businesses to halal clothing and fashion shows to halal children's books and television programs, even halal Internet and halal cat food. Some medical academic journals are also using Islam and Muslims to diversify the field of mental health based on religious following. A Target store in Austin, Texas, used a photo of two young girls wearing *hijab* on the front of an application for local store grants. And an item of clothing that could be making a comeback in Iran is the necktie for men, symbolically a Western (non-Islamic) accessary item that is forbidden by some Islamic religious leaders. A designer has created a tie he considers more in line with the Islamic Shi'i tradition.

Journal of Muslim Mental Health cover. The inscription at the top, "Identifying the mental health care needs of Muslims in North America and the global Muslim community," raises questions about why such a journal targets Muslims. Photo by the author.

Target store flyer, Austin, Texas, 2007. This flyer about Target's local store grants features two young girls dressed in Islamic clothes listening to music, a smart marketing strategy. Photo by the author.

Iranian designer's "Islamic tie." Hemat Komaili's design resembles Zulfiqar, the famous sword of Ali Ibn Abi Talib, first Shi'i imam, to represent Islamic values in an article of Western clothing often prohibited by religious leaders in Muslim countries. The Arabic writing on it is a well-known saying: "There is no brave youth except Ali, and there is no sword which renders service except Zulfiqar." Bulletin website news and Shahrzad News.

The trend toward all things Islamic is ushering in cultish "Muslim" religious personalities, that is, self-proclaimed religious experts who offer highly opinionated Qur'anic interpretations and busily create online fatwas, religious decrees. Hence, a new industry is taking shape, the Islamic culture industry, and its ramifications are far-reaching.

Muslim immigrants in non-Muslim-majority nations—whether in the European Union, Australia, Canada, or the United States—often demonstrate their religiosity by carefully selecting and purchasing halal-certified foods. Second-generation Muslims, especially those born in Western nations who have developed value systems different from their parents', are of particular interest to marketers. It is this younger group of second-generation Muslims who will comprise the most lucrative segment of future halal consumers.[12] In determining best marketing practices and strategies, companies and entrepreneurs bent on offering Islamic products must educate themselves as to key factors underpinning Muslim consumerism. Given a soaring birth rate, the Muslim population is expanding rapidly in many regions of the world. Until recently, global marketing essentially dismissed the Muslim consumer even though research demonstrated that "Muslims are actually more brand aware than the general population . . . [and have felt] largely ignored by marketers."[13] Using a common brand—in this case, a certified halal logo—promises to be an effective strategy in connecting Muslims dispersed among multiple cultures together into a single global community. Indeed, consumerism plays a vital part in social roles, Marian Salzman contends: "Brands and products can unite different peoples in shared experiences and values, providing common reference points—or they can divide them. As uncomfortable as it may sound, where there is consumerism, there is the potential for bridging divides."[14]

Numerous academic publications, including ones associated with marketing and consumer affairs, have discussed emerging halal global markets and the long-term repercussions. Consumer studies have offered detailed requisite guidelines for creating Islamic-branded products that align with Sharia—guidelines that help companies develop their particular brand's image and reputation.[15]

What, if any, are the hazards in labeling a product or service halal or "Islamic"? Nazia Hussain, director of cultural strategy at Ogilvy and Mather Global, explains, "There is no such thing as a Muslim brand because brands can't have a religion but they can align themselves with the values of that religion."[16] In establishing a nominally Islamic brand, marketers make every effort to align their products or services with some of the core principles or values of Islam. Those core principles include belief in the oneness of God (*tawhid*), belief in the Prophet Mohammad as the last prophet of God, belief in the Qur'an as the true words of God, and belief in destiny and divine decree.

It should be noted that multinational corporations as well as individual entrepreneurs assume a certain amount of risk when framing their appeals to Muslim consumers. These companies may receive harsh criticism as the ideological battle continues over Islam and terrorism carried out by radical Islamic factions.[17] A decision by Best Buy electronics retailer to carry Muslim greeting cards resulted in heated controversy in the United States, as described in a *Los Angeles Times* article:

> When Best Buy carried "Happy Eid al-Adha" greeting cards for the important religious holiday celebrated by Muslims, people around the country posted contrasting views on the Best Buy website: "You insult all of the heros [*sic*] and innocent who died in 911 by celebrating a holiday of the religion that said to destroy them!" wrote one. Many others said they would no longer shop at Best Buy.[18]

Islamic resurgence fueled by information technology has opened the door to the commercialization of Islam. In this book I examine the process of Islamic commodification and analyze how the phenomenon is affecting the religious, cultural, and economic lives of Muslim consumers. A new demand for Islamic consumer goods has arisen where no demand previously existed, resulting in products being marketed under the auspices of Islam and blessed by the watchful eyes of ayatollahs, ulama, and muftis. Furthermore, this book focuses on the development and marketing of Islamic commodities I view as Brand Islam, working at the level of fetish, as Muslim consumers, perhaps especially Muslim middle-class consumers,[19] attach mystical and religious significance to what might otherwise be considered inutile and mundane objects.

I have investigated the significant role of Islam as a commodified religion, with pietism as a marketing tool and persuasive means utilized in selling goods and services to concerned Muslims. I have explored innovative print media, scholarly publications, and the Internet and online strategies for capturing consumers, through which a new meaning for "Islam" has emerged, since Muslims represent a major untapped niche market. I use the term "commodification" in the sense of transforming an idea, a value, or an object into a commodity for the purpose of economic gain and commodification of Islam as, in Greg Fealy's assessment, "turning the religion and all its symbols into a commodity capable of being bought and sold for profit."[20]

I also use "commodification" as a valued service, object, or idea used to exploit a targeted market—Muslims. This type of marketing environment of labeling goods and services Islamic is occurring in Malaysia, where the government now uses a halal bar code for religiously permissible products.[21] Traditionally, halal requirements have been applied to food and drink but now are also being applied to medical services, banking and financial services, insurance and real estate providers, hotels, the tourism industry, commercial aspects of popular pilgrimages and shrines, music industry products, sportswear, lingerie, fragrances, cosmetics, hair and skin care products, and a host of other accoutrements—transmuting the mundane into powerful symbols of religious correctness and piety.

By using the term *commodification*, I do not intend to downplay the importance of genuine religious motivation behind such businesses. My intention is rather to understand how the religious symbols of Islam are used to promote and market products and services to consumers.

At the same time, it is noteworthy that in Muslim-majority nations such as Indonesia, the resurgence of Islam is beginning to play a role within the context of neoliberal globalization,[22] particularly within the contemporary consumer market, halal or otherwise. Daromir Rudnyckyj explains, "In Indonesia, religion is not a 'refuge' from or resistance to neoliberalism, nor is it a retreat into 'magic and mystery' in response to global capitalism."[23] Rather, it is leading to an ethic of individual self-policing based in Islamic practice, an ethic that holds true whether in the public, private, or governmental sectors.

Theoretical Perspective

The framework for this book rests on two theories: the theory of reasoned action (TRA) and the theory of planned behavior (TPB), both of which may be applied to consumer behavior and choices. TRA asserts that the most important determinant of behavior is behavioral intention. TPB is mainly concerned with individual motivational factors as determinants of the likelihood of a specific behavior.[24] TPB is widely used to study consumer behavior and is, in fact, based directly on TRA.

From an Islamic perspective, the worshipper consciously acknowledges and engages in *tawhid al-talab wa'l-qasd wa'l-iraadah* (oneness of goal, purpose, and will).[25] Religious precepts, therefore, reinforce behavioral intention and support consumer motivation to exercise free will when seeking out, purchasing, and using halal-certified items.

From an economic perspective, and based on Marx's theory of consumer fetishism, TRA and TPB also demonstrate that halal purchasing is an intentional behavior, especially when the brand name and halal logo together are visible and recognizable to the consumer. Many studies that discuss Muslim consumer behavior have used the theory of planned behavior as an analytical tool.[26] A survey of these studies reveals that the increased demand for halal products and services may be understood through a social psychology model describing the role of religious considerations in consumer purchasing decisions. In short, the consumer of ostensibly Islamic goods and services does so with conscious intention and, as a result, fulfills an internal, affective need.

One could argue that the theories of Karl Marx, including consumer fetishism, laid a framework for understanding the subjective nature of human consumer behavior and are still applicable today. Marx's exploration of the interrelation of capitalism, patriarchy, and colonialism remains relevant as we attempt to understand the complex intersection of capitalism and halal consumerism.[27] At this intersection one finds widespread concern on the part of Muslim consumers that the products and services they are purchasing are indeed authentically halal. Obviously not every Muslim is concerned about the halal lifestyle. However, those who are concerned, especially Muslims living in non-majority-Muslim nations, make conscious choices, as explained by the reasoned action and planned behavior theories. Many of these individuals are living in Western cultures—the same cultures that have exercised colonial power and dominance. For the minority-Muslim communities, it is essential to determine and decide if the commodities they are being offered as halal are bona fide. In Muslim-majority nations like Indonesia, Iran, Malaysia, Pakistan, and Saudi Arabia, halal is not an issue simply because the assumption is that in these regions everything is halal. In reality, this may or may not be true, but the question is nevertheless a non-issue.

Religion, Consumer Behavior, and the Marketing of Piety

Differences in cultural and religious values have had a significant impact on product innovation and directed the creation and adoption of new products, and not just within the Islamic market.[28] The growing

US religious publishing market was valued in a 2006 report at approximately $7.5 billion. Inarguably the primary driving force behind these religious publications is, the report finds,

> evangelical Christians, who have successfully established a powerful political presence and alternative media platform to compete with secular society, and who are now entering the mainstream of popular culture. Yet attributing growth solely to evangelicals would be a mistake. For buyers of Catholic, Jewish, Islamic, Hindu, Buddhist, and New Age religious publications are also fueling the market.[29]

The marketing of spirituality and religion is commonplace, even in secular consumer environments, and therefore holds no surprise. However, some would suggest that true spirituality has nothing to do with conspicuous consumption, that the selling of products and services to promote spirituality directly contradicts core precepts upon which spiritual and religious practices are founded.

Nevertheless, religion as a key cultural element in the twenty-first century markedly influences consumer behavior and purchasing decisions.[30] While this type of influence is not entirely new, there is a discernible gap in research and publication on the relationship between Islam, specifically, and consumer consumption. Djamchid Assadi has studied the correlations between the monotheist religions of Judaism, Christianity, and Islam and their respective adherents' consumer behaviors. His results indicate a definite link between the consumer and the consumer's religion and choice-of-purchase behaviors.[31] Oriah Akir and Nor Othman focused on Malaysian consumer shopping behavior. One of their major findings indicated that although consumer behavioral theories can be applied globally, consumer preferences and purchase decisions are often influenced by cultural background and norms and, in the case of Muslims, strongly affected by the Islamic principle of halal and purity.[32]

In recent years much has been written about Islamic concerns regarding veiling and the halal fashion industry (Turkey and Indonesia being the leaders), the halal food industry, and more recently, halal tourism. In terms of tourism, packaged halal holiday getaways such as halal honeymoons are being arranged in Muslim majority and non-Muslim-majority nations.[33] The *Economist* reported in 2013, "Crescent Tours, a London-based travel agent, books clients into hotels in Turkey that have separate swimming pools for men and women, no-alcohol policies and halal restaurants, and rents out private holiday villas with high walls."[34] Muslims in greater numbers are searching for Muslim-friendly hotels and resorts in which to spend their money. Although Muslims constitute one of the largest tourist markets in the world, the value of this genre of tourism has yet to be clearly defined. The hospitality industries in several non-Muslim-majority countries have begun recognizing that Muslims prefer to stay in halal-friendly hotels and are providing this service. Among the countries quick to cater to Muslim tourists are China, Sri Lanka, Thailand, Argentina, South Africa, and Belgium. The public and private sectors in these more Muslim-friendly destinations often play instrumental roles in assisting local firms to export goods and services to Muslim nations. The commerce seems to benefit all parties involved.[35]

Beyond the commercial and leisure aspects of Islamic tourism, there is a more substantial religious justification for travel. The Qur'an teaches that when an individual travels, she or he experiences firsthand the natural wonders of God and develops humility in the face of Allah's miraculous creation.[36]

Say, [O Muhammad], "Travel through the land and observe how He began creation. Then Allah will produce the final creation. Indeed Allah, over all things, is competent."
QUR'AN 29:20

The rapidly growing Muslim travel market requires that hoteliers today offer their Muslim guests unusual amenities, specifically in alignment with Islamic religious code—including prayer rugs, Qur'ans, halal food and drink, and ensuring that alcoholic beverages are removed from minirefrigerators in the guests' rooms. Some luxury hotel chains from St. Moritz, Switzerland, to Berlin, Bangkok, and Budapest even provide Arabic-language TV channels and a marker, or *qiblah*, indicating the correct direction to Mecca for praying. One finds not only gender-segregated exercise sessions but also special prayer rooms "for the guests' personal staff and security team" in these Western hotels.[37] It should be noted that US hoteliers lag behind their European counterparts in offering services to this significantly expanding customer base.

As economic conditions and educational opportunities improve among Muslim populations, larger numbers of individuals are journeying to the West and Asia. In fact, the total Muslim travel market has now superseded the German and Chinese markets, traditionally the largest segments of the travel industry. It is no surprise that the Persian Gulf nations represent 37 percent of Muslim travel expenditures.

Countries catering to these more affluent travelers must have adequate economic resources and be willing to invest them appropriately; these travel destinations must invest in shrewd branding and marketing strategies to continue attracting loyal and well-heeled Muslim tourists.[38] Like any other service industry, successful halal tourism depends on customer satisfaction, loyalty, and word-of-mouth recommendation.[39] Figures cited at the Halal Tourism Conference 2014 in Granada, Spain, suggest that the halal travel industry is worth $128 billion excluding hajj and other core religious pilgrimages such as Umrah.[40] Halal tourism loyalty is becoming a crucial issue for destination regions such as Malaysia where the quality of products and services has increased repeat tourist visitation.[41] A quick online search for halal hotels and travel services in Western and Eastern European nations, including surprising destinations such as Bosnia and Herzegovina, reveals numerous agencies equipped to arrange halal accommodations, restaurants, and entertainment. More nations are joining to attract Muslim tourists. In 2014 in Moscow, a hotel began offering special prayer rooms, copies of the Qur'an in the rooms, and other halal service to lure more Muslim tourists. A Malaysian news article quotes hotel staff members:

> "Around 70 per cent of our guests are from overseas and 13 per cent of these—or some 5,000 people—come from Muslim countries, especially Iran," said Lyubov Shiyan, marketing director at the Aerostar hotel. . . . [Another said,] "If we now add in the number of tourists and businessmen coming to Russia from the Middle East, Turkey or Iran then we're talking about a truly enormous number of potential customers."[42]

Competition and innovation have become the name of the halal game, whether one is referring to Islamic tourism or to the hawking of Islamic souvenirs. Savvy entrepreneurs along with giant corporations are seeking ways to maximize halal profits through a plethora of resources, from marketing gurus and scientific and psychological publications and manuals to consumer-behavior studies, anthropological assessments, journals, and magazines. All are asking the same question: how best to accommodate and take advantage of the recently "discovered" mother lode of Muslim consumers. Here a consultant describes Mecca as an ideal environment for marketing to Muslims and the prime time to do so, during the annual pilgrimage of the hajj. Shelina Janmohamed, a senior strategist on building brands with Muslim consumers, advises,

> Islam is the only religion where it's compulsory to undertake a pilgrim-
> age at a specific time, in a specific place, with specific rituals so that
> it's in unison with other Muslims. Any brand hoping to have an im-
> pact in the Muslim world needs to understand the power of this oc-
> casion in the collective Muslim consciousness along with the values it
> embodies.[43]

Ms. Janmohamed warns that devious techniques, although effective, may be unproductive during this annual umma gathering: "Any brand plastering itself across a hajj convoy risks a serious backlash." One can see her point in that some pilgrims would find the splash of material-ism offensive during this important spiritual journey. After all, the hajj is intended to transform one's life, purge the heart of greed and covet-ousness, and allow a Muslim to become more devoted to Allah. Janmo-hamed continues, however, to emphasize that opportunities for market-ers do exist at the hajj but that these "must be handled subtly and with pure intentions."

Marketers within the corporate world do not need to restrict them-selves to a mindset of pure intentions. With today's varied lifestyles and global mass consumption, corporations are increasingly targeting niche markets, focusing on products with an added ethical, religious, or cul-tural value. This added value of any given product often means that consumers are willing to pay higher prices. With the growing affluence and relatively high birth rates that are providing Muslim communities worldwide an appreciably increased purchasing power, well-known cor-porations like Nestlé, Colgate-Palmolive, Carrefour, and Unilever are investing significant resources into serving the thriving Muslim mar-ket. A study in 2011 reports, "Nestlé's halal sales are estimated to be in excess of $3 billion annually. Tom's of Maine, an American natu-ral care products company, recently sought halal certification."[44] Ac-cording to the company website, "Nestlé Malaysia's Halal Policy out-lines information on ingredients, sourcing, production, packaging and transportation of Nestlé halal product . . . [and Nestlé Malaysia] of-fers policy guidelines, know-how and expertise on halal to other Nestlé markets."[45] On July 10, 2009, Colgate-Palmolive posted a news release on its website detailing all product items that did not contain any raw animal products and that were, therefore, deemed halal.

Qur'anic Guidelines, Consumerism, and Halal Literacy

Adhering to Islamic principles in no way means adopting an ascetic or bare-bones lifestyle. Indeed, most Muslims believe that living a comfortable life and acquiring material goods are entirely sanctioned as long as one acquires wealth in accordance with Sharia and Qur'anic guidelines. Islamic interpretations on consumerism vary, though, based on the interpreter's perspective. Qur'anic verse 17:31 warns against excesses of consumerism:

> O children of Adam, take your adornment at every masjid, and eat and drink, but be not excessive. Indeed, He likes not those who commit excess.

Hossein Godazgar suggests that nationalist concerns also influence Islamic attitudes toward consumerism:

> Islamism, as a political ideology and distinguished from Islam as a religion, is explicitly neither in agreement with consumerism nor enthusiastic in tackling green issues. . . . It is not surprising that postrevolutionary Iranian authority, in an anti-western, anti-capitalist ideological mood, has opposed consumerism as the core of political liberalism . . . [and] anti-consumerism served the country's economic interests while it was suffering from severe economic sanctions.[46]

Generally speaking, in terms of commerce and consumerism, a business journal report finds that Islamic principles offer the devout practitioner a "practical value system for sound business decision making while laying down a strict ethical code of conduct for classifying and evaluating business and marketing behavior."[47] The Prophet Mohammad himself is often cited for his exemplary business practices early in life. According to the principles of Islam, then, marketing ethics merit special attention.

When those ethics are purposefully breached, Muslim consumers have a right, if not a responsibility, to engage in what may be labeled "halal literacy." Qur'anic verse 35:28 states, "It is only those who have knowledge among His servants that fear Allah." Based on that verse, Salehudin asserts that Muslims with a superior knowledge of halal should be more scrupulous about the types of products they purchase and consume. Salehudin's study, focusing on Muslim consumers and their process of selection, strongly suggests the importance of individual awareness and understanding of halal commandments.[48]

Malaysia, as one of the leading Muslim nations taking up this mantle, is investing heavily in research as well as publishing scientific findings concerning products falsely claimed to be halal. Most of these sham products involve meat and meat by-products. Fraudulent marketing claims have been uncovered exposing supposedly reputable international companies claiming to be halal certified. The Islamic Food and Nutrition Council of America (IFANCA) stated online in 2012 that Unilever used an IFANCA halal logo without authorization on its Knorr products.[49]

Converting to halal standards including production, research, transportation, and so forth at a national or state level is fraught with challenges. The Malaysian government has undertaken this very project, converting the entire state of Penang to halal standards, a process that demands exclusion of all those industries failing to meet rigorous requirements. This exclusivity means that questions inevitably arise concerning the role that money and politics play in the process of coveted halal certification. It also suggests that, on occasion, superior and higher-quality products may be dismissed, undermining the advantages of a competitive and open marketplace.

In Malaysia and elsewhere, Muslims like other consumers generally trust the food products they purchase. Most are genuinely surprised to discover that a vegetarian sausage mix contains pork or that organic burger meat labeled "GM free" or "organic" contains genetically modified soya and chemical preventatives. Imam Salehudin contends that halal literacy encourages Muslims to cultivate "the ability to differentiate permissible (halal) and forbidden (haram) goods and services [an ability] which [comes] from better understanding Islamic laws (Shariah)."[50]

John Ireland and Soha Abdollah Rajabzadeh studied consumers in the United Arab Emirates (UAE) who voiced concern about fraudulent halal products permeating the market;[51] not surprisingly, these consumers were pushing strongly for rigorous halal certification. A total of 86.5 percent of participants in the study expressed "'great concern' that at least one category of items [from their shopping list] was not halal."[52] Muslims living in European nations apparently harbor the same concerns.

Young Muslims residing in Western nations are pushing forward a specific consumer agenda, demanding goods and services that are authentically halal. Ahmed Ameur, a member of the faculty of law and business at the University of Abdelhamid Ben Badis in Algeria, has observed that Muslim youth in the European Union are exerting tremendous influence over the potential halal market.[53] Sharmina Mawani and Anjoon Mukadam observe that by insisting on halal products, young Muslims may be communicating personal values and beliefs in which "objects are removed from the physical, emotional and relational settings in which they are fabricated and redefined in new terms."[54] Mawani and Mukadam suggest that the phenomenon transpiring outside of indigenous lands may be explained in part by mass immigration, which often results in "harsh attitude towards 'others' in the creation of the hybrid identity which otherwise might not have developed among minority ethnic communities."[55] This consumer behavior represents what Pamela Nilan calls "clear evidence of the hybridity of social and cultural identity practices."[56]

Such a hybrid identity, evidenced among European Muslim communities and contributing to an increased demand for halal consumer goods, is often portrayed as a threat to traditional Western values. Others view the trend as a logical extension of the capitalist system. After all, capital is always on the prowl for new and emerging niches in the marketplace. Why should the tsunamic surge in the production and purchase of halal items be any different? Özlem Sandikci, assistant professor of marketing at Bilkent University, coolly describes this phenomenon as "an untapped and viable consumer segment" increasingly visible in the global market.[57] Despite hostile Western attitudes toward Muslim groups—fueled by an array of conservative media and elected officials—at the end of the day it will be supply and demand that determine the extent to which the halal phenomenon proliferates in all markets, whether East or West.

As Islamic marketing intensifies, unusual products are beginning to surface. In Malaysia one can now buy halal bone china. The reader may ask what makes this particular bone china halal. As it turns out, three factors are involved in the certification: the use of only halal animals' bone ash, not that of pigs; the use of earthen clay; and the intensity of heat. According to Sharia, high temperatures such as those generated by the sun are important in the purification process. Purifying, too, is earth, which is sometimes used in place of water for ablution. Thus, if the heat of the sun is acceptable as a cleansing agent, then the heat of a kiln at temperatures between 1,200°C (2,192°F) and 1,400°C (2,255°F) presumably makes the product unquestionably pure, so that pig bone should not make any difference since the earthen clay and the high heat intensity are the purifying agents. However, some would question such logic. Among these is Alicia Izharuddin:

The line between the sacred and the consumable profane have blurred, and true to the dictum that Islam is "a way of life," anything which supports the notion of good Muslim personhood can now be made halal. The explosion of consumer goods imbued with spiritual meaning is a new phenomenon spurred on by the broadening middle classes disenchanted with meaningless consumerism. Now consumer goods can have real intrinsic, spiritual meaning. But how did everything beyond consumables (and indeed items beyond meat) become halal?[58]

Beyond the astronomical revenues generated by the business of halal certification and beyond the sheer uniqueness of Islamic goods and services, additional factors deserve careful consideration. Which specific consumers are being targeted, and why are these consumers interested in the product? How is the product being used? Is the consumer using it to satisfy a need for cultural identification, as a status symbol, or as a signal of piety to others? Do halal products serve as political statements? If so, then to what extent is "political Islam" responsible for products popularized and utilized by the Muslim majority? Are Muslims pushing their way of life onto the global market, or is this trend the inevitable result of shrewd marketing strategies? Questions such as these have led to the research and writing of this book.

The reader will note that the case studies in this book at times would focus more on Iran. This is, in part, due to the fact that I am profoundly interested in the contradictory nature of Iranian lifestyle. Although ruled by an iron-fisted theocratic government, the majority of Iran's population is comparatively highly educated and comprised of young, Internet-savvy individuals who are often liberal in their political outlook. Even with government filters and obstacles, young Iranians still manage to maintain a consistent online presence, opening doors to discussion of their government's authoritative role in every aspect of Iranian life. Furthermore, being an Iranian citizen, I have had ample opportunity to interview key individuals, observe and document Iran's contradictory social behaviors, and analyze firsthand the significance of these contradictions. I was born in Iran and, therefore understandably, have had personal access to the sociopolitical processes of that nation. In addition, I am fluent in Persian, which allows me to access sources in the original language.

CHAPTER I

Islamophobia and Western Culture

How did the phenomenon of Brand Islam emerge as a powerful marketing strategy? In part, this new economic movement may be understood as a reaction to the upsurge of Islamophobia following September 11, 2001. The politics of defending Western civilization have been responsible for promoting and exaggerating xenophobic responses to all things Islamic. Ironically, this political backlash has pushed many Muslims, including secular Muslims, to find security by identifying with anything and everything Islamic or halal. And the global marketplace has enthusiastically responded.

Xenophobic response to September 11, 2001, generated heated political debate as well as activist movements against Islam and the very concept of halal initiatives. Anti-Islamic sentiments allowed savvy politicians in the West to put forward fear-based initiatives. Xenophobic propaganda, whether targeting Muslims or other groups, often plays directly into the hands of a conservative electorate and, more often than not, assures candidates or legislators engaged in such activities increased chances of campaign victories. Islamophobia, in particular, transforms all Muslims living in the West into enemies within any given nation's boundaries. Individuals are easily manipulated by fear. Looking into examples and ramifications of xenophobic practices that target Muslims sets the stage for examining Western responses to the halal phenomenon.

To begin with, let us clarify the terms "xenophobia," "Islamophobia," and "Islamoparanoia." Xenophobia refers to an irrational fear toward individuals from cultures and countries other than one's own, that is, an inherent fear or distrust of foreigners or strangers. A xenophobic person generally has inimical perceptions of any given group of people that may threaten to sully, sabotage, or destroy her or his own social and cultural identity. The xenophobe may be suspicious of immigrants and may wish to restore and purify his or her own native culture by taking an aggressive or antipathetic posture toward foreign persons and cultures.

"Islamophobia" is a more recent term. Although various phrases describe hostility toward Muslims, "Islamophobia" is now the most widely used term. Robin Richardson has found that the word may be traced back to the early twentieth century: "The first known use of the French word Islamophobie appeared in a book by Alphonse Etienne Dinet, a painter who was a convert to Islam, written in 1916 and published some two years later."[1] Since the 1980s this term has been applied repeatedly in media and academic settings to individuals who fear Islam or Muslims in general and perceive Islam as a palpable threat to Western culture.

"Islamophobia" might be taken to mean much the same thing in the United States, the United Kingdom, and Australia, but as lived and practiced in each of these nation-states, it has been created out of different national histories of racism."[2] Furthermore, it should be noted that associating race with Islamophobia is illogical and counterproductive, since Islam consists of many diverse groups from a wide variety of genetic and cultural backgrounds. In fact, Islam thrives on seven continents, is represented by almost every race, and includes populations that speak numerous languages. True, Islam is a homogenizing, unifying force in that most Muslims adhere largely to the same foundational principles and precepts. However, Muslims do not all follow Islam in precisely the same way; the differences in perception and practice add to the diversity already established by geographical, genetic, and cultural variations.

As for the term "Islamoparanoia," one need only refer to the neoconservative political agenda that emerged post-9/11 in the United States. In reaction to the attack on the World Trade Center Twin Towers, a report was issued in 2012 by the American Council of Trustees and Alumni (ACTA)—interestingly enough, founded by Lynne Cheney, wife of then vice president Dick Cheney—entitled "Defending Civilization: How Our Universities Are Failing America and What Can Be Done about It." The original version of this report cited comments from 117 university faculty members, staff, and students in reaction to the attacks. The report, Joel Beinin notes, "maintained that criticism of the Bush administration's war on Afghanistan on campuses across the country was tantamount to negligence in 'defending civilization' and proof that our universities [were] failing America."[3] This type of document could only have been disseminated in a climate of extreme paranoia.

All three terms have emerged from classic Orientalism and represent a contemporary genre of manufactured fear.[4] In short, Muslims have become the scapegoats for various crises and are easily targeted, given their mosques, minarets, and distinctive aspects of appearance such as *hijab* worn by women and beards worn by men.[5] Sometimes the uninformed may assume any man who wears a turban must be a Muslim. However, Sikh men often do, as well as men in India and some other South Asian countries where traditional cultures require male head coverings that resemble turbans.

Exploiting Islamophobia for Political Gain

The act of grouping all Muslims together as a homogeneous entity is a convenient strategy that gained momentum following the tragic events of 9/11. Indeed, the suicide attacks in New York City prompted a vitriolic surge in Islamophobia throughout the West, and by "the West," I mean Europe, Australia, and New Zealand, as well as the United States. Muslims in the United States felt particularly vulnerable and, almost overnight, witnessed a shift in the popular media's portrayal of Islam as the personification of evil. Very little mention was made of the sixty Muslims who died in the Twin Towers attack.[6] The media hardly reported this news or considered the relevance of interviewing family members grieving as deeply as non-Muslims. Mehr Amanullah, the widow of an assistant vice president at Fiduciary Trust who died in the South Tower, is quoted in *USA Today*: "Nobody cares that Muslims were victims as well as non-Muslims."[7]

On the heels of 9/11, the mosque—that most obvious symbol of Islam—became an easy target. Acts of arson, insulting graffiti, and hate messages ensued. Events described by Laura J. Nelson in a *Los Angeles Times* report on opposition to a mosque in Murfreesboro, Tennessee— a case finally resolved in federal court—exemplify how the so-called war on terror has often subsumed the real issue of Islamophobia:

[S]ome neighbors objected to the new [Islamic] center, and harassment began. First came menacing phone calls. Then a construction vehicle caught fire. Someone scrawled "Not welcome" in violet spray paint on a coming-soon sign. A bomb threat in September 2011 resulted in the federal indictment of Javier Alan Correa, 24, who is awaiting trial. . . . Opponents sued to block the mosque. Among their contentions: The planning commission did not follow proper procedure; Islam was not a real religion; and its devotees had no 1st Amendment right to religious freedom.[8]

Nelson points out that over a seven-year period at least twenty churches had been constructed in Murfreesboro, all without objection.

Of the many court cases and legal actions brought against construction of new mosques and Islamic community centers in the United States, perhaps the most controversial has been the Park51 center. In May 2010, the Lower Manhattan Community Board No. 1 approved construction of an Islamic community center by a 29–1 vote, with 19 abstentions. Original plans for the fifteen-story center included a prayer space for as many as two thousand worshippers and a plethora of community programs. Because of its location two blocks from the World Trade Center site, the media immediately dubbed the project "the Ground Zero mosque." The rhetorical question arose of how many blocks distant from the World Trade Center would have been an appropriate distance. Would three blocks have achieved approbation? Logically, is it not an arbitrary decision for distance to be a primary criterion? What distance would have convincingly signaled that New York City's Muslims are indeed morally sensitive and sincere and that they have only one objective in mind—to create a center to serve their community?

In July 2011 the American Center for Law and Justice (ACLJ), a conservative legal group, attempted to overturn a ruling supporting the Ground Zero mosque construction. Brett Joshpe, representing the ACLJ, stated that the ACLJ "remain[ed] confident that this mosque will never rise above Ground Zero."[9] However, the ACLJ, filing a lawsuit on behalf of an ex-firefighter, failed at the New York Supreme Court level to overturn the city's Landmarks Preservation Commission ruling— which sanctioned the demolishing of a 150-year-old Park Place building so that the center could be constructed.

Park51's grand opening was celebrated in September 2011. In January 2013, however, developers were still raising money to complete the mostly vacant center. Doors were opened to accommodate religious services held four times a day, Fox News reported in May 2012, but all other community programs were suspended.[10] Other media likewise were quick to report that the center functioned only as a mosque a year after it opened. Among them was the *New York Post*: "Gone are the Arabic classes, workshops in calligraphy, talks on the genealogy of Muslims in America, film screenings and art exhibits."[11]

American conservative groups and right-wing politicians have remained vigilant, eyeing Islamic centers with suspicion and, whenever possible, finding self-serving ways to ride the surging tide of resentment toward Muslims. In one instance, the African American business executive and 2012 presidential candidate Herman Cain went out of his way to make mosques and specifically the construction of the one proposed in Murfreesboro a campaign issue. Cain said in a Fox News interview that prohibiting construction of the Murfreesboro mosque "would not be discriminating based upon religion."[12]

Cain joined forces with numerous critics opposed to the mosque construction, all claiming that Muslims intended to impose Sharia law in the United States. When asked whether he, as someone who had faced racial prejudice, was willing to restrict people because of their religion, Cain replied,

> I'm willing to take a harder look at people that might be terrorists.
> That's what I'm saying. Look, I know that that there's a peaceful group
> of Muslims in this country. God bless them and they are (free) to wor-
> ship. I have no problem with that. If you [look] at my career, I have
> never discriminated against anybody because of their religion, their sex,
> or origin, or anything like that. I'm simply saying I owe it to the Amer-
> ican people to be cautious because terrorists are trying to kill us. And
> so, yes, I'm going to err on the side of caution, rather than on the side
> of carelessness.[13]

It is ironic that Herman Cain's thoughtless comments hinted that by being an American one couldn't be a Muslim. Unfortunately, the tragedy of 9/11 has allowed ultraconservatives to push forward their "cautious" agendas, some of them brazenly and openly announcing that Muslims are unwelcome and others, like Cain, promoting fear when the opportunity arises for self aggrandizement.

John R. Bowen, in his 2012 book, *Blaming Islam*, points to numerous myths surrounding Muslims and Islam and alludes to intense discussions around Islam's incompatibility with Western values. Bowen emphasizes "how exaggerated fears about Muslims [cause individuals to] misread history, misunderstand multiculturalism's aims, and reveal the opportunism of right wing parties who draw populist support by blaming Islam."[14] The ignorance and fearmongering that quickly surfaced concerning the building of the mosque in Tennessee, for example, appealed to those individuals uncomfortable with the idea that US constitutional rights apply to minorities such as Muslims as well as to Christian majorities.

A January 2007 mosque-related incident near Katy, Texas, reported by Fox News underscores how extreme and often ludicrous circumstances emerge when emotions run high and cultural values clash. The incident involved Craig Baker, a pig farmer and owner of a marble company, and Kamel Fotouh, president of the five-hundred-member Islamic Association in Katy, Texas. Fotouh, a proponent of construction of a new mosque adjacent to Baker's family farm, said the Islamic Association intended to build it because the other mosques in the Houston area did not "provide the kind of environment" local Muslims wanted.[15] Baker, whose family had owned the farm for two centuries, felt insulted by Fotouh's suggestion during a town meeting that Baker move his pig farm farther away from the mosque. In retaliation, Baker began staging elaborate pig races on Friday afternoons, the Islamic world's holy day of the week.

Fotouh, refusing to be intimidated by the pig races, moved forward on mosque construction. Meanwhile, property owners from neighboring areas joined the bandwagon by avidly supporting and attending the pig races. The antimosque parties claimed that the mosque would be out of place, increase traffic in the neighborhood, and significantly depreciate their property values. In 2010 the *Houston Chronicle* reported that the pig races had finally come to an end, but resentments remained: "A 'no trespassing' placard is posted at the entrance to the mosque property on Baker Road, and a wooden sign with a large cross and Star of David is staked where the races once were held."[16]

Muslim Integration beyond the United States

Although the religion of Islam is practiced worldwide by people of virtually all races and in nations with varied languages, histories, and cultural backgrounds, anti-Islamic sentiment abounds globally, especially where so-called democratic Western governments claim to promote, preserve, and protect human rights. In Belgium, politicians have found creative ways to exploit the tide of Islamophobia. Filip Dewinter, Belgium's leader of the far-right Vlaams Belang party, publicly displayed campaign posters of his nineteen-year-old daughter clad in a bikini with a burqa over it. Dewinter was responding to the Islamic fundamentalist group Shariah4Belgium opening Belgium's first Sharia court.[17] Events like this represent a clash of cultures, certainly, but also demonstrate what happens when both sides engage in extremist behaviors. When far-right European values come up against fundamentalist Islamic values, unrest is bound to occur. In such instances, where are the much-needed voices of moderation and balance? Are individuals with tolerant, mediating viewpoints simply choosing to remain silent, or are they consistently drowned out by aggressive, fundamentalist rhetoric?

Whichever the case may be, discriminatory behaviors and practices continue to plague Muslim communities within the European Union nations. A 2006 report by the European Monitoring Centre on Racism and Xenophobia (EUMC) contends that

> Islamophobia, discrimination, and socio-economic marginalisation have a primary role in generating disaffection and alienation. Muslims feel that acceptance by society is increasingly premised on "assimilation" and the assumption that they should lose their Muslim identity. This sense of exclusion is of particular relevance in the face of the challenges posed by terrorism.[18]

The growing phenomenon in European Muslim communities of alienation and radicalization, especially among youth, has led the European Union to carefully reexamine its integration policies. The EUMC investigated "how to avoid stereotypical generalisations, how to reduce fear and how to strengthen cohesion in . . . diverse European societies while countering marginalisation and discrimination on the basis of race, ethnicity, religion or belief."[19] The EUMC report, conducted in Muslim communities in ten member nations, addressed a number of concerns, such as women's issues, employment, housing, and education, and underscored the rich diversity Islam encompasses:

> European Muslims are a highly diverse mix of ethnicities, religious affiliation, philosophical beliefs, political persuasion, secular tendencies, languages and cultural traditions, constituting the second largest religious group of Europe's multi-faith society. In fact Muslim communities are no different from other communities in their complexity.

Discrimination against Muslims can be attributed to Islamophobic attitudes, as much as to racist and xenophobic resentments, as these elements are in many cases inextricably intertwined.[20]

The report offers suggestions for remedying discriminatory practices against Muslims; however, these proposals seem more like good intentions than concrete practical agendas for governments and policy makers to adopt. That is, no specific directives are provided for the implementation of progressive programs, such as early childhood educational programs in public schools that would guide both Muslim and non-Muslim children toward understanding and honoring the beauty of other cultures and religions. Just this one innovative step might lay strong foundations for breaking generational chains of hatred. To date, no such governmental programs or policies have been enacted in the European Union.

When a minority community consistently experiences discrimination and is made to feel part of a second-class citizenry, resentments are inevitable. If left unaddressed and unresolved, potentially volatile issues will continue to fuel distrust between Muslims and their non-Muslim European counterparts. Although the EUMC report succeeded in identifying explicit xenophobic practices aimed at Muslim communities in Europe, it failed to arrive at workable, pragmatic solutions or explore the long-term consequences of Islamophobia. In my opinion, the most immediate concern is the effect on Muslim youth in European environments as their numbers increase. What assumptions can be made regarding these young people growing up among Islamophobes? What might be the outcomes of their experience? What might one project about their future choices and behaviors? Vibrant communities whose individuals are integrated into the national cultural fabric produce stable, productive citizens. Conversely, children growing up without a sense of social belonging, with feelings of alienation from the dominant culture, tend to face their futures with uncertainty and diminished expectations.

The demographics are clear. Muslim populations in Europe, such as South Asians residing in Great Britain, are growing exponentially, both in first and second generations. Poynting and Mason point to a "rise of anti-Muslim racism in Britain and Australia, from 1989 to 2001, as a foundation for assessing the extent to which the upsurge of Islamophobia after 11 September was a development of existing patterns of racism in these two countries." They also suggest that this pattern has by no means been limited to Britain or Australia but that other Western societies have demonstrated similar patterns of behavior as well.[21]

The Mosque, That Most Obvious Symbol

From London's docklands to the rolling hills of Tuscany, from southern Austria to Amsterdam and Cologne, the issue of Islamic architecture and its impact on citadels of "Western civilization" has become increasingly contentious.

In June 2008, in a joint survey conducted by a Dutch television network and the newspaper *Nederland Dagbald*, 65 percent of respondents supported a ban on large mosques.[22] In the same year in Austria, the governor of Carinthia province, Jörg Haider, representing the far right, called for a ban in Carinthia on mosque construction. Haider identified himself as "a pioneer in the battle against radical Islam for the protection of our dominant western culture."[23] The province of Carinthia succeeded in passing a law that effectively banned the construction of mosques by requiring that any "extraordinary architecture" be evaluated and approved by a commission before construction could begin. Governor Haider urged resistance to approval: "I can only recommend to all to have the courage to stand up effectively against this Islamisation that is creeping through Europe and represents a totally different culture."[24] A year earlier the bishop of Graz in Austria expressed his opinion about mosque construction: "Muslims should not build mosques which dominate . . . [towns'] skylines in countries like ours."[25] In other words, mosques are unfit to be integrated into Austrian urban planning.

A *New York Times* article in 2009 reported that the Swiss government imposed a national ban on the construction of minarets, an architectural feature unique to mosques. This unusual Swiss referendum was created by a far-right political party and sanctioned by the government.[26] Some may claim that this policy does not reflect attitudes of the average Swiss citizen but rather represents its imposition by powerful right-wing lobbyists. Yet a referendum outcome that supports a ban is revelatory: it mirrors the will of the people and the political majority and signals national sentiment toward a targeted religious group. Another incident in Switzerland, perhaps equally telling, was the resignation of Alexander Müller from the Swiss People's Party. His resignation occurred after a tweet sent from his Twitter account (which he initially denied) called for a repeat of the tragic 1938 Kristallnacht, or Night of the Broken Glass.[27] Müller's tweet reads, "Maybe we need another Kristallnacht . . . this time for mosques." Previously Müller had tweeted, "We should take this pack [Muslims] out of the country. I do not want to live with such people." The Swiss constitution irrefutably guarantees freedom of religion. Soon Germany followed Switzerland's direction. Several weeks after Swiss voters banned the construction of minarets, the *New York Times* reported, "a German right-wing group is hoping to use a new European Union law to hold a minaret referendum across the 27-member bloc."[28]

Even in the Czech Republic, where Muslims constitute a tiny part of the population, one finds antimosque campaigns—perhaps the most visible and vitriolic being AntiMešita (AntiMosque), led by Valentin Kusák. With big plans for himself politically, Kusák had to dig deep to find an issue around which the ordinary Czech might rally. His issue: the power of Muslims to blemish the Slavic way of life. "The Czech Statistical Office has no official numbers on the country's Muslim population, but estimates put it at around 15,000, a number that would account for not more than 0.1 percent of the population."[29] The Haradec Králové Regional Authority provided financial support to the antimosque movement. Kusák's AntiMešita is an organization of individuals whose primary focus is to collect petitions railing against mosques specifically and the spread of Islam in general.[30] This antimosque movement is building momentum, as indicated by a SANEP national poll; the poll revealed that 75.2 percent of Czechs opposed mosque construction in the Czech Republic.[31]

In 2009 in the Finnish city of Kotka, Finns Party councilor Freddy van Wonterghem put forward a proposal "to ban buildings 'harmful to the cultural identity of the city.'" The buildings in his proposal were none other than local mosques. A 2012 report also cited city zoning chief Lars Olsson, who insisted "that current laws don't provide for a ban on building mosques and says public debate is instead needed on Finns' attitudes toward newcomers and representatives of different faiths."[32] The idea of a ban is problematic and runs counter to Finland's constitution. At least two chapters in the Finnish constitution refer to the right to construct places of worship as a right that cannot be denied to any group of people. The Finnish constitution, like those of all Western nations, states matter-of-factly that protection of human rights and equal treatment under the law are paramount. These guarantees include basic freedoms of each citizen to practice the religion of his or her choice.

On the subject of minarets, Israeli Prime Minister Benjamin Netanyahu came forward in December 2011 to support a law banning mosques from using loudspeakers in the call to prayer.[33] Knesset member Anastasia Michaeli, who initially promoted the bill, referred to specific complaints in Upper Nazareth about the volume of the muezzin's *azan*, or call to prayer. A muezzin is an individual responsible for calling the public to prayer five times a day from a mosque's minaret, or tower. Netanyahu's position on this issue echoed the legal precedent set in France. It should be noted that Netanyahu faced stiff opposition from three prominent ministers of his own Likud Party, including Limor Livnat, who suggested instead that Israel follow the example of Britain, where "the volume of the Muslim call to prayer is subject to limits drawn up by noise pollution legislation, though it is most often enforced only in the case of specific complaints."[34]

When prominent politicians like Netanyahu begin to challenge the legality of religious traditions that have been honored for fifteen centuries and lawmakers like Dutch parliamentarian Geert Wilders intentionally formulate derogatory remarks about Islam, one cannot ignore the potential short- and long-term consequences. In July 2012, reflecting remarks by Wilders, Colorado state senator Kevin Grantham, a Republican, made the following statement in an appearance at the Western Conservative Summit in Denver:

> You know, we'd have to hear more on that [construction of new mosques], because, as Wilders said, mosques are not churches like we would think of churches. . . . They [Muslims] think of mosques more as a foothold into a society, as a foothold into a community, more in the cultural and in the nationalistic sense. Our churches, we [Christians] don't feel that way, they're places of worship, and mosques are simply not that, and we need to take that into account when approving construction of those [mosques].[35]

Senator Grantham's assumption that all Muslims see the mosque as a foothold into a society and a community and perceive their houses of worship in a cultural and nationalistic sense is simultaneously arrogant and mind-boggling. One wonders if the senator ever made a single effort to speak directly with any Muslims regarding their personal opinions about the meaning and function of mosques. Or was he blindly following the pronouncements of that well-known European Islamophobe Geert Wilders? Also, did Senator Grantham conveniently forget the First Amendment to the US Constitution, in which religious freedom is guaranteed to all—including American Muslims?

In France, home to Europe's largest Muslim population, two thousand mosques have been built, half of those since 2001. With the growing presence of Muslim worshippers sometimes pouring out into the streets, particularly in the nineteenth arrondissement of Paris, Interior Minister Claude Guéant was able to pass legislation outlawing street prayer in September 2011. Guéant warned that "police will use force if Muslims, and those of any other faith, disobey the new rule to keep the French capital's public spaces secular."[36] Guéant suggested that the ban could eventually be applied to other regions in France, including Nice and Marseilles, where prayer in the streets has become a contentious issue.

Before enactment of this law, in December 2010, the forty-two-year-old daughter of Jean-Marie Le Pen, outgoing leader of the National Front and an individual convicted repeatedly on charges of racism and anti-Semitism, had stoked reactionary fervor at a political rally. She alluded to "ten to fifteen places in France where Muslims worshipped in the streets," describing these areas as occupied territory and likening this activity to "the Nazi occupation of Paris in the Second World War . . . without the tanks or soldiers."[37] Although President Nicolas Sarkozy and his ruling Union pour une Mouvement Populaire (UMP) were quick to condemn the comments, no doubt Marine Le Pen ignited sufficient nationalistic fervor to push through the legislation banning street prayers.

Spain, once a Moorish stronghold, is also no stranger to Islamophobic activities. In the summer of 2012, just east of Madrid in Torrejón, which is home to approximately ten thousand Muslims, municipal authorities approved a site for a new mosque. A spokesperson for Torrejón's Muslim community, Farid Bahoudi, explained that the small building previously used as a mosque was nothing more than "the ground floor of a drab block of flats near the main square in town"[38] Although the proposed site had met with approval, the media stirred up sufficient controversy to unite political activists from both the radical left and far right in defending their home turf from encroaching Muslims, who, as usual, found themselves caught in the middle. The mosque brouhaha fed directly into social discontent around Spain's immigration policy in general and Muslims in particular. Bahoudi stated, "We've tried to overcome ignorance to show people the truth about who we are and show them the reality of Islam and the reality of coexistence. But instead of wanting to integrate with us, the locals here would rather we moved elsewhere."[39] The situation in Torrejón shines light on widespread integration challenges in Europe, particularly as the media continues to portray Muslims as obdurate fundamentalists stubbornly refusing to assimilate into the rest of population. The *Irish Times* reported local residents' views about the mosque construction:

> "How would you like it if two or three hundred 'Moors' came wandering in and out of your street to pray each day?" says one man who lives on the same street as the proposed site for the new mosque and who prefers not to give his name.
>
> Francisco Morena, a pensioner who is sitting on a bench near the proposed site, knows little about the new mosque project. But when told about it, he says: "When we go to other countries, we have to behave the way people do in those countries. But it seems as if here it's the other way round: we have to accept what the foreigners want."[40]

The reference to all Muslims living in Spain as foreigners throws an ironic light on the discussion. Is it possible that many Spanish citizens are unaware of the rich Moorish influence on Spain's culture, of the importance of Islam's contribution to art, science, and literature? Do they understand that being a Muslim does not necessarily translate to being a foreigner or an immigrant from another land? Spain's constitutional law, specifically in Articles 14 and 16, clearly provides every Spanish citizen the basic right to worship according to individual conscience, regardless of ethnic, national, or religious background.

Article 14 [Equality]
Spaniards are equal before the law, without any discrimination for reasons of birth, race, sex, religion, opinion, or any other personal or social condition or circumstance.
Article 16 [Religion, belief, no state church]
(1) Freedom of ideology, religion, and cult of individuals and communities is guaranteed without any limitation in their demonstrations other than that which is necessary for the maintenance of public order protected by law.

In Western European nations, then, antimosque sentiments are easily framed around the argument that national and cultural identities are threatened. This type of rhetoric appeals to the uninformed and to those citizens particularly prone to manipulation by the power élite. Marisa Caroço Amaro suggests that political parties in the West often take advantage of xenophobia to obfuscate more immediate and critical issues, such as failing economies and budget deficits.[41] Furthermore, Amaro stresses, more traditional parties tend to remain passive and silent, thereby validating xenophobic behaviors. This silent indifference gives rise to slogans and speeches that turn immigrants and minorities into scapegoats, with blame heaped on them for whatever financial or social ills the nation faces. This pattern, repeated across history and one that wreaked havoc in twentieth-century Europe, begs to be acknowledged and addressed. Regarding mosque construction in Switzerland, Amaro makes an excellent point about diversity and the importance of working together to encourage mutual respect in Western nations:

> Minarets should not be unilaterally banned; however, it is perhaps reasonable to suggest that mosque leaders and architects work with municipal leaders or urban planners to raise understanding and to create places of worship that blend into the Swiss aesthetic. Diversity should be embraced both by citizens and immigrants arriving to Europe. Once diversity is accepted as something normal, perhaps the integration debate can be redefined to avoid unnecessary divisions.[42]

Diversity and tolerance cannot remain abstract notions in reports and studies; rather, individuals and communities must work together and move determinedly toward social activism. Otherwise, our differences—the same ones that deserve celebration and contribute to the richness of human experience—will consistently thwart global stability.

Voices of Tolerance, Indifferent or Silenced?

Dislike and distrust between Muslims and the West has generally been a two-way street. The Pew Global Attitudes Project reported in 2006 "that the U.S. draws its most negative assessment from Muslim nations."[43] The Pew Research Center study found that six out of ten Americans viewed Islam unfavorably, and "more than half of the American public now believes the terrorist attacks over the last few years are, or soon will be, part of a major civilization conflict between Islam and the West."[44] When Western figureheads of state, like the queen of England, demonstrate cultural sensitivity towards Muslim practices, even a deliberate show of sensitivity can fan the flames of Islamist intolerance toward values of freedom and liberty. Tawfik Hamid, a formerly radical Muslim who abandoned extremism to embrace moderate and peaceful interpretations of Islam, finds Queen Elizabeth's 2010 visit to the UAE a perfect example.[45] The queen chose to conform to the Muslim dress code by simply covering her hair and wearing a long outer coat.

Sheikh Yasser Burhani, one of Egypt's leading Islamic scholars, jumped on the queen's gesture as justification for furthering a repressive, fundamentalist Salafi Islamic position. Burhani, who favors a Sharia-controlled nation "where women are stoned for adultery, gays are beheaded, and non-Muslims are humiliated as second-class citizens,"[46] wants to dictate by law that all female tourists wear the *hijab* and avoid immodest bathing suits on Egypt's beaches and that male and female tourists abstain from drinking alcohol. Burhani's response to the Queen's deference to local custom is nothing more than a skewed interpretation of mutual tolerance and respect between East and West.

Historian Bernard Lewis has said that current and future prospects for viable, working relationships between Islam and the West seem unlikely.[47] It should be noted that, generally speaking, Lewis is a well-respected scholar, although many in academia consider his methodology (Orientalism) outdated. In my opinion, Lewis's scholarship is solid, even though some of his personal and political views are disturbing. Professor Richard W. Bulliet, a preeminent scholar of Middle Eastern history at Columbia University, has written about the Middle East, voicing ideas that are diametrically opposed to those of Lewis. Bulliet maintains that differences between Islam and Christianity may be reconcilable. Opposed to the "clash of civilizations" theory, he strongly asserts, "Americans to this day continue to misread the Muslim world and to miss the opportunity to focus on common ground for building lasting peace."[48]

Similarly, Fawaz A. Gerges argues that after 9/11, two political perspectives framed US foreign policy, and both of them sabotaged diplomatic efforts between the United States and the Muslim world: accommodationists favor policies that reflect an imperialist viewpoint, and confrontationalists view Islam as America's archenemy and Judeo-Christian values as presently under attack.[49] In this configuration, Lewis is considered a confrontationalist thinker who views Islamic radicals as believing that Sharia applies to Muslims wherever they reside. Any Muslim committing an offense against Islamic law, therefore, whether in Albany, New York, or Albania, is subject to the same consequences and must be punished accordingly. Lewis contends that this position is opposed to that of Sunnis:

> The majority Sunni view is that Muslim law only applies in countries under Muslim government. What happens outside is no concern of the Muslim authorities. What is never discussed at all—it is never considered—is an offense committed by a non-Muslim in a non-Muslim country. That, according to the unanimous opinion of all of the doctors of the holy law, is of no concern to Islamic law.[50]

The obvious notion that non-Muslims living in non-Muslim nations should be off the Islamist radar is unfortunately anything but obvious in some circles. Why? Because Muslim extremists do not buy into it, choosing instead to promote fear and unrest by interpreting Sharia and Qur'anic precepts through their own narrow lenses of perception. These deluded individuals believe it is their right and duty to punish any non-Muslims residing in the West whom they consider to be blasphemous.

Three cases in point are the fatwas issued against Danish cartoonist Kurt Vestergaard, Dutch film producer Theodoor van Gogh, and twelve people working for *Charlie Hebdo*, a weekly satirical newspaper in Paris. *Charlie Hebdo* has been the target of two terrorist attacks, presumed to be in response to a number of controversial cartoons featuring the Prophet Mohammad which appeared in the publication. Vestergaard, whose caricatures of the Prophet Mohammad offended Muslim sensibilities, has warned that the West must not allow itself to be held hostage to the threat of Islamic retribution. As a result, Vestergaard has been the target of multiple assassination attempts. Theodoor van Gogh, whose film *Submission* openly criticized the treatment of women in Islam, was murdered by a Dutch-Moroccan Muslim in 2004. *Charlie Hebdo*, Vestergaard, and van Gogh, creative enterprise and visual artists, are examples of non-Muslims judged and condemned by radical Islamists in non-Muslim nations.

In Spain, partly in response to the controversy around Vestergaard and van Gogh, changes are being made to the annual Moros y Cristianos Festivals. These folkloric celebrations, held primarily in southern Valencia, commemorate the Reconquista, during which Spanish forces battled with and ultimately ousted the Moors (Muslims). Changes to these village festivals reflect growing fears of retribution by radical Islamic factions. One tradition that is particularly offensive to Muslims worldwide includes mocking, insulting, and burning an effigy of the Prophet Mohammed called La Mahoma. Paul Belien writes in a 2006 post for the conservative *Brussels Journal*, "The village of Bocairent near Valencia decided this year to discontinue the century old tradition of mocking and burning effigies of Muhammad. Bocairent does not want to risk becoming the target of suicide bombers."[51] In the Spanish town of Vienna, tradition demands filling a puppetlike image of Muhammad's head with gunpowder and detonating it with a cigar. The town's annual Reconquista reenactment also entails dragging a Mohammad-like doll through the streets. Although activities of this nature are being strongly reconsidered and in some villages dropped from the celebrations, the president of the Union of Festive Associations of Moors and Christians, Francisco Lopez Perez, told US National Public Radio (NPR) in 2006 that "the Muhammad puppet has become a beloved figure in the celebrations and must continue to be part of them. However, I asked participants to take out any rituals that might offend people of other faiths."[52]

Clearly Perez found it more convenient to pay lip service to objections being registered than to propose practical solutions to avoid offending people of other faiths. The president of the Islamic community in Vienna, Spain, responded that "Muslims understand perfectly that the Muhammad figure is a local tradition" and added that the Muhammad figure "does not refer to my faith."[53] While this extremely tolerant view may hold true for many Muslims in Spain, one cannot make universal assumptions. A local Muslim in a Vienna café did not share that view:

> I've seen this Muhammad, and I don't like the way he's treated. . . .
> But what can I tell you? They lack respect. They have to learn to show respect, like we Muslims respect Jesus and all the religions.[54]

The reevaluation of popular Spanish Reconquista traditions is a move in the right direction—whether a result of honoring Muslim sensibilities or spurred by deep concern about radical Islamist response. However, Sina Lucia Kottman, in her "Mocking and Miming the Moor," finds that not all enthusiastic festival participants agree:

The retrenchment of the [Reconquista] feasts has subsequently been the object of emotional disputes in regional and national media and cyber-space. . . . [Some] defend their tradition as nothing more and nothing less than an age-old cultural practice, a deep expression of local identity and clearly not intended as an attack on Muslims. . . . [K]een public and political debates about the significance of local cultural practices, the political correctness of tradition, freedom of expression and affronts to collective or individual sensibilities continue.[55]

Nevertheless, decisions in Spanish communities to reconsider and perhaps discontinue burning effigies of Muhammad has had an impact on other European carnival celebrations, such as the Mardi Gras parade of Aalst, Belgium. Belien reports that there is good reason to believe participants will no longer dress in burqas or pose as the Prophet Muhammad:

The authorities in Oldenzaal [Netherlands] have decided that mocking Muhammad will not be tolerated. "We will be very strict," they told the media. Similar prohibitions have also been imposed in the province of Limburg, where carnival (this year from 26 to 28 February) is a very old tradition. Participants can mock whomever they want, except Muslims. "Making allusions to the cartoon crisis will not be tolerated either," the organizing committee of a carnival parade in Brabant said.[56]

While Europe has managed to maintain a number of ancient racist traditions, higher educational levels and expanding global awareness are calling these traditional activities into question, especially when measured against the need to promote values of human dignity and cultural sensitivity.

This brings one back to the question of whether the same rules and consequences for which Muslims are held accountable, such as insulting the Prophet, are applicable to non-Muslims. Lewis observes that Europeans have been insulting the Prophet Mohammad for a very long time. He refers to the first part of Dante Alighieri's fourteenth-century epic poem *Inferno* in which Dante, guided by Virgil (28th Canto), recognizes the Prophet Mohammad

in the course of his eternal damnation. He is punished—I quote Dante's words, as a *seminator di scandalo e di scisma*, a sower of scandal and of schism. Now, this is very insulting. In the great Cathedral of Bologna there is a wonderful set of pictures painted, if I remember rightly, in the 15th century depicting scenes from Dante's Inferno, including some very graphic pictures of Mohammed being tortured in hell by the devil—very graphic.[57]

Some years ago, leaders of the Italian Muslim community in Bologna sent a polite request to cathedral authorities expressing their concern about the paintings, requesting that the paintings be covered. Although the cathedral administration took the request under consideration, no further steps were taken. That is, the paintings remain on public exhibition even today.

In a report by the European Network against Racism (ENAR), during 2009–2010 Italy ranked "runner-up" behind Denmark in terms of occurrences of mistreatment, attacks, and racially based violent acts in European nations.[58] It is not surprising, therefore, that prominent political figures in Italy might openly oppose new mosque construction and take actions that are purposefully antagonistic. Roberto Calderoli of the Northern League Party, an official government minister, proposed a "Pig Day" protest to oppose the construction of a mosque in Bologna. By guiding a pig on a leash around the site in protest, Calderoli believed that the site would become unsuitable and "unclean" for Muslim worshippers. Insisting that mosques are "potential centers for harboring terrorist cells," Calderoli announced, "I place myself and my pig at the disposal of those who are against this mosque."[59]

In the face of Calderoli's highly disrespectful behavior, a voice of reason and moderation rose to defend Italian Muslims. Paolo Ferrer, Italy's welfare minister from the Communist Refoundation Party, expressed his disgust regarding Calderoli's comments and Pig Day proposal. Offering a public apology to the community of Muslims, Ferrer said, "I apologize to Muslims living in Italy on behalf of all civilized Italians."[60] Ultimately Calderoli was forced to resign his position when

he provoked the wrath of Muslims by appearing on television wearing a T-shirt decorated with the notorious Danish editorial cartoons that mocked the prophet Mohammed and led to violent protests around the world. In his latest jab, the Northern League leader said that he planned to eat pork as the Islamic season of Ramadan began, simply to annoy Muslims.[61]

Whether in Italy or in Denmark, cultural racism has attained a startling level of popular support—and manifests as anti-Muslim and anti-refugee attitudes, Karen Wren notes:

Cultural racism has found fertile territory in a post-industrial Europe experiencing economic crisis and social disintegration, but its manifestations vary between countries. Denmark, a country traditionally regarded as liberal and tolerant, experienced a fundamental shift in attitude during the early 1980s that has seen it emerge potentially as one of the most racist countries in Europe. Paradoxically, liberal values are used as justification for negative representations of "others."[62]

Equipped with this knowledge Muslims would do well to remember that in multiple instances throughout his life the Prophet Mohammad taught tolerance and moderation, chiefly through personal example. Perhaps that is why the Prophet is referred to as Rahmat lil-'Alimeen—"a mercy to all the worlds." In this time of global unrest and division, Muhammad Wajid Akhtar advises, "Muslims have a choice . . . [to] either use . . . limitless love for the Prophet to burn the world to avenge him or to reunite, refocus and re-build the world in honor of him."[63]

It is noteworthy, given the many irreverent references to and behaviors toward the Prophet Mohammad—whether Dante Alighieri's epic poem, the Spanish Moros y Cristianos tradition of burning the Prophet in effigy, or the creation of caricatures that mock the Prophet in contemporary media—that one rarely hears of Muslims behaving disrespectfully toward Moses or Jesus. Even though one may be free to insult the religion or belief system of others, it is nevertheless prudent to keep in mind what it feels like when the tables are turned.

While freedom of speech in the West can reach seemingly intolerable limits, such as the 2010 threat by pastor Terry Jones of the Christian Dove World Outreach Center in Gainesville, Florida, to burn the Qur'an, international outrage and pleas for reasonable solutions from world leaders can and often do make a difference. Indeed, voices of moderation forced Jones to withdraw his threat to desecrate the Qur'an. Unfortunately, in 2012 American soldiers embroiled in the war in Afghanistan openly destroyed the Qur'an, resulting in a series of violent protests. Clearly both sides of the East-West equation must find non-aggressive outlets for their fears, resentments, and frustrations. Otherwise, mutual understanding and respect for each other's religious and cultural practices will never be possible.

Sensational reports—whether from Katy, Texas, or Kabul, Afghanistan—demonstrate the growing pressure and antagonistic sentiments resulting from Muslims living in Western environments and Westerners temporarily residing in Eastern countries. In the West, one finds a tendency to generalize about Muslims. In the East, few Muslims find reason to speak favorably of the West. Against this backdrop of mutual suspicion, Islamophobes find fertile territory to convincingly portray all Muslims as agents of terror, members of extremist factions, and/or representatives of an increasingly violent Middle East. All Muslim women are oppressed and need saving. All Muslim men are unreasonable and illogical at best, scheming and misogynistic at worst. All Muslims are secretly furthering terrorist agendas to sabotage the Western way of life. Because of these ongoing generalizations, it is no wonder that Muslims worldwide are jumping on the halal, or religiously permissible, bandwagon. It is not only their adherence to religious piety but also their search for identity and security that lie at the heart of the halal industry.

CHAPTER 2

Islam and the Halal Food Industry

Islam is not the only religion to prescribe dietary regulations, perhaps similar to Orthodox Jewish dietary law. To receive the coveted halal label, Islamically sanctioned food products must pass through multiple channels of approval. Here I address the roles that ulama, religious scholars, play in this process and how their interpretations of Qur'anic verses serve to regulate the halal food industry. Detailed regulatory criteria may vary from one Islamic nation to another, and halal certification agencies not only differ one from the other but also often require different standards; therefore, no single global halal standards exist. This places tremendous responsibility and pressure on the individual consumer and reliance on consumer loyalty to particular Brand Islam products.

Throughout history, religious affiliation has influenced individual lifestyle and personal choice. Across cultures and societies, the impact of religious dictates is clearly observed in the types of foods proscribed. Judaism sets forth kosher dietary laws that, like those of Islam, forbid consumption of pork. In Hinduism and Buddhism, pork and beef are taboo. Catholics abstain from red meat on Ash Wednesday and on Fridays during Lent. Seventh-Day Adventists value vegetarianism and the avoidance of pork, shellfish, and other foods described in biblical text as unclean. Mormons follow dietary guidelines as part of their religious practice that include abstinence from tea, coffee, and alcohol.

While it is thus not unusual for religions to establish dietary restrictions, what is unusual is the unprecedented demand for and global marketing of religiously sanctioned foods in the twenty-first century. The key players in this scenario—manufacturers, distributors, and retailers of halal foods—are realizing impressive profits. My aim is to explore the

Islamic concept of halal as it pertains to food production and consumption and, more specifically, to discuss the emerging roles, challenges, and geopolitical consequences of halal food production, marketing, and certification.

Halal, Haram, and *Mashbooh* Guidelines

In terms of food, halal designates food and drink deemed permissible for consumption by Sharia, or Islamic law. Food and beverages must be sourced and prepared in specific ways to meet Sharia standards. Any food products considered unfit to eat are termed haram, or religiously forbidden. The list of haram foods includes all pork products, the meat of carnivorous animals and birds of prey (particularly those that feed on dead animals), animals without external ears (such as snakes and worms), animals with certain hooves, meat from sick or dead animals, and any food products that have come into contact with or been contaminated by any of the above directly or by non-halal processing such as using utensils or surfaces that have been contaminated by haram products.

Alcoholic beverages are considered haram, as is any food containing even minute traces of alcohol, such as chocolate bars or candies filled with liquor. One further classification of food and drink, beyond halal and haram, is *mashbooh*, or "doubtful food."[1] While no religious prohibitions exist against consuming this group of products, Muslims are nevertheless advised to avoid them. According to Islamic law, food and drink normally considered haram might be reclassified as halal under special circumstances. This is particularly true in certain medical situations or when an individual's life is at stake. For example, medicines prepared and compounded with alcohol may be used for the duration of time that a patient requires them.

Islamic law regarding consumption of food and drink is drawn from several sections of the Qur'an, among them Qur'an 5:4 and Qur'an 5:90 (prohibition of intoxicants), Qur'an 35:12 (permissibility of seafood), and Qur'an 6:145 (prohibition from eating animal carcasses or the blood from such carcasses or the flesh of swine or animals that have been slaughtered without invoking Allah's name).

The detailed prescription for slaying animals and the permissibility of different ingredients—according to Qur'anic guidelines as well as those derived from *ahadith* (words of the Prophet Mohammad and his companions)—have been adhered to by religious leaders and scholars throughout the history of Islam.[2] However, at present, countless processed foods available to global consumers are tainted with preservatives, colors, and artificial flavors the origins of which are often unknown. Many such ingredients, whether plant, animal, or chemical, either did not exist or were unknown or unavailable in ancient times. Therefore, devout Muslims often face enormous challenges in following halal guidelines, especially when eating in restaurants and other public spaces or when purchasing food and drinks at grocery stores.

The following statements make clear what the Qur'an proscribes in terms of forbidden food and drink:

QUR'AN, SURAT AL-MĀ'IDAH (THE TABLE SPREAD), CHAPTER 5, VERSE 4

Prohibited to you are dead animals, blood, the flesh of swine, and that which has been dedicated to other than Allah, and [those animals] killed by strangling or by a violent blow or by a head-long fall or by the goring of horns, and those from which a wild animal has eaten, except what you [are able to] slaughter [before the animal touches it], and those which are sacrificed on stone altars, and [it is prohibited] that you seek decision through divining arrows. That is grave disobedience. This day those who disbelieve have despaired of [defeating] your religion; so fear them not, but fear Me. This day I have perfected for you your religion and completed My favor upon you and have approved for you Islam as religion. But whoever is forced by severe hunger with no inclination to sin—then indeed, Allah is Forgiving and Merciful.[3]

QUR'AN, SURAT AL-MĀ'IDAH (THE TABLE SPREAD), CHAPTER 5, VERSE 90

O you who have believed, indeed, intoxicants, gambling, [sacrificing on] stone altars [to other than Allah], and divining arrows are but defilement from the work of Satan, so avoid it that you may be successful.[4]

QUR'AN SURAT AL-AN'ĀM (THE CATTLE), CHAPTER 6, VERSE 145

Say: I do not find in that which has been revealed to me anything forbidden for an eater to eat of except that it be what has died of itself or blood poured forth or flesh of swine—for that surely is unclean—or that which is a transgression, other than [the name of] Allah having been invoked on it; but whoever is driven to necessity, not desiring nor exceeding the limit, then surely your lord is forgiving, merciful.[5]

QUR'AN SURAT FATIR (ORIGINATOR) CHAPTER 35, VERSE 12
And not alike are the two bodies of water. One is fresh and sweet, palatable for drinking, and one is salty and bitter. And from each you eat tender meat and extract ornaments which you wear, and you see the ships plowing through [them] that you might seek of His bounty; and perhaps you will be grateful.[6]

In regions with large Muslim populations, the ulama and other religious leaders constantly offer new opinions as to what foods are permissible for Muslims to consume, what services they may seek, and which products they may use. Using the shield of Sharia, the ulama, along with regulatory religious organizations, can seriously hamper the promotion, sales, and consumption of existing products while at the same time supporting and promoting development of other products.[7] Riaz and Chaudry explain, "The basic principle is that all things created by God are permitted with a series of exceptions that are specifically prohibited." One can imagine how such statements are open for interpretation. These same authors continue with the following warning: "To make lawful and unlawful is the right of God alone. No human being, no matter how pious or powerful, may take this right into his own hands."[8] This statement is a thoughtful reminder that acting arbitrarily to convert haram items into halal and vice versa is comparable "to ascribing [ourselves as] partners to God."[9]

The concept of permissible foods is not limited to Islam or even contemporary faiths. Pre-Islamic cultures and religions also recognized distinctions regarding meat from different animals. Zoroastrianism, the ancient religion of Persia (present-day Iran), cultivated a significant respect for nature so that killing certain animals was forbidden. Zoroastrians protected the bull, as they believed it was the first animal in God's creation. Another pre-Islamic religion, Judaism, has declared kosher restrictions since ancient times, especially regarding the ritual of slaughter. The original intent of kosher ritual slaughter was, like Zoroastrianism, to ensure humane treatment of animals. Islamic precepts follow the same intention.

The Islamic method of slaughtering animals (*dhabihah*, also spelled *zabiha*) requires that Muslims perform a specific ritual process.[10] The methodic details of slaughter arise from Islamic tradition rather than from direct Qur'anic mandate. The animal to be slaughtered must be fed and watered first and stressed as little as possible. Anything fed to the animal, fish, or bird must be from halal sources and devoid of any haram ingredients. If any of the above steps is skipped, the meat of the slaughtered animal is considered haram. *Dhabihah* involves a swift, deep incision with a sharp knife to the neck, cutting the jugular veins and carotid arteries on both sides, and leaving the spinal cord intact. The knife must be exceedingly sharp so that slaughter can be accomplished in one stroke. This process must be carried out with respect and compassion, causing the animal as little pain and suffering as possible. And the animal must be slaughtered in the name of Allah.

At present, most Muslim nations import chicken that has been slaughtered mechanically. One interesting aspect of the mechanical slaughtering technique initiated and developed in the West is that, according to Riaz and Chaudry, "a Muslim while pronouncing the name of God switches on the machine."[11] Ulama are divided in their opinions regarding whether this step makes the chicken meat authentically halal. Highly pious and halal-minded Muslims, particularly in Sharia-based countries, hardly ever buy imported chicken. Instead, they purchase from reliable local butchers who use only small-scale, nonmechanized slaughter methods. Riaz and Chaudry suggest that standards differ from one Islamic community to another. Poultry feed is a good example. The feed for halal poultry "should be devoid of animal byproducts or other scrap materials, which is a common practice in the West. Some halal slaughterhouses use an integrated approach, for example, where they raise their own chickens on clean feed."[12] In the United States, Muslim retailers of halal poultry prefer to purchase their birds from the Amish, a religious group of Christian church fellowships. Amish church members, who eschew many technological advances, do not feed animal by-products to poultry.

Since the halal meat industry is such a lucrative market in the West and constantly expanding, standard safety and hygienic regulations and licensing requirements—as well as frequent, unannounced health department inspections—are applied. When selling halal meat, slaughterhouses must meet further specific criteria required by halal industry regulations. These would include the method of transportation from farm to slaughterhouse, packaging, storage, and how the packaged meat is sold in the market. Given all these steps, halal meat should not come into contact with any harmful adulterations or anything considered haram. When the meat is sliced or ground, it is critical that the knife, butcher's board, and grinding equipment as well the butcher's hands and gloves not touch any haram item such as pork or meat from animals that have been slaughtered in a non-halal manner.

Because of these strict criteria, many Muslims in the West are especially distrustful of fast-food chains that claim to sell halal products. After KFC, formerly Kentucky Fried Chicken, announced that a designated number of its British fast-food restaurants would begin serving halal chicken, the Halal Monitoring Committee (HMC) of Britain along with several Muslim community groups and the Lancashire Council of Mosques spoke out, expressing concerns that the KFC chicken did not qualify as halal. The primary issue was the use of mechanical slaughter. KFC consulted the Halal Food Authority of Britain, the country's oldest regulatory organization, which declared machine slaughter as halal. The monitoring committee and the Lancashire Council of Mosques disagreed, stating that the slaughter must be done by hand, and they backed up their claim by referring to a study the committee conducted in 2009 consisting of a poll of Muslim religious leaders. The results indicated that 94 percent of the religious leaders disagreed with the practice of machine killing. Controversy continues in the United Kingdom concerning the use of stunning animals before they are slaughtered, a practice carried out at halal slaughterhouses.[13]

Fast-food halal. This photo of a "KFC—Now Serving Halal Orignal [sic] & Crispy" sign was posted on the anti-Muslim site Bare Naked Islam, http://www.barenakedislam.com.

Protest of KFC halal in England. This "Koran Fried Chicken?" placard appeared at a demonstration by British National Party members. Image from Islamophobia Watch, November 15, 2011, http://www.islamophobiatoday.com /2011/11/15/.

English Defence League poster. The EDL's call to ban halal meat throughout the United Kingdom here particularly targets Shazia Saleem's marketing of her halal-prepared traditional British and Italian dishes. When the EDL's poster appeared online in 2014, it unleashed a storm of anti-Islam hate comments on social media. Image from TellMama, http://tellmamauk.org/tag/ieat/.

An Islam 4 Infidels decal. I4I promotes anti-Islamic bigotry in Australia. Its "About" page says the website "is run by patriotic Australians who see the grave danger that islam poses to our civilization and our culture." Decal sales purportedly go toward the website founder's electoral campaign for Parliament with an eventual aim of "a referendum on whether we want to pay a Halal tax or not." Image from Islam 4 Infidels, http://islam4infidels.com/.

Halal faces difficulties throughout the Western world. Aggressive campaigns against halal meat, among various Islamic schools of thought and Muslim lifestyles, are daily occurrences used also in political elections and anti-immigrant laws.

At the same time the Western world is catering to the demands of the Muslims. Air France flights to and from Morocco serve meals guaranteed to contain no pork or pork products. Halal vitamins are

AIR FRANCE

garantit ce repas sans viande de porc.

guarantees that this meal does not contain pork.

Sunulan yiyeceklerin içinde
domuz eti bulunmadığını garanti eder.

005386

AIR FRANCE

تضمن أن هذا الغذاء خال ٍ من لحم الخنزير

اس کھانے میں سور کا گوشت نہیں ہے ۔

تضمین می کند که این غذا بدون گوشت خوک می باشد.

Pork-free meals in flight, guaranteed. On an Air France flight from Paris to Rabat, Morocco, each tray of food was accompanied by this card printed on both sides in various languages guaranteeing that the meal does not contain pork. Photo by the author.

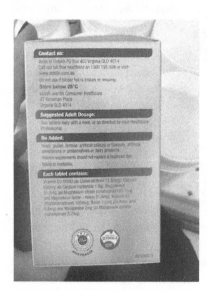

Halal vitamins. This multivitamin product bears the Australian Federation of Islamic Councils' AFIC Halal Australia stamp. Photo by Sogol Shirazi, Melbourne, Australia.

US halal beef jerky. This is a product of the Halal Jerky company of Corona, California. Image from company website, http://www .thehalaljerky.com.

Ganocafe Mocha packet, marked with the halal logo. This Gano Excel USA product can be purchased online. Photo by the author.

Halal chicken masala. Spices like this National brand example can be purchased with halal certification from India. Photo by Smeeta Mishra, New Delhi.

Golden arches above a halal McDonald's. The McDonald's Lebanon website lists its halal policies; http://m.mcdonalds.com .lb/. Image from Bare Naked Islam, http://www.barenakedislam.com.

manufactured in Australia, and halal beef jerky is made in California. It is evident that producers of a large range of food products in different parts of the world are recognizing the purchasing power of Muslims who strictly follow religious dietary rules.

Another fast-food chain, McDonald's, has been under fire in Britain for a very different issue—not revealing to the general public its use of halal chicken in 1,200 British outlets. A McDonald's spokesperson responded in a *Daily Mail* article, "As a result of your enquiries, our investigation has confirmed that some halal chicken has entered our supply chain without our knowledge, and we apologise to our customers for this."[14]

Why the fuss? First of all, some general consumers object to certain aspects of halal slaughter such as killing the animals without first stunning them, cutting the animals' throats, and invoking the name of God just before killing them. Secondly, non-halal consumers wanted to know how and why halal chickens entered the McDonald's supply chain in the first place. To obtain halal-certified chickens, a company must pay huge certification fees for inspection and paperwork. Critics asked how McDonald's, known the world over for selling food products cheaply, could possibly profit from using halal chickens without passing costs on to its customers. One plausible explanation is that McDonald's deceived its Muslim customers in the first place, possibly through false advertising. Perhaps it was, in fact, not serving halal chicken. When general consumers queried why they were not informed about the chicken being halal, McDonald's was caught in a dizzying web—apologizing in two directions at once. This is not the first time that a fast-food company has issued apologies for using halal meat or foodstuffs in the West, as we shall see.

Ulama, Certification Standards, and Contradictions

The primary challenge that suppliers and exporters of halal food products continually face is the glaring absence of universally agreed-upon standards. Islamic clerics often put forward contradictory interpretations of what is and what is not halal. Indeed, an item deemed halal by one set of fatwas might be considered haram according to another. These discrepancies in religious opinion may result in a company or corporation being rejected when applying for the all-important halal certification seal. Thus, the potential for profit as well as for bribes and corruption often lies in the hands of a powerful few.

Furthermore, national profit motives can override religious dictates, allowing a product's haram classification to be changed to halal. The issue of caviar, a precious and lucrative commodity in Iran, is an example. The Islamic Republic of Iran's religious clerics zealously approached this issue, as Houchang Chahabi explains:

Caviar . . . posed a delicate problem. Shiite jurisprudence considered it *haram* (forbidden), but since its production and export were a state monopoly, caviar procured the Iranian treasury millions of dollars in revenue. Trading in what is forbidden under the *shari'a*, the Islamic Republic faced the alternative of either reneging on its promise of applying divine law or depriving itself of valuable export earnings. Moreover, caviar is the epitome of luxury and culinary refinement in Western culture, for which alone must have rendered it suspect in the eyes of the populists who took power soon after the [Islamic] revolution [of 1979]. To find a way out of this dilemma, the status of caviar under religious law was revisited. At the end of a laborious process involving both clerics and fisheries experts, the traditional ruling was reversed, and caviar was declared *halal* (permitted).[15]

Another item in Iran that flies mysteriously under Sharia radar is beer. While only nonalcoholic beer is available through legal outlets, alcoholic beer and other alcoholic beverages are regularly smuggled into the country and consumed. Wine and other alcoholic beverages are sold legally in the Armenian (Christian) neighborhoods. At the same time, nonalcoholic local beer breweries are well established in Iran. This halal Iranian beer, which superseded the alcoholic beer consumed prior to the 1979 Islamic Revolution, is known by the Arabic term *ma'al sha'er* (juice or extract of barley).

For ulama to agree on what foodstuffs are halal or haram in their own nation is one thing. The real difficulty arises when ulama of one country disapprove the validity of another country's halal products, creating ambiguity and mistrust around the authenticity of halal certification. Thus consumers are left with questionable choices. Islamic re-

Halal "beer." This kind of nonalcoholic malt beverage with a variety of fruit flavors is very common in Iran. The pomegranate example here is from the Nik Rose Chenaran company in Iran. Photo posted on Flickr by Uncornered Market.

Label from a "50% halal" dry soup package. Manufactured by Mie Yabi, this "Rasa Ayam Babi" soup mix is identified as a product of Indonesia "with technical help" from a Japanese firm. Image from Chemicals for Peace Not War, https://wanibesak.wordpress.com/tag/mie-yabi-pas-susunya-rasa-ayam-babi/.

ligious authorities tend to cast aspersions on many organizations that provide halal approval in the West. This means that halal food producers in the West have to go the extra mile to seek the clerics' approval, which requires spending extraordinary amounts of time and money. These costs are passed on to consumers. In the United States, halal foods may be prohibitively expensive for some Muslim consumers. In general, Sharia-compliant (halal) food items are costly. Tariq Javid, manager of a halal restaurant in Virginia, told the *Halal Journal*, "If someone is selling Halal food cheap, I will think, it's not Halal."[16] Ironically, some products find their way in the market with labels such as 50 percent halal; that does not make sense at all but reveals how the word "halal" is associated with value in sales.

The halal food industry faces another challenge, Mian Riaz explains, when halal certification is issued for a particular product and is only valid for the duration of time stated on the certificate. This means the certification must be renewed on a regular basis:

A batch certificate issued for each consignment is valid for as long as that specific batch or lot of the product is in the market—generally, up to product expiration date or "use by" date. In a separate case, if a certified product is made according to a fixed formula, a certificate may be issued for a one-, two- or three-year period. The product remains halal-certified, as long as it meets all the established and agreed-upon production and marketing requirements between the company and the halal-certifying organization.[17]

Each time a certification is renewed, an additional fee is charged.

According to the International Halal Integrity Alliance (IHIA), an international nonprofit organization, five kinds of entities may certify halal food products.[18] These include mosques, nongovernmental organizations (NGOs) or private group initiatives, semigovernmental or government-related entities, Islamic and Muslim associations, and certification bodies under Islamic and Muslim associations. The IHI freely admits to the contradictory nature of halal endorsements: "The absence of a credible reference centre for information has resulted in industries and consumers being bombarded with various interpretations of the meaning and application of Halal, which often contradict each other."[19]

As a result, in some countries, especially those where a majority follow Sharia, religious and regulatory authorities are setting national halal standards. Indonesia, with a population that is 88 percent Muslim, is one of these nations.[20] In January 2011, the Indonesian Ulema (Ulama) Council (Majelis Ulama Indonesia, MUI), Indonesia's highest authority on Islamic affairs, claimed that it would "set a single national halal standard to replace the 41 world-class institutions . . . promoting their different standards in Indonesia."[21] The same *Jakarta Post* article reported that

> food, medicine and cosmetics analysis body (LPPOM MUI) head Lukmanul Hakim said that the 41 institutions had different standards, with only eight referring to the MUI. . . . According to the Food and Drug Monitoring Agency (BPOM), there were currently 113,515 halal-registered products in the nation, 36 percent of which were certified as halal by the MUI.[22]

Other Muslim-majority countries like Malaysia are following Indonesia's example of self-monitoring. In 2008 the Halal Industry Development Corporation of Malaysia was given a government mandate to start issuing halal logos and certificates. The corporation was set up with the objective of positioning Malaysia as a global halal hub and accelerating the development of the halal industry worldwide.[23]

However, halal authorization did not stay out of the hands of religious authorities for long, a halal website reports:

> From Jan. 1, 2012, only the Halal logo issued by the Malaysian Islamic Development Department (JAKIM) can be used and will be recognised. Minister of Domestic Trade, Cooperatives and Consumer Affairs Datuk Seri Ismail Sabri Yaakob said this was a follow-up to the enforcement of the Trade Descriptions Act 2011, approved by Parliament in July, and which would come into force on Nov 1. "This means that food premises, hotels and others which, prior to this, were using halal logos not issued by JAKIM will need to make fresh applications because the existing logo is void after January 1 [2013]. No other parties can recommend or issue halal certificates or make self-declarations concerning the halal status."[24]

The same report indicated that if any business—restaurant, market stall, factory, hotel, or other—used a halal logo other than the one issued by JAKIM, it would face heavy fines and its principals could be incarcerated. These penalties include the equivalent of about $79,000 for corporate bodies and $31,600 and/or three years in jail for individuals.[25] Since JAKIM is now the single entity granted responsibility for halal logo issuance in Malaysia, some individuals have questioned exactly what is in it for JAKIM and have voiced concern about unethical practices. JAKIM has defended its policies by issuing the following statement: "(JAKIM) does not commercialise its halal certificates, as its application fees cover the costs of research and laboratory tests on the status of product ingredients, said Minister Datuk Seri Jamil Khir Baharom in the Prime Minister's Department."[26] Consumer skepticism and, at times, cynicism continue to undermine the legitimacy of JAKIM's monopoly on the halal certification process.

In May 2011, Malaysian Muslims were advised against drinking Barbican beer, a popular drink. JAKIM and the state Islamic affairs councils deemed it haram, prohibiting its sale to Muslims and claiming that it contained 0.5 percent alcohol rather than the permissible 0.01 percent. In Johor state Mufti Mohd Tahrir Samsuddin said the "National Fatwa Council had decided that the permissible alcohol content in food and drinks according to Islamic law was under 0.01 per cent."[27] Interestingly, within two months, the National Fatwa Council reversed its ruling and announced that Barbican's nonalcoholic beer was consumable for Muslims. The council explained that the low alcohol content was, after all, incidental and not intoxicating.[28] One can imagine that Muslim consumers are often confused. On any given day, they may be told a particular beverage is haram, and the next day the same product is pronounced halal. No wonder fatwas issued by Malaysia's National Fatwa Council run the risk of appearing arbitrary and even on occasion contradictory.

Questions and discussions regarding genuine halal certification continue to produce differences of opinion among Muslim nations. A recent disagreement between Indonesian and Malaysian ulama regarding civet coffee illustrates this point. The particular coffee in question is made from coffee beans consumed by the Asian palm civet, a small nocturnal mammal, and related civets. The coffee berries pass through the animal's digestive tract, where they are processed with proteolytic enzymes and eventually defecated. Civet coffee, or *kopi luwak*, is regarded as a high-quality coffee among Indonesians and Malaysians. Indeed, the Indonesian Ulema Council considers *kopi luwak* a delicacy and unquestionably halal, which means that to trade or consume this coffee locally and internationally does not break any religious codes. However, in Malaysia, where demand for civet coffee is also growing, the JAKIM halal certification has been rejected. Why, one might wonder, is this coffee declared halal in Indonesia yet haram in Malaysia? Could it be because Sumatra, Indonesia, is the largest regional producer of this lucrative commodity, a connoisseur's coffee with global demand? The Gourmet Coffee Lovers website describes it as such: "Civet Coffee is one of the world's rarest coffees, as well as the most expensive, selling for up to $600 per pound on the world coffee market."[29] A post on another blog offers this information on prices: "One small cafe in Queensland, Australia has Kopi Luwak on the menu at $50.00 (US$33.00) per cup. Brasserie of Peter Jones department store in London's Sloane Square started selling a blend of Kopi Luwak peanut and Blue Mountain called Caffe Raro for £50 (US$99.00) a cup."[30]

Two major Indonesian Islamic organizations—MUI and Nahdlatul Ulama (NU)—debated whether to issue a fatwa on the consumption of *kopi luwak*. However, the government-backed Indonesian Ulema Council (MUI) recognized this product as halal and gave official approval. An article on the fatwa debate describes strategies to make civet coffee halal:

In the near future the [Malaysian] Board of Ulamas will be having a meeting with representatives of the largest Muslim organisation in Indonesia, with 100 million members. Maʿaruf Amin has already announced that Luwak [Civet] coffee is halal, and therefore permitted. However, the beans do have to be washed properly and they are not allowed to be damaged.[31]

"Damaged" means the broken beans should not be mixed with the unbroken beans. Ultimately, civet coffee was categorized as *mutananis*—meaning essentially that washing and handling it carefully removed the *najes* (impurities) and made it halal. This implies that the coffee bean itself is not inherently haram or impure.[32] Before this ruling was finalized, that is, when ulama threatened to issue a fatwa against the use of civet coffee in Indonesia, civet coffee prices skyrocketed, and its production rose by 30 percent.[33] This obvious relation between religious ruling and potential market value of any given commodity seems irrefutable. At the time of this writing, civet coffee has yet to receive halal status from the National Fatwa Council in Malaysia.

Following the lead of Malaysia and Indonesia, Iran, Turkey, and Egypt continue to develop and maintain their own halal standards,

Back of a box of Nougaz candy. *Gaz* is a traditional pistachio- or almond-filled candy from Iran. Among the logos on the box, one is a halal certification. Photo by the author.

overseeing the production of new items as well as creating new standards accordingly. This nationalist approach to certification almost certainly sets the stage for differences in religious opinion regarding the halal/haram issue.

In the United States, IFANCA, the Islamic Food and Nutrition Council of America, is a nonprofit Islamic organization that certifies halal food products in more than fifty countries. Headquartered in Chicago, IFANCA has representatives in Canada, Europe, China, Malaysia, India, and Pakistan. Its website describes the council's global reach: "IFANCA's halal certification symbol, the Crescent 'M', can be found on thousands of products around the globe. In addition, IFANCA maintains close working relationships with many Islamic centers and Islamic organizations throughout [the United States] and [the] world."[34] IFANCA has been recognized and endorsed by the following religious and governmental organizations:

- Malaysian Department of Islamic Development (JAKIM)
- Central Islamic Committee Office of Thailand
- Majelis Ulama Indonesia (MUI)
- Majlis Ugama Islam Singapura (MUIS)
- Muslim World League, Saudi Arabia
- USDA/FSIS International Programs
- United Arab Emirates (GSM)

However, in November 2000, Mohammad Mazhar Husseini, co-founder and executive director of IFANCA, resigned from the organization complaining about the halal certification process—a process he started decades ago. In an interview with Sound Vision, an Islamic information website, Husseini said of IFANCA, "They are interested in charging fees and certifying products and getting commission." Eat Halal website, in a 2009 article, cites Husseini from that interview and continues:

[Husseini] noted that in earlier years the organization was more education-oriented and community based in offering workshops and organizing seminars on Halal food issues, something that no longer takes place.

Offering more insight into the practices creating problems in the halal food industry, a book published in 2003 by Mian Riaz and Muhammad Chaudry, entitled "Halal Food Production," agrees that a number of the products that international companies are marketing as Halal are not as permissible as one might think.[35]

Husseini explained that IFANCA had been engaged in halal certification since the early 1990s—for small nominal fees. In later years, however, certification became the organization's main and most profitable activity.[36]

A Global Phenomenon

The Pew Forum on Religion and Public Life projected the global Muslim population to increase by about 35 percent between 2010 and 2030, from 1.6 billion to 2.2 billion. This rapid increase, based on a relatively high birth rate and growing affluence, translates to an increasingly lucrative Muslim consumer market. Because Muslims are expected to choose Islamically sanctioned substances and activities, these restrictions are being reflected in increasingly competitive marketing activities.[37] Few would argue that producing and distributing halal food in the twenty-first century has become a highly profitable business.

Agriculture and Agri-Food Canada has reported that by 2011 the halal food market grew to an estimated $632 billion annually. This means that 17 percent of the entire global food industry is based on halal potential. The organization reports, "Several multinationals, such as Tesco, McDonald's and Nestlé, have recognized this, and have expanded their halal approved product line. . . . [I]t is estimated that these multinationals control 90% of the global halal market."[38]

Reliable estimates suggest that 70 percent of Muslims worldwide follow halal standards and that 75 percent of Muslims follow dietary rules in the United States, meaning that even after having migrated, most Muslims still choose halal products.[39] Furthermore, Muslim halal consumers in the United States and Canada tend to be educated and affluent and thus generally more able to afford high prices for halal foodstuffs. Marketing halal food to Muslims living in the West, therefore, has become a multibillion-dollar industry, often accompanied by cutthroat competition.

In addition to the United Kingdom, Canada, and the United States, surprisingly large Muslim populations reside in other countries, including Argentina, which is home to at least 1 million Muslims. The largest emerging halal markets are India, with 177 million Muslims; China,

Table 2.1. Global halal food market size by region (US$)

Region	2009	2010	% Change
Africa	150.6 billion	155.9 billion	3.5%
Asia	400.0 billion	418.1 billion	4.5%
Europe	66.6 billion	69.3 billion	4.1%
Australia/Oceania	1.2 billion	1.6 billion	33.3%
Americas	16.1 billion	16.7 billion	3.6%
Total halal food market	634.5 billion	661.6 billion	4.3%

Sources: International Halal Integrity Alliance; Islamic Chamber of Commerce and Industry; 6th World Halal Forum, Kuala Lumpur, April 2011, http://worldhalalforum.org/; Agriculture and Agri-Food Canada

with 23 million; and Russia, with 16 million.[40] To meet the demand for emerging markets such as these, producers in Turkey and elsewhere aim to become major halal suppliers. In Turkey's case, the primary focus is on the European Union. Table 2.1 presents the 2009–2010 halal food market in various regions of the world.

The ramifications of the growth in halal food production and distribution are reflected in European economic reports. In France alone, the halal food market more than doubled from 2007 to 2012, to $7 billion.[41] The Halal Media network cites eye-opening data: "[T]he French Halal market is witnessing noticeable development contributing to as much as 5.5 billion Euros in 2010 . . . that approximately 4.5 billion were spent on food products and about one billion Euros at the restaurants . . . [and] the Halal market is targeting not just the seven million Muslims in France alone but also the overall 17 million Muslims throughout Europe."[42] Indisputably, France and other EU nations have established themselves as important links in the international halal import/export food chain.

Gaining Consumer Confidence

Whether East or West, the global food industry is increasingly supplying a huge demand for halal foods and must demonstrate that products are worthy of the halal certification label. When multinational corporations market halal foods, they risk opposition and criticism by devout

Muslim consumers questioning the legitimacy of halal products, especially products manufactured and produced in Western or non-Muslim-majority nations. Manufacturers and retailers are realizing that winning the trust of Muslim consumers as well as that of halal regulatory organizations may not be so easy. However, the often laborious and costly process of qualifying for the coveted halal certification logo promises skyrocketing profits as well as all-important consumer loyalty. Earning consumer trust and confidence has become a high priority in importing and exporting halal foodstuffs. Increasingly, the special care and handling of food is being afforded significant attention in the European halal market. An Agriculture and Agri-Food Canada report offers examples:

> In Europe the Port of Rotterdam in the Netherlands is a key halal entry port into the EU, as it dedicates a warehouse for halal products to ensure they do not come into contact with alcohol or pork. Several European companies, including Tahira Food (UK), Mecca Foods (Germany), Isla (France) and Halaland (France) are major halal food exporters and producers.[43]

With consumer approval in mind, Campbell Soup of Canada announced the addition of fifteen halal-certified products targeting Canada's growing Muslim community. The introduction and marketing of this halal line very shrewdly takes advantage of shifting Muslim demographics:

> "Campbell Canada is committed to making a difference and providing products that meet the diverse dietary needs of all Canadians," said Mark Childs, Campbell Canada's vice-president of marketing. "When we challenged our employees to develop new products linked to our vision of *Extraordinary, authentic nourishment for all*, the ideas they provided reflected the diversity of Canada, including the growing need for accessible, affordable and nourishing Halal-certified foods. With the passion, energy and commitment of the Campbell team we were able to launch our Halal-certified products."[44]

Another corporate giant, Kellogg's, which opened its first plant in the United Kingdom in 1938, has also entered the halal market. Most likely, its UK market analysts projected huge profits based on the number of Muslim children consuming sugary cereals for breakfast. In 2011 Kellogg's UK received certification from the Halal Food Authority

Campbell's soups in Canada. When Campbell Canada began offering halal-certified foods there, Americans started a Facebook page in 2010 called Boycott Campbell's Soup. Image from Houston Press, http://www.houstonpress.com/restaurants/why-id-rather-eat-halal-food-including-campbells-soup-6406111.

(HFA) for its plants in Manchester, Wrexham, and Bremen, England. The halal logo now appears next to the Royal Seal of approval on more than thirty Kellogg's cereals and snack bars.

For Muslim consumers, the question remains whether they can trust that food and beverages marketed and labeled as halal are, in reality, 100 percent halal. Especially with processed food, often the ingredients listed do not reveal hidden information, such as the sources of preservatives or coatings. The following list describes haram ingredients that may be hidden in packaged foods. It is known that many E numbers refer to contents with unlisted haram ingredients; generally, these are additives derived from animals and insects. While in no way a comprehensive compilation of haram substances, the list may give consumers pause for thought.[45]

HARAM INGREDIENTS HIDDEN IN PACKAGED FOODS

Bone phosphate—E542: This is an anticaking agent made from degreased steam extract of animal bones. It raises two concerns: Is the source animal halal or haram? And even if it were permissible to consume the source animal, was that same animal haram because basic halal slaughter standards were not met?

Cochineal/carmine—E120, E122: This is a red dye consisting of the dried bodies of female cochineal insects. Traces of this item are common in foods such as Tabasco sauce and were found in food items sold by Starbucks chains.[46] In June 2012 Starbucks promised to replace this coloring agent with lycopene, a tomato-based extract. In January 2012, the US Food and Drug Administration (FDA) began requiring food manufacturers to disclose use of this additive in their lists of ingredients.[47] In the past, failure to disclose these ingredients affected an "unaccounted number of consumers who are highly allergic to cochineal extract and its primary chemical ingredient, i.e., carminic acid. . . . [T]he coloring has been tied to dozens of cases of anaphylactic shock and near-death incidences."[48]

Gelatin: This is an odorless, tasteless, gluelike substance obtained by boiling the bones, hooves, and other waste parts of animals. Vegetarian alternatives exist, such as agar and Gelozone. Since slaughtering methods of the source animal cannot be known, Muslim consumers have no assurance that gelatin within a given food item has been sourced from halal animals and meets Islamic guidelines.

Glycerine—E422: This can be produced from animal fats, synthesized from propylene, or derived from fermentation of sugars.

L-cysteine: This is a flavor-enhancing agent manufactured from human hair, animal hair, and chicken feathers.[49]

Magnesium stearate: This can be made from animal fat and is often found in medicines.

Chymosin or rennin: This enzyme found in rennet is produced in the lining of a cow's stomach. It is often used in the manufacture of cheese.

Vanilla extract: Alcohol is the solvent of choice for producing the extract. Derived from the vanilla bean, the extract is normally kept in a solution containing alcohol.

Whey: Cream, butter, cheese, drinks, syrups, and powders are some of the products made from whey. The health hazards of using whey protein in the form of powder or liquid are connected to the hormones and other drugs fed to the animal producing the milk from which whey is derived.

Shellac—E904 Lac:[50] This is derived from the scarlet, resinous secretion of a number of species of insects of the superfamily *Coccoidea*. Vegans, vegetarians, and Muslims are among the groups voicing objections to eating insects. Other consumers may simply oppose ingestion because of personal health concerns or ethical issues.

Emulsifiers—E470 to E483: As described earlier, E numbers often denote haram derivatives from animals and insects.[51]

Given that this is only a partial list, one can understand why Muslim consumers voice concern about the accurate listing of hidden ingredients, food sources, and processing methods. It may take an army of nutritionists, chemists, and concerned citizens to ultimately bring about this type of change. Whether the consumer is a vegetarian, vegan, kosher-conscious Jew, halal-conscious Muslim, or individual suffering from food allergies, all would benefit from stricter labeling standards, particularly of processed foods.

One of the world's leading food brands, Mars, is responding rapidly to consumer concerns. Mars executives apparently well understand the importance of consumer satisfaction. A section of the Mars UK website on product suitability for several consumer groups revealed the company's well-considered marketing strategies.[52] The page, which has been removed, listed corporate policies and goals by consumer category headings: vegetarian, halal, kosher, and allergens. The Mars corporate approach demonstrated sensitivity to consumer preferences at all levels—moral, religious, and medical—and reflects growing concern about hidden ingredients in food. In the twenty-first century, consumers are increasingly educating themselves to protect their health and the health of their families.

Whether Muslim or not, reading about L-cysteine in this *Natural News* article might alter one's decision to buy:

While the thought of eating dissolved hair might make some people uneasy, most Western consumers ultimately have no principled objections [to] doing so. For Jews and Muslims, however, hair-derived L-cysteine poses significant problems. Muslims are forbidden from eating anything derived from a human body, and many rabbis forbid hair consumption for similar reasons. Even rabbis who permit the consumption of hair would forbid it if it came from corpses—and since much L-cysteine comes from China, where sourcing and manufacturing practices are notoriously questionable, this is a real concern. In one case, a rabbi forbade the consumption of L-cysteine because the hair had been harvested during a ritual at a temple in India.[53]

Leaders in the food industry, especially those savvy corporate executives hoping to establish an edge in the halal market, would do well to continue paying close attention to consumer preferences and concerns.

Legitimately Halal or Not?

Across the globe, pious Muslims continue to question the legitimacy of halal foods. Surimi-based food products are one example. *Surimi* is the Japanese word for "ground meat," although seafood products, mostly fish, are the main ingredients. Surimi is not a new technique; rather, it has been used in Japan for centuries as a means for preserving fish. In the process today, fish is mechanically deboned and washed, then mashed to a thick, wet substance. To this mixture meat plasma is added as well as cryoprotectant to ensure long shelf life when frozen.[54] Surimi is a highly processed food product, with monosodium glutamate, MSG, used as a flavor enhancer and an assortment of starches and gums added to create the expected texture. Surimi enables producers to take cheap fish and upgrade it to a taste and texture reminiscent of the most expensive seafood available, specifically crab and lobster.[55] Researcher Nurul Huda and colleagues give a brief early history of surimi's industrial-scale production:

> The technology became popular and gained favorable response after being introduced in the US market in 1980. In 1994, surimi production was about 400,000 tons a year and about one million tons of surimi-based products are produced annually. They are widely marketed in Japan, USA, Korea and European countries.[56]

Surimi goes into artificial crabmeat, a very popular ingredient in Asian foods like sushi. Muslim consumers must ask whether surimi is a halal food, since ingredients deemed haram are added during the manufacturing process.

Another questionably halal food is a popular Indonesia snack—beef jerky, or *dendeng*. The *Jakarta Globe* has reported that in an investigation by BPOM, the national food and drug monitoring agency, beef jerky was found to contain pork despite its halal labeling. The head of

BPOM, Husniah Rubiana Thamrin, said "her agency conducted a second test on 34 products collected randomly from supermarkets and found that four contained pig DNA. . . . [T]he BPOM has issued an order to all its offices nationwide to raid establishments that sold the tainted beef products and confiscate them."[57] Although the confiscated items were registered with health agencies, it was discovered that the Indonesian Ulema Council had not certified those products, and therefore, the halal labeling was fraudulent. Indeed, manufacturers had mixed pork with the beef jerky to cut costs.

In a country with the vast majority of Muslim citizens, selling pork as a halal-labeled product is a serious crime: "Municipalities could charge businesses with violating the Consumer Protection Law, which carries a jail term of up to five years and a Rp 2 billion ($186,000) fine."[58] Still, the craze for halal packaged food is increasing despite the rising incidence of food crimes.

Foods like surimi and *dendeng* are enjoyed by a significant number of Muslims. For producers to continue selling these items in Asian countries and elsewhere, they must find ways not only to have them certified halal but also to win back consumer confidence.

Halal Certification as Big Business

Issuing halal certificates means big business and big money for Muslim- and non-Muslim-majority nations alike. In China, with the world's second-largest emerging Muslim population, food companies are eagerly jumping into the fray. China has had multiple false starts in the halal market, however, primarily because its accreditation procedures have fallen noticeably short. Due to fraudulent products with which China has flooded the market in general, Muslims are wary that China's halal food production is not trustworthy and certainly not in accord with Islamic principles. In 2008, for example, a high-profile scandal involving milk resulted in the death of six infants and sickened more than 300,000 consumers.[59] Another case in 2008 involved frozen vegetables sold by Whole Foods Market in the United States that were labeled as organic produce from China. As it turned out, the organic certification from China was not traceable.[60] Chinese food producers, not wanting to fall behind in the halal market, are soliciting help from Malaysian companies like Master Malaysia Global that are supporting Chinese efforts to master food production according to halal principles and to meet Malaysian halal standards.[61] Building success with the Malaysian Muslim population may be Chinese producers' best hope for competing successfully and legitimately in the halal global market.

China's food industry is only one among many in non-Muslim-majority nations vying for shares in the halal market. These national industries' agendas depend entirely on halal certification, a process that generates profit in two directions: for the agency issuing certification and for the company receiving it. The issuing agency receives a plethora of fees for applications, legal contracts and renewals, and so forth. In Britain, the Halal Monitoring Committee "is a non-profit organisation and its objective is to serve the community. However, to operate such an enormous system without costs and overhead is nonsensical. Therefore fees are applied to the businesses wishing to be certified."[62] As if anticipating complaints, the organization offers assurance that costs will be kept to a minimum. Halal Australia has a nonrefundable application fee of $100 (Australian) and an assessment fee of $200. These fees are just to get the wheels turning; certification will not be cheap, and more than likely, costs will pass to the consumer.

In Muslim-majority nations such as Indonesia, agencies are vying fiercely for halal certification authority. Halal Focus reports, "The Indonesian Ulema Council (MUI) has criticized Nahdlatul Ulama's (NU) plan to draft halal and honesty certifications for its members."[63] Nahdlatul Ulama, also spelled Nahdatul Ulama, is a traditionalist Sunni Islam group that funds hospitals and schools and helps combat poverty in Indonesia. The issuing of halal certifications by NU is subject to government fees because the government does not subsidize the office as it does MUI. The MUI agency claims to represent all Islamic organizations, inclusive of NU. However, NU members heatedly question that assumption. Meanwhile, the two Muslim organizations continue striving for more political power. Unfortunately, such power plays for halal certification authority tend to discredit both groups, fueling suspicion and mistrust among consumers.

In 2009, the Indonesian government announced that it "would no longer recognise New Zealand halal certification authorities."[64] This announcement presented new opportunities for yet another agency, Al-Rasoul Halal Certification, a company claiming to offer New Zealand exporters an "internationally accepted halal certification." Al-Rasoul Halal Certification agency guaranteed that the certificate would be acceptable to Islamic countries, especially those with a history of distrusting halal products imported from non-Muslim-majority nations. The

New Zealand Federation of Islamic Associations strongly objected, insisting that the Al-Rasoul Halal Certification agency lacked requisite resources to carry out inspections in New Zealand. The federated associations leveled the same objection at the Indonesian certifier.

Meanwhile, the Indonesian Ulema Council commented that a "product will be able to be sold as halal there [Indonesia] only if it has the council's own halal certification."[65] It is apparent that the Indonesian Ulema Council is not willing to share halal certification profits with any other organization and controls all exports to Indonesia—a country that constitutes the largest number of Muslims on earth. In the past, fatwas did not affect cases in Indonesian civil courts, and even the religious courts rarely relied on fatwas when making decisions. As 2012 economic journal article details how the council has gained influence:

> MUI has nonetheless been effective in using fatwa to influence state policy on Islamic legal traditions in a way that favours its own increasingly conservative orthodox positions on social and doctrinal issues.
> This has led to an important shift in recent years, as new regulation has made certain fatwa issued by MUI in relation to banking and halal certification enforceable as binding law. . . . MUI has a comprehensive formal role in relation to halal food labeling and advertising in general.[66]

Indonesia's decision to hand over halal certification to religious authorities sets a disturbing precedent. By rejecting all halal certifications except those issued by MUI, Indonesia's government has created a religious monopoly through which economic gains are tightly controlled and manipulated.

Essentially, Indonesia has proclaimed itself the exclusive arbiter of halal law and, in doing so, has set itself apart from all other Muslim agencies and Sharia-based nations. This action may well be taken as an insult by the rest of the Islamic world community since any opinions concerning halal authenticity—other than those proscribed by Indonesian authorities—are now, by default, considered invalid.

What began as a few *ayat*, or verses, in the seventh century intended to guide individuals toward spiritual and physical well-being have unexpectedly translated into a twenty-first-century phenomenon. Out of those Qur'anic verses a gigantic global food industry has emerged, driven by fraudulent manufacturers, cut-throat competitors, profit mongers, and corrupt politicians. In the end, it is the Muslim consumer, exploited and confused, who stands to lose the most.

CHAPTER 3

Halal Slaughtering of Animals:
Perils and Practices

The act of intertwining Brand Islam with religious observance exploits one of the core principles of Islam; namely, the act of *'ibaadah* (worship) of Allah. *'Ibaadah* refers to more than worshipping Allah. It infers that Muslims are abiding by all of his rules and recommendations. Purchasing and consuming halal products is one of the keys to *'ibaadah*. Another essential component is the method of *dhabihah*, or Islamic slaughter. Because the name of God must be invoked at the moment of slaughter, all meat and meat products labeled halal must follow this basic *dhabihah* regulation.

In non-Muslim-majority countries, purchasing halal meat or meat products often signals affiliation with or belonging to the greater Muslim community, the *umma*. Equally important if not more so is the core Islamic principle of *tawhid*, meaning "divine unity." For the devout Muslim, every small act engaged in throughout the day, including the act of eating, becomes a reminder, an experience of unity with Allah, that is, *tawhid al-'ibaadah* (worship).[1] In other words, the individual must choose what is deemed to be halal, as commanded by Allah, and avoid all that is haram, or forbidden. In attempting to maintain a unified relationship with the Divine, those individuals who intentionally choose to purchase and consume halal products, including meat, are purposefully practicing their act of *'ibaadah*.

Many of the cultural clashes in Western Europe today center on halal issues—especially the slaughter of animals according to Islamic law, or *dhabihah*. The Islamic act of slaughtering is preceded by the prayerful word *bismillah* (in the name of Allah). *Dhabihah* is not simply ritual sacrifice but rather a powerful acknowledgment, as stipulated by the Qur'an, of Allah's domination over all things and provision of daily sustenance to all believers. As seen from this perspective, *dhabihah* is a necessary act of gratitude. The following Qur'anic verses make this point clear:

SURA 6:118
So eat of (meats)
On which Allah's name
Hath been pronounced.
If ye have faith
In His signs.

SURA 6:121
Eat not of (meats)
On which Allah's name
Hath not been pronounced:
That would be impiety
But the evil ones
Ever inspire their friends
To contend with you
If ye were to obey them,
Ye would indeed be Pagans.

Devout Muslims in the West, especially those who follow halal dietary dictates, are caught in the struggle between animal rights activism and the preservation of religious rights and freedoms. The practice of ritual slaughter without initial stunning has created heated debate, spurred many scientific studies, and resulted in philosophic clashes among academics holding opposing opinions, scientists working in regulatory and meat industries, and meat-processing companies. Numerous studies have been conducted gauging and comparing the different levels of pain experienced by animals when electrically shocked or when subjected to a rapid slashing of the throat. In 1978 a German veterinary publication reported that halal slaughtering causes less pain to calves and sheep than slaughtering animals after stunning by a "captive bolt," a term for the industry's standard procedure.[2] However, in another scientific study thirty years later—addressing both *shechita* (ritual slaughter according to Jewish dietary laws) and halal slaughter—research findings contradict the 1978 German study: "The combination of false aneurysms and collateral routes to the brain present a risk of sustained consciousness during religious slaughter in cattle."[3] This study indicates that if such aneurysms occur, the animal can feel pain and suffering ensues until the animal is completely dead. Such studies provide the media, politicians, and certain activist organizations plenty of information to use factually or in a biased manner when advancing particular agendas.

The politics of slaughter are receiving increased attention, particularly where Muslim culture has been imported to the West. In Europe particularly, politicians focus on the issue of Islamic slaughter to demonstrate barbaric and savage Muslim practices. Indeed, cultural tensions between Europeans and Muslims residing in Western Europe are intensifying. Oxford University scholar Tariq Ramadan asserts, "Over the last two decades Islam has become connected to so many controversial debates . . . it is difficult for ordinary citizens to embrace this new Muslim presence as a positive factor."[4] Moreover, cultural tensions in Western Europe are spawning anti-Muslim movements such as the coalition of Danish and English activists called Stop the Islamisation of Europe (SIOE). Widespread fear over possible demographic shifts and concerns that Muslims will eventually "take over" are giving rise to new political policies, such as Denmark's 2014 ban on the religious slaughter of animals for kosher and halal meat.[5]

Here I examine three key issues: the role that halal slaughter plays in Western political systems, the subject of halal labeling and certification, and the increased use of science and technology to detect fraud, especially in the meat industry.

Islamic Slaughter and Western Politics

In January 2013, animal rights activists gathered in Warsaw to protest ritual slaughter. Protesters demonstrated against the "reintroduction of kosher and halal slaughter methods, after Poland's Supreme Court ruling banned the practice [in] December [2012]."[6] Two reasons were given for reversing the ban. According to the agriculture ministry, Poland stood to lose millions of dollars by prohibiting halal- and kosher-slaughtered products to be exported to Saudi Arabia and Israel. At the same time, Polish government officials meant to avoid offending Poland's small Jewish and Muslim communities. As evidenced by the ongoing protests and political clashes in Poland, this issue has gained significant momentum in Eastern and Western European environments.

Already by July 2011, the International Halal Integrity Alliance officially responded to the question of religious animal slaughter, given that the issue had arisen time and again in the media and various political arenas:

> The issue of animal welfare in religious slaughter is most often taken at face value where only the negatives are highlighted and up-played leading to a worldwide outcry and marginalization of the Jews and the Muslims worldwide. . . . Clearly in the matter of religious slaughter, animal welfare goes beyond the slaughter boxes alone, and balanced information that looks at both sides of the coin should be made available to all for a fair judgment of the situation without sidelining the religious rights of the Muslims and Jews across the world.[7]

On June 28, 2011, the Dutch Parliament voted to ban ritual slaughter. After the news was announced, the chief rabbi of Holland, Racobs Binyomin, responded that the ban was comparable to the laws during the Nazi occupation imposed in Holland that banned the kosher slaughtering of animals.[8]

In a 2006 *Journal of Law and Religion* article, Israeli law professors Pablo Lerner and Alfredo Mordechai Rabello acknowledged both sides of this type of ban, in that "the right to freedom of religion or belief requires nation-states to respect the rights of religious minorities that engage in ritual slaughter, even if they recognize the importance of avoiding unnecessary suffering of animals. . . . [H]owever, we must respond to the legal reality that religious freedom rights are not absolute and can be qualified where there is a strong enough state interest."[9] It should also be noted that European nation-states all ratified the Universal Declaration of Human Rights (UDHR), a document that recognizes freedom of religious practice.

In the Netherlands halal food gained an important share of the market before being banned.[10] Indeed, halal food products are still sold in Dutch supermarkets and served in hospitals. School administrators have included halal food choices on children's lunch menus. This trend toward halal availability is being questioned not only by animal rights groups but also by those who fear Islamization of the Dutch nation.[11] Inarguably, animal rights groups in the Netherlands and elsewhere have proven the most vocal opponents to ritual slaughter, contending that for humanitarian purposes animals must be stunned before they are slaughtered. Their core argument is that kosher and halal slaughter causes the animal unnecessary suffering.

The standard response to these concerns is that banning kosher and halal slaughter necessarily infringes on religious rights. In addition to Holland, Sweden, and Luxembourg, the non-EU members Norway and Switzerland have banned ritual slaughter. The issue of animal slaughter without stunning the animals has become complicated by allegations of anti-Semitism and xenophobia. However, "the EU, which bans the killing of non-stunned animals, allows religious exemptions."[12] In the *Official Journal of the European Union*, the EU directive states these exemptions in the section titled "European Convention for the Protection of Animals for Slaughter," Article 17:

1. Each Contracting Party may authorize derogations from the provisions concerning prior stunning in the following cases:
   * slaughtering in accordance with religious rituals,
   * emergency slaughtering when stunning is not possible, slaughtering of poultry and rabbits by authorized methods causing instantaneous death,
   * killing of animals for the purposes of health control where special reasons make this necessary.[13]

One can clearly detect a loophole, if not a contradiction, in the EU's regulatory position regarding the freedom of religious practices.

Jewish people in Germany have faced unique challenges, historically, regarding kosher slaughter. One is hardly surprised to learn that "the Nazis vilified the Jewish method of slaughtering animals . . . [and] the notorious Nazi propaganda film 'The Eternal Jew' shows gory scenes of Jews slaughtering animals."[14] Rabbi Reuven Yaacobov of Berlin suggests that kosher and halal slaughter styles are more humane than the industrial slaughter practices followed in Germany.[15] While the German government allows contemporary Jewish communities to practice kosher slaughter, less tolerance is demonstrated toward the Muslim community. Because slaughtering of animals without prior stunning has been banned in Germany since 1995, German halal butchers face difficulties practicing their craft. In 2002 a halal butcher challenged the ban and won his case in court. In 2011 he finally received a legal permit to slaughter thirty sheep and two cows a week in accordance with halal procedure. Still, he continued battling extensive bureaucratic regulations and requirements and facing opposition by German animal rights activists.

In France, the offering of no-bacon burgers at Quick, a fast-food chain, has sparked heated criticism among French politicians who argue that this practice deprives non-Muslims of their right to a normal menu. What is missing from this rhetoric is the rights of Muslims who cannot eat from Quick restaurants serving a non-halal menu. Do they have any rights or choices in a situation such as this? Out of 346 Quick restaurants in France, only 22 sell halal items.[16] That leaves 324 Quick restaurants with non-halal menus intact.

Meanwhile, French politicians using such discriminatory rhetoric evade discussion of the advantageous economic outcome from Quick restaurants serving halal burgers. Equally important, they do a superb job of obfuscating the truth behind the situation. A *Bloomberg* writer notes state involvement in the company's decision as contradictory:

> If it's a savvy business decision—Quick says sales doubled at restaurants that have tested the concept—the move has also opened a new chapter in the perennial war over how much society should accommodate Muslim traditions. . . . Quick is 94-percent owned by a subsidiary of the state-controlled bank Caisse des Depots et Consignations. Some critics find it absurd that the French state—which has such a strict interpretation of secularism that it does not allow girls to wear Muslim headscarves to school—is technically behind the operation.[17]

Stéphane Gatignon, mayor of the Parisian suburb Sevran, expressed his own concerns about Quick's decision to offer a halal menu. Gatignon, who "is a member of the environmentalist party Europe Ecologie, says he is worried the Quick in his town will become a Muslims-only hangout, preventing ethnic groups from mingling."[18] His professed concern is an important reminder that many French citizens assume that all Muslims are foreigners who speak the same language and, equally presumptuous, that a French citizen cannot be a Muslim. This is analogous to the assumption that all Catholics are from the same nation, speak the same language, and when congregating, exclude everyone else from social intercourse. That such an uninformed statement could come from a French municipal government official is revelatory.

Yet another government official, Interior Minister Claude Guéant, insisted, "We don't want foreign town councillors making halal food obligatory in canteen meals . . . or regulating mixed bathing in swimming pools."[19] During the 2012 French elections, the issue of halal meat proved to be a hot topic. Mohammed Moussaoui, head of the

French Council of the Muslim Religion, voiced concern about the issue of halal meat entering the campaign because "it creates tensions in the society." Rabbi Bruno Fiszon said that labeling meat only by the way it was slaughtered "would lead to stigmatization."[20] Others have contended that if new regulatory standards are set in place requiring that meat be labeled with the method of slaughter, the same standard should apply to all meat products. Doing so would send a message of fairness to the consumer, who would be able to gauge the quality of animal products based also on method of slaughter. Package labeling would clearly state slaughtering methods used in the meat industry: gassing, electrically stunning before slaughtering, and killing by blows to the head. Some observers have pointed out that concern for animals does not appear to be the basis for anti-halal regulations: "Yunus Dudhwala, chairperson of the Halal Monitoring Committee in Britain, said he believed that animal welfare was a 'red herring' because there was little interest shown in factory farming methods and the conditions of animal transportation prior to slaughter."[21]

If Australians took an example from the French, then the Australian government would have to document on packaging labels the approved method of killing a joey, a young kangaroo—either bashing it over the head with a heavy object or chopping its head off with an axe. Large fish like salmon are sometimes bashed on the head with a wooden bat, and many are seriously injured but still conscious when they are cut open.[22] Other cruel practices including submerging live lobsters into boiling water. If the aim of labeling methods of slaughter is to inform the consumer, then the fair thing would be to label all the other commonly used legal techniques to kill animals before they are sold at market. It is hard to imagine labels saying, "This salmon clobbered on the head" or "This chicken gassed" or "This cow electrocuted first before throat cut." Occasionally the first attempt at stunning does not work, so the animal is stunned a second time. Thus the label might read, "This lamb stunned twice (due to technical difficulties)." Would consumers appreciate such information on their meat packaging? Perhaps the gruesome reality about how animals are slaughtered would reduce the huge consumption of animal flesh—motivating poultry, fish, and meat industries to avoid clear labeling since doing so would likely affect consumers' purchasing decisions. Indeed, comprehensive labeling practices might significantly increase the number of people who would choose alternatives to meat. Is it reasonable to require detailed labeling information only for those animals slaughtered according to halal or kosher standards? In the name of religious freedom, perhaps we must recognize differences in tradition and respect the diverse opinions of others, even when it comes to the processing of meat.

Halal products have a significant market in France, which has the largest Muslim population in the European Union—between four and six million. Despite economic gains gleaned from emerging halal markets, the French continue to exploit the issue of Islamic slaughtering in order to achieve political favor. A 2012 *Guardian* article reports that Nicolas Sarkozy, the twenty-third president of France, waffled on this topic:

> Sarkozy, in a major election speech, proposed a change to the law to impose transparency on the way animals were killed, a U-turn on his earlier comment that this was not an issue. This statement provoked anger not only among Muslims, who felt they were being used as an electioneering tool, but also Jews whose kosher meat follows the same ritual ways of killing as halal meat. Richard Prasquier, the head of the Jewish representative council in France, condemned the claims. He had been, until then, a staunch Sarkozy supporter. Nathalie Kosciusko-Morizet, spokeswoman of Sarkozy's campaign, distanced herself from the controversy.[23]

During periods of economic uncertainty, as has certainly been the case in France, politicians would do well to consider what is best for their nations' economic growth. Instead, time and energy are spent in endless tirades about the growing presence of Muslims. One might argue that the fuss over bacon burgers is actually a cover-up for Islamophobia. The halal food industry, along with the face veil (*niqab*), headscarf (*hijab*), and Muslim men's beards have become daily topics in European media and politics. Along with the issue of mosque construction, these topics promise to continue dominating headlines and permeating campaign speeches.

The concern over Islamic slaughtering practices reflects a shared angst, an awareness that the French Muslim population is growing exponentially. It is reasonable to assume that ultimately, Muslim citizens will defy French traditional authority and insist on preserving their own customs, dress codes, food, and rights as guaranteed constitutionally. Indeed, many view Islam as an invasive culture with the potential power to destroy European civilization. One cannot escape the irony here. French government officials apparently and conveniently fail to recall centuries past when France freely invaded Muslim-dominated regions, established colonial rule, and coerced entire populations to adopt French customs. Now descendants of former subjects have chosen France as their homeland, and the French government and non-Muslim citizens will have to come to terms with that fact rather than categorize all Muslims as invaders and destroyers.[24]

As in France, issues surrounding halal meat are coming to the fore in the United Kingdom. British ministers have succeeded in enacting a requirement that all meat slaughtered according to Islamic custom must be accompanied by proper permits before it may be sold in the market.[25] As part of a sweeping 2010 coalition, "members of the European Parliament, by a vote of 559 to 54, passed Amendment 205 to the food-information regulation, which requires all meat from ritually slaughtered animals to be labeled: 'Derived from animals that have not been stunned prior to slaughter.'"[26] With the label attached to European packaged meat, more challenges and controversies have arisen around the halal issue.

In Britain, the idea of serving halal meat as part of the school lunch menu has met with angry response. Some parents took matters into their own hands in 2010, sending warning notes home to other parents to heighten awareness of what is transpiring in school cafeterias. "Don't let the Muslims force their barbaric ways on us," advises an anti-halal leaflet in London's Harrow borough, which is 7 percent Muslim.[27] This leaflet, distributed by an unnamed group outside a school in Harrow, protested the arbitrary decision to serve only Islamic-approved halal meat at all high schools in the area. Parents were not consulted or asked for their approval. As a result, an anti-halal blogger wrote, many parents staged a furious protest objecting to their children having "no option but to eat meat slaughtered following Islamic teachings specifically for Muslims."[28]

The BBC reported in March 2013 that pork DNA surfaced in halal chicken sausages being served at a primary school in Westminster, central London: "Tests on a sample from Burdett Coutts School revealed the presence of lamb and pork DNA in lean minced beef" used to make the sausages.[29] These incidents underscore two important points: because of the highly sensitive nature of the halal slaughtering issue, non-Muslim parents must be consulted before the implementation of a halal-only policy for school lunch menus; and for Muslim parents, it is essential to be able to trust the labeling of halal food items.

Adulterated halal foods served to Muslim prisoners in England have made headlines as well. Pork DNA has been detected in halal meat pies and pasties served in English prisons, the *Daily Mail* reported in February 2013: "This is not a matter of dietary preference but of Islamic law. There are clear hospital and prison rules that Halal meat must be on the menu."[30] In the United Kingdom, then, one begins to see emerging sociological patterns around halal foods and meats indicative of the lack of trust moving in both directions between Muslims and non-Muslims.

Blogs and Halal Meat

Islamophobic campaigns against Muslims and their dietary requirements are especially vituperative on the Internet. One cannot overestimate the power of social media to stir antagonism. Again, the irony in online messages such as "Muslims should go home" is that most Muslims are already home, including those residing in the West as citizens. Many are second- or third-generation citizens, and some claim more ancient roots. No matter where Muslims call home or where they were born, online attacks labeling them as the enemy easily manipulate the minds of millions of non-Muslims—and promise to be far more damaging than political rallies or grassroots protests.

On an Australian blog Michael Smith expresses his frustration around halal slaughter and government regulations in a 2009 comment:

> lets get politicans to ban this practice as they have in NZ [New Zealand]. It is slowly deviding aussie in to religious groups, next step, their own law, then jailing people who go outside their law, as opposed to our law. stand up aussies, and get in touch with your local pollie.[31]

Blog posts such as this reveal much about the mindset of some citizens toward Muslims and perhaps broader public opinion as well. Conservative activist and blogger Pamela Geller, author of the widely read blog American Thinker, spearheaded a boycott of food giant Campbell Company when Campbell's attempted to distribute halal soup in Canadian markets. A 2010 article in the *Washington Post* reports that Geller claimed to have no problem with the availability of halal or kosher food but adamantly suggested a link between the Islamic Society of North America (ISNA)—an entity responsible for halal certification and labeling in the United States and Canada—and Middle East terrorist organizations, including the Muslim Brotherhood and Hamas.[32] Geller and her organization are listed online by the Southern Poverty Law Center as a US-based anti-Muslim hate group.[33]

Pamela Geller's website and her American Thinker blog are of particular concern because she uses the Internet as a tool for rumormongering and making serious claims without referencing or validating her sources. In her blog, Geller provides insights regarding Butterball turkey, a commonly purchased halal food item found in most American supermarkets. She calls upon "good Americans" (non-Muslims) to take a stand against halal turkeys:

> Did you know that the turkey you're going to enjoy on Thanksgiving Day this Thursday is probably halal? If it's a Butterball turkey, then it certainly is—whether you like it or not. In my book *Stop the Islamization of America: A Practical Guide to the Resistance*, I report at length on the meat industry's halal scandal: its established practice of not separating halal meat from non-halal meat, and not labeling halal meat as such. And back in October 2010, I reported more little-noted but explosive new revelations: that much of the meat in Europe and the United States is being processed as halal without the knowledge of the non-Muslim consumers who buy it. . . . In a little-known strike against freedom, yet again, we are being forced into consuming meat slaughtered by means of a torturous method: Islamic slaughter. The same Islamic law that mandates that animals be cruelly slaughtered according to halal requirements also teaches hatred of and warfare against unbelievers, the oppression of women, the extinguishing of free speech, and much more that is inimical to our freedom. Don't support it on this celebration of freedom. Join our Facebook group, "Boycott Butterball."[34]

Geller's message starts with halal turkeys and ends with a diatribe on the mistreatment of Muslim women and threats to American freedoms. "Americans" in Geller's discussion apparently excludes Muslim Americans. Geller's main concern is Butterball, a corporation attempting to capture a segment of American consumers with special needs. Why blame Muslims for this marketing decision? Butterball is not owned or operated by Muslims, nor does any Muslim stand to profit financially from Butterball's choices. Living in a free market economy, Geller has the option to purchase turkey from a variety of companies and is under no obligation to buy Butterball. One wonders if, in an effort to market her own book, she found Muslim bashing and corporate criticism useful. As with any opportunist, pursuing a scapegoat agenda may be the quickest way to get attention and to promote her own materials. According to the Southern Poverty Law Center page about Geller,

> in January 2012, Geller formed Stop the Islamization of Nations (SION), a new international organization, with herself as executive director. SION joins with the European anti-Muslim group that inspired it, Anders Gravers' Denmark-based Stop the Islamization of Europe (SIOE). The new organization intends to create a "common American/ European coalition of free people to oppose the advance of Islamic law." It will also publicize the names of politicians, activists and others who promote the alleged Islamic agenda in the West.[35]

Countless blogs with various political, racial, and hate-filled agendas abound on the Internet. These include a variety of Islam-bashing sites on which ordinary citizens actively participate—virtual spaces for bigots who use the privacy of blog zones as bully pulpits, never having to expose their true identities.

One of the more infamous public bloggers is Joe Kaufman, whose absurd statements following 9/11 about the US government's right to use nuclear weapons in response and whose questionable ties to extremist organizations have earned him significant notoriety. He was even skewered on *The Daily Show* by Jon Stewart, at which time Kaufman was, ironically, leading a group called Americans against Hate. In March 2013 Kaufman contributed an article published on a website called *Frontpage Mag* entitled "Can Buying Food Contribute to Terrorism?" The article states that because certification agencies are linked with jihadist organizations, halal-certified products in the United States must be avoided at all costs. Kaufman calls into question Campbell's decision to obtain halal certification from the Islamic Society of North America and the company's subsequent alliance with IFANCA, one of the largest American halal certifying groups. Of the many commenters responding to Kaufman's article, here is a sampling:[36]

KAFIR4LIFE
We don't hire muslims. We refuse to shop in their stores. We don't shop in stores that hire muslims, but tell management as to why. muslims can be dangerous. Sometimes they explode, sometimes they try to kill you. Not all the time . . . sometimes. It's not possible to differentiate be-

tween the ones about to explode from the ones that will explode later. It's a safety issue. Concern for my life and my family's life comes first. Some muslims cannot be trusted to not explode, some muslims cannot be trusted to not murder, but you cannot tell which will and which will later. Best to avoid muslims.

BRUJO BLANCO

It is apparent that the Muslims want to incrementally impose their religious laws on us. This can very well reach a point that these religious laws will become our laws. They do not believe in the free practice of religion. Dearborn, MI is siding with Muslims in their religious disputes with Christians. Arrests have been made.

ADINAK

Islamic front groups operate like Mafia cartels, hydra-like. They have FRONT groups all over the world. In other words, through partnering with legitimate entities they gain a veneer of "kosher" certified, or in their case, halal.

In effect, not only does the above effectuate public mainstreaming, but it is much easier to launder their proceeds. And launder they do. How do I know this? Well, peek within—http://adinakutnicki.com/about.

This is where I cut my Islamic "teeth" . . . "tracking and tracing" . . . following the money trail . . .

POUPIC

Fight back. Every time you see the sign for Hallal on anything, don't buy it. Fighting Islamic terror should be everybody's business.

MONEY JIHAD

IFANCA also maintains tax-exempt status with the IRS although the disclosures in its tax returns indicate that it is an ordinary for-profit business: http://moneyjihad.wordpress.com/2012/01/24/for-pr. . . . In addition to the terrorist ties, they are tax evaders too.

One can easily see that a "community" of uninformed, right-wing commenters and bloggers can create confusion rather than clarity, damaging the image of all Muslims and furthering the misperception that behind halal labeling is a Muslim global conspiracy of terror.

Halal Fraud and Misrepresentation: A Meaty Matter

Like any other segment of the general population, American Muslims are vulnerable to market exploitation. A 2011 investigation by the district attorney's office in Anaheim, California, provides a clear example. In November 2011, the DA's office determined fraud on the part of a local supermarket selling meat as halal. Anaheim Super King Market had been labeling generic meat and mixed meats as halal in an effort to appeal to the Muslim consumer. Eventually, the Orange County District Attorney's office announced a $527,000 settlement with Anaheim Super King Market, the *Orange County Register* reports:

> The investigation began in early 2010. Anaheim Super King Market didn't admit fault. . . . The market now must only purchase meat that is clearly labeled halal on the invoice and packaging and must ensure that halal meat is properly segregated. The settlement money doesn't go to individual victims, because it would be too difficult to determine who exactly was victimized, a D.A.'s spokeswoman has said. Instead, the money goes into a fund to help prosecute fraud cases. Several Muslims said they should be entitled to compensation and are considering filing claims.[37]

This type of fraud, selling dubious meat products as halal, can happen anywhere at any time. However, the unique aspect of this fraud is its direct connection to religion. Muslim consumers select halal food items based almost exclusively on label information. If the label itself is inaccurate, what are the consumer's options? Because halal products can command high prices and generate impressive profits, there is always the danger of fraud.

Authentic and consensual halal certification is requisite. When two Islamic groups clash as to which food qualifies as halal, it can be difficult to determine which group Muslim consumers can believe. A battle for authority is raging among halal labeling entities, making food choice even more difficult for the consumer. Controversy surrounding the KFC company decision in Britain in 2010 to serve halal chicken extended beyond Muslim-bashing when Muslims also responded suspiciously to the announcement:[38]

> On the one hand, non-Muslim groups [set up] Internet petitions against KFC's move to sell halal-only products in the trial at 74 of its

outlets across the country. On the other, Muslims themselves [ques-tioned] whether, in fact, the poultry . . . sold [was] truly halal.[39]

The problem pivoted around KFC's decision to use stunning proce-dures before slaughtering the birds. When it publicly announced this decision, KFC spared itself the ire of animal rights groups but offended certain Muslims who insisted that the chicken could not be labeled ha-lal. An article in *The National* noted that the fast-food chain was also "summoned to a meeting with the Lancashire Council of Mosques (LCM) after it was 'inundated' with calls from Muslims asking how ha-lal KFC's 'halal' really was."[40] A non-Muslim consumer commented,

> I think to have halal forced on us and to not have a choice is wrong.
> They are saying the food is blessed, but that is not my religion. They
> have also taken out all their pork and bacon products. Surely, this is dis-
> criminating against people who do eat pig in this country.[41]

Ultimately, DNA India reported, due to a "boycott by angry custom-ers," KFC scrapped its halal-only menu.[42]

Across the globe in China, in early 2013 the Uyghurs, a Muslim mi-nority, rose up in opposition to Chinese companies passing off goods imported from Muslim countries as halal:

> The products with foreign labels marking them Islamic-compliant are
> popular among Uyghurs who distrust the certification by China's state-
> run Islamic body, sources in Xinjiang said. One company contacted by
> RFA Uyghur Service, Tianren International Ltd., admitted it had been
> producing food products domestically and mislabeling them as certified
> halal goods from Malaysia, a predominantly Muslim country. . . . The
> issue is often overlooked, [as] Han Chinese "do not respect the religious
> rights of the Uyghur Muslims," which is a by product of the Chinese
> government "oppressing Uyghur religious freedoms."[43]

On the island of Fiji in 2011, the Consumer Council of Fiji cau-tioned restaurants, food producers, and retailers against making spuri-ous claims. The warning came after authorities found cases of fake halal products available for sale.[44] The government stepped in to require halal certification documents for any item labeled halal. The same ruling now stands for restaurants in Fiji that publicly advertise halal on their menus or indicate halal availability anywhere on premises.

Scandals abound involving misrepresentation of halal labeling, particularly where meat is concerned. In January 2012 in Cape Town, South Africa, a newspaper reported wrongdoing on the part of Orion Cold Storage: "a video surfaced of an employee at the meat distribution company relabeling uncertified products and pork as halal. Orion management denied the allegations, claiming it had been set up."[45] The imported pork products reportedly had been deliberately relabeled and sold as halal. Criminal halal practices such as these are not unusual in the meat industry. Pork proteins that signal contamination to Muslim consumers are occasionally detected in chicken products because of the type of feed provided to the poultry. In such cases, the poultry is no longer halal, even though it has been slaughtered according to halal requirements.

Hazel Croall, professor of criminology at Glasgow Caledonian University, United Kingdom, suggests that crimes committed against consumers tend to receive less public attention than other white-collar or corporate crimes; consumer crimes may be viewed as trivial in comparison. As a result, consumers of food products are often left in the dark, unable to accurately identify potentially harmful ingredients or corroborate the authenticity of ingredients listed. Croall has observed that

> in Britain, some large supermarkets such as Tesco and Asda, part of the Walmart chain, [are] amassing a string of convictions for different offences. Advertisements by 'household names' such as McDonald's and Estee Lauder have been criticized by the British Advertising Standards Authority (ASA). . . . Large food manufacturers . . . are generally opposed to extensions of food labeling laws. The impact of criminalization falls more severely on smaller businesses whose activities can more readily be defined as "unscrupulous" or dishonest.[46]

Giant chain corporations may deceive consumers purposefully and effortlessly. These actions, like those of organized criminals, cannot be justified or overlooked and potentially cause harm to an unsuspecting public. These profitable deceptions, whether in the form of counterfeit items, toxic products, or "meat laundering," may result in public health hazards.[47] John Pointing and Yunes Teinaz have found that in the United Kingdom, illegal trade in haram meat amounted to $2.5 billion, largely due to the absence of regulatory systems controlling organized food crime.[48] Their discussion targets loopholes in British law and suggests how these laws could be amended to prevent criminal action. The authors cite a case as far back as the 1980s of food-based crime in the United Kingdom:

> The criminals involved were responsible for recycling up to 1,000 tonnes of rotten meat, originally intended for use as pet food, into the human food chain . . . [and] over a period of more than 10 years, a substantial proportion of the meat was exported, including to Muslim countries as Halal.[49]

In April 2013, Dutch authorities were busily addressing horse-meat scandals in restaurants and other food establishments after horse meat was marketed as 100 percent beef. BBC News reported, "In total, 132 companies in the Netherlands and some 370 more around Europe [had been] affected by the discovery."[50]

While law enforcement raced to keep up with the horse-meat scandal, still other scandals emerged, one of them in Norway, where pork was identified in halal beef kebab meat and in pizza toppings all labeled halal. The Norwegian Food Safety Authority discovered that some products contained large amounts of pork, even though labels said that they were 100 percent beef. Ragnhild Arnesen, spokesperson for the Norwegian Food Safety Authority, warned in 2013, "We consider this to be serious and have begun criminal proceedings against two producers—Kuraas, the company that sold pork as halal meat—and another producer, Norsk Mesterkjoett, whose products were labeled 100 percent beef but contained more than 60 percent pork."[51]

In 2002 Saudi Arabia ordered all Saudi food markets to pull European-produced chicken from their shelves and from storage. Saudi authorities suspected, correctly so, that artificial hormones had been used in poultry feed. The phenomenon of exports from Western nations to Muslim-majority regions of meat that has been tainted with either artificial hormones or contaminated feed is shamefully prevalent.

An article published by Johan Fischer, associate professor in the Department of Society and Globalization at Roskilde University, Denmark, references a 2001 food scandal in Indonesia:

> The Indonesian Ulemas Council (MUI; Jakarta, Indonesia) accused a Japanese company of using pork products in the production of the flavour enhancer monosodium glutamate (MSG), and demanded that the Indonesian government take appropriate action. It was a serious accusation: if true, the company would have violated halal rules. . . . As a

consequence of the scandal, several employees of the company were arrested and a public apology was issued.[52]

This company's practices, immoral and unethical, were undertaken for one reason only—to save money on production. The company blithely substituted the pork derivative bactosoytone in place of a beef derivative. This incident was especially embarrassing for the MUI since it had certified all the company's food products as halal. Indeed, "the scandal seemed to undermine or question the legitimacy of these religious scholars in the eyes of millions of Muslim consumers."[53]

What resulted was a domino effect, forcing many other companies to apply for halal certification. Although many of these companies enjoyed long histories of business relationships with Indonesia, consumer outrage left no other option. Either the companies seriously complied with halal regulations or they ran the risk of losing a secure and profitable market position. One such entity, the Danish company Novozymes, manufactured enzymes for a wide range of applications, particularly in the areas of food, pharmaceutical, and scientific research. Fischer notes,

> Customers of Novozymes became more aware of the validity of halal certifications, and the company eventually chose to have its products certified by the Islamic Food and Nutrition Council of America (IFANCA; Chicago, IL, USA).[54]

When consumer confidence is shaken, it is often difficult to regain and, in some cases, impossible. Halal branding is an uncertain business, given numerous fraudulent halal indictments, and is at risk of being hijacked, in the words of a Halal Focus writer, "by political narratives where 'halal' is used as a football for deeper ethnic and religious tensions."[55]

A 2013 study of Belgian Muslim consumers by the journal *Meat Science* tested which consumers were likely to regard the halal label favorably:

> Cross-sectional data were collected through a survey with 202 Muslim consumers in Belgium. Findings indicate that more acculturated and female consumers are more in favour of purchasing certified halal labelled meat in a supermarket.[56]

This segment of the population is more willing "to pay a price premium (of 13 percent on average) for halal meat," provided supermarkets offer assurance that verification is authentic and that appropriate controls have been exercised—that is, that the halal meat label means what it says. This particular consumer expects to see halal meat clearly marked and separated from the non-halal meat section. In short, the study concludes that the level of importance consumers attach to a certified halal label and the level of trust they place in that status makes them more willing to pay higher prices.[57]

Protecting the Consumer: Halal Certification

Given potential profit margins, an impressive number of international food-based corporations are going halal. Mohd Nasir and colleagues of the faculty of computer science and information technology at the University of Malaya reports that, given the proliferation of halal-certified companies, Muslim consumers are more concerned than ever about the valid halal status of foods purchased. In Malaysia, with over 60 percent of the population claiming allegiance to Islam, JAKIM, the Malaysian Islamic Development Department, has introduced a halal logo and has adopted SMS, short message service, for cell phone texts and images. A concerned consumer can send the bar code on the packaged food item to JAKIM via SMS to check its halal status. The consumer receives a reply by e-mail or text. JAKIM has also set up a web portal to educate consumers regarding halal information. Individuals can use the portal for two purposes—to check the halal status of products and to make consumer complaints. Manufacturers and retailers also can use the web portal to apply online for halal certification.[58] The portal's biggest drawback is the time lapse; consumers may not be able to get information about their purchases as quickly as is needed, especially during peak hours.

In a 2009 study focusing on another technology for validating halal products, radio-frequency identification (RFID), the authors concentrated on industry readiness to implement RFID technology in Malaysia.[59] RFID provides information more quickly than other known approaches. Participants in the study reported that existing systems such as bar code and SMS are not as reliable and fail to return information to consumers in a timely manner. The study indicated that "99 percent of the respondents strongly agreed that [RFID] . . . application should be a new alternative in validating Halal status for all consumers."[60] On the down side, the RFID system, while gaining consumer trust, may result in an increasing number of phony logos. The study authors have found that "the advancement of technology has contributed to the production of fake halal logos."[61] One is left with the impression that perhaps in some cases Islamic authorities may be easily corrupted if the price is right and more than willing to grant halal status to unqualified companies.

Numerous other technologies are being developed that can be applied to testing halal food credibility. Some procedures are quite sophisticated, requiring significant research monies. Fourier transform infrared spectroscopy (FTIR) has been applied to detect lard adulteration in many packaged foods that contain fat, such as potato chips. Because lard is the cheapest source of fat, manufacturers may be prone to choose this haram ingredient. Other sources of contamination may include animal casings used in meat or cheese products. A DNA-based polymerase chain reaction method has been applied to detect this type of contamination and is considered very reliable.[62]

Yet another method for detecting contamination in meat products is a pork detection kit developed in 2010 in Japan.

> Pork detection kits are immunochromato graphic assays using nano-sized colloidal gold particles to detect adulteration of pork in food samples. The assays can detect pork in both raw and cooked food. These assays allow rapid detection of pork in food samples at low cost without using any special equipment or requiring skilful techniques (Ali, Hashim, Mustafa, Che Man, & Islam, 2012). Unlike the existing testing methods such as PCR, which require special equipment and laborious procedures involved in the identification of specific sequences within it by RFLP analysis, southern blotting or sequencing, gold nano particles can be used to detect target sequences just by observing colour change. Ali et al. (2012) have pioneered the identification of pork adulteration using gold nano particles. They have successfully identified pork adulteration in beef and chicken meatballs using 20 nmgold particles as colorimetric sensors. The method is thus suitable for conducting preliminary screening of large numbers of routine samples before using an existing method for confirmation, which can enable an enhanced surveillance programme of the halal meat product supply.[63]

Many other efforts have been initiated in the fields of spectroscopy and chromatography as well as differential scanning calorimetric (DXC) technologies to detect and quantify pig derivatives in food products.[64] Scientific analyses continue to be developed using a wide array of biological and chemical techniques as well as computer technologies to confirm halal authenticity.

To date, no specific testing has been developed to detect blood plasma in food products. Islam prohibits consuming the blood of any animal, even if that animal has been slaughtered by halal standards. Therefore, the presence of plasma in meat products makes them unsuitable for Muslim consumers. The Qur'an clearly prohibits the consumption of blood, as cited earlier. One can appreciate that serving 100 percent halal meat for dinner is a tall order. Numerous regulations must be met, beginning with the farm of origin and extending to the abattoir, from packaging and transportation to the storage facility. All steps in this process are pivotal and must be monitored closely to guarantee the purity of halal meat.

Producing Halal Meat: Complexity and Challenge

At present, quality control of halal meat in non-Muslim-majority countries is sketchy. None of the steps taken by the meat industry to assure halal compliance are visible to the consumer, and therefore they cannot be verified before the actual purchase takes place. Thus it is understandable, as reported in the journal *Agriculture and Human Values*, that "consumers prefer transacting with Muslim butchers; that is, individuals of known reputation with similar moral and religious obligations."[65]

As food sources are developed to feed a burgeoning global population, multiple considerations such as genetically altered foods must be central to the discussion of public health and safety. Whether in Islamic or other regions, Muslim consumers will find themselves faced with special challenges and questions. For example, are genetically modified foods considered halal? In terms of certification and labeling, will Islamic authorities continue using reliable and sometimes costly techniques to analyze and authenticate halal meat and other food products? Will certification be honest or driven by corruption? Can Muslim consumers trust that Islamic authorities are protecting their welfare, not only in nations where Islam dominates but also in areas where Muslims reside as minorities?[66]

In the absence of trustworthy regulatory mechanisms, it comes as no surprise that some individuals lean toward vegetarian or vegan diets, especially when eating out. This trend is evident in the expanded menus of many high-end restaurants that now include vegan and vegetarian options. Indeed, anyone who now boards international flights is offered food choices as diverse as vegan, vegetarian, halal, and kosher.

Whether Muslims or not, many individuals are concerned about the treatment of animals in factory farms, no matter which slaughtering technique is employed—halal, kosher, or otherwise. As long as Muslims and non-Muslims insist on eating meat, a logical balance must be struck in terms of developing and implementing the best possible processes to slaughter animals humanely while respecting individual religious practices.[67]

CHAPTER 4

Marketing Piety: *Hijabi* Dolls and Other Toys

The concept of segmented marketing, which implies targeting specific consumers according to culture and religion, is not new. What is new is designing and implementing strategies that specifically target Muslim consumers, their preferences, emotional responses, and religious orientation. Brand Islam products hold powerful sway over adults and children alike and represent one more evolutionary step in the development of segmented marketing.

Here I examine toys that particularly target Muslim children and, most importantly, appeal directly to their parents. I also explore the increasingly innovative and, on occasion, manipulative advertising strategies used to attract consumer attention. These strategies weave religious ideology into the manufacture and packaging of consumer products. Toys are a vivid example of how mundane products are referred to or labeled as halal or Islamic.

In response to this phenomenon, I pose several questions. How do contemporary religious ideologies fuel the successful marketing of Brand Islam products for the very young? What strategies do companies set in place to strengthen parental loyalty to their products? In what ways do marketers attract—and ultimately exploit—the religiously devout individual?

Many consumer products such as toys, dolls, comic books, and certain video games explicitly target young children. While advertising and marketing strategies must appeal directly to the child, generally speaking it is the parent who writes the check, and therefore, the parent must be invested in or convinced of the value of that product. This rule holds true with "Muslim" (Islamically sanctioned) toys that, although introduced relatively recently in the global marketplace, already enjoy a unique position and are reaping impressive profits.

Exploring these questions leads one to discover a thriving industry of children's toys that focus on Islamic values. Games for both children and adults have been developed, such as the Mecca to Medina board game,[1] various quiz games such as Sawab (good deed) Quest,[2] and products from companies such as Baba Salam Educational Islamic Toys + Games. All are designed to educate, motivate, and test an individual's understanding of and dedication to key Islamic precepts—in other words, teaching the religion of Islam while entertaining players and participants.

Also new to the marketplace is an alternative to the American doll Barbie: *hijabi* (veiled) dolls sold with Islamic accessories. Spin-off items such as tiny prayer rugs, miniature copies of the Qur'an, and prayer beads are also packaged for child's play. It is no exaggeration to say that new entrepreneurs and their carefully considered marketing techniques have successfully challenged the monopoly of Barbie, that all-American cultural icon. Morris Kalliny and Angela Hausman have asserted that "Barbie dolls are easier to criticize than other products since they are viewed by religious leaders as exerting a societal force contrary to the teachings of the religion."[3]

Indeed, dolls are fast becoming symbolic centerpieces of a debate about the significance and implications of religious commodification. By intentionally appealing to concerned Islamic consumers—comparing and contrasting Barbie's morality, looks, and accoutrements with the more conservative *hijabi* dolls—savvy entrepreneurs have transformed an innocent, fanciful plaything into a powerful symbol for religious correctness and piety. A quick perusal of the Internet finds these dolls referred to by a variety of labels—Muslim dolls, Islamic dolls, burqa dolls, *hijabi* dolls, *chaduri* dolls, and veiled dolls. No matter the label, with the global Muslim population approaching two billion, the promise of profits from mullah-approved Barbies looms large.

While other, more mundane products also created for children are designed to snag the Muslim parent's attention and interest,[4] it is primarily the *hijabi* dolls that are setting record profits, in part because religious authorities condemn Barbie and in part because of consumer vulnerability and aggressive marketing. Marketers can only succeed in their efforts to promote the halal *hijabi* dolls by contrasting Barbie's haram status. When Barbie was created and introduced into the market, no one imagined she would ultimately wield enough power to influence policy within certain Muslim regions. By inviting government interference, regulation, and ultimately, importation bans, Barbie has single-handedly exerted tremendous political power effortlessly and without any participation on the part of her manufacturer, Mattel. Barbie is even blamed for a low rate of birth in Russia, Valerie Sperling has observed: "Putin's envoy to the Central Federal District, for instance, recently asserted his [Putin's] intention to start a campaign against Barbie dolls, believing for some reason that they play a role in the falling birthrate."[5]

One can find important policies drafted in response to Barbie, as described in a 2003 CBS report: "Saudi Arabia's religious police have declared Barbie dolls a threat to morality, complaining that the revealing clothes of the 'Jewish' toy—already banned in the kingdom—are offensive to Islam."[6] One of the most interesting aspects of this report was that Barbie was imbued with religious affiliation; the doll is referred to as "Jewish." The Jewishness of Barbie is mentioned several times in the same report:

> "Jewish Barbie dolls, with their revealing clothes and shameful postures, accessories and tools are a symbol of decadence of the perverted West. Let us beware of her dangers and be careful," said a message posted on the site.
>
> A spokesman for the Committee said the campaign against Barbie—banned for more than 10 years—coincides with the start of the school year to remind children and their parents of the doll's negative qualities. Speaking to The Associated Press by telephone from the holy city of Medina, he [the spokesman] claimed that Barbie was modeled after a real-life Jewish woman.[7]

Ironically, ascribing the Jewish religion to Barbie is the same as calling the *hijabi* dolls Muslim.[8] Reportedly the Saudi *muttawa*, or religious police, are permitted to confiscate Barbie dolls and fine the seller, and yet one can purchase a Barbie doll in the kingdom for about $27. Taking advantage of political strife between Israel and the Arab world, Saudi government officials may have assumed that calling Barbie a Jewish doll would solidify citizen allegiance.

Toys as Social Markers

Observations by Gregory Starrett in a 1995 issue of *American Anthropology* shed light on the meaning of objects in relation to the human psyche and the objects of commodity:

[O]bjects are meaningful not in their individual relations to human purpose, but in their collective consumption, their relations to other objects as a field of signifiers. Insofar, then, as religious commodities are to be understood as material things, they have two networks of signification in which they can act as markers of difference: first, with regard to other objects defined as religious, and second, with regard to the field of commodities as a whole.[9]

There is no doubt that the number and variety of religious commodities, including dolls and other toys, offered to the general pubic has expanded not only as a result of innovative product development but also due to carefully considered marketing techniques, media advertising, and packaging design. Booming and struggling economies alike have registered an increased demand for these commodities. Pradip Thomas notes that "the globalization of religion has led to a massive global trade in on-line and off-line [commodities]."[10] Environments where one predictably finds religious commodification include shrines and pilgrimage sites. While individuals on pilgrimages are primarily searching for moral and spiritual illumination, they also tend to purchase religious memorabilia. Particularly in economically challenged, so-called developing nations, worshippers willingly invest what little money they have in items marketed as religiously supportive or significant.

Regardless of a nation's economic standing, its cultural and social orientation may be inferred from examining the toy and game market for children. Why? Because this specific market tends to mirror adult worldviews and parental preferences. Doris Wilkinson has found that

> toys and dolls reflect and emit a configuration of social images about ideas, indigenous folkways and rules of behavior. . . . [D]olls capture what little babies and girls who resemble them anatomically should look like and the definitional mode in which they should consider themselves. They create mental representations of images to be expected.[11]

The anthropomorphic qualities of dolls naturally reflect social norms. Their physicality mirrors collective psychology and values. Dolls also function as tools for self-identity, cognitive development, and fantasy.[12] In the United States, the hawking of Christian-based religious toy figures other than dolls is nothing new. In 2007 the American giant retail corporation Walmart added Biblical action figures to its toy products line, including representations of Jesus. In 2007 BBC News reported that Bible action figures were being sold in 425 Walmart stores across the United States. The reporter ponders the potential market for this line of toys:

> So will the 12in (30cm) Jesus doll quoting scripture or the 3in (8cm) figure of Daniel in the lion's den open up children's imaginations—and their parents' wallets? The founder of One2believe, Mr. David Socha, firmly believes in the success of these products and has expressed confidence in the demand for "God-honouring" toys that reflect Christian teachings and morality.[13]

These toys—including a three-inch action figure of Daniel in the lion's den, a twelve-inch talking Jesus doll, and a thirteen-inch Samson action figure—are aimed at three- to twelve-year-old children and packaged with related Bible stories. One of the most obvious elements of the One2believe action figures, as described by David Socha in the BBC report, is their strong appeal to conservative and fundamentalist consumers:

> If you go in a toy aisle in any major retailer, you will see toys and dolls that promote and glorify evil, destruction, lying, cheating. In the girls' aisle where the dolls would be, you see dolls that are promoting promiscuity to very young girls. Dolls will have very revealing clothes on, G-string underwear . . . [while] something faith-based . . . is not only fun to play with but also is solidifying a person's spiritual wherewithal and their spiritual journey.[14]

Figures from the Association for Christian Retail show a steady, lucrative increase in the sale of Christian products from $4 billion sold in 2000 to more than $4.6 billion in 2006.

A similar trend should not be surprising, then, in the Muslim children's market. The post-9/11 fascination with Islam and with the Muslim woman's practice of veiling has given rise to numerous publications examining the *hijab* from different aspects. What is worth examining here is the concept of using Muslim women's piety to manufacture an entire product line of dolls dressed in various styles of regional Islamic veils—face veil, burqa, chador, *abaya*, head scarf, and others—and to market them globally with the subtle promise of enhancing families' religious fervor, propriety, or status. A number of these dolls sans veil have been available in toy stores for a while, but attaching the veil suddenly made them expressly appropriate for Muslim consumers. Indeed, prior to introduction of the "doll veil," Sukmawati Suryaman, an Indonesian engineer, had already come up with the brilliant idea of purchasing Barbie dolls from China and simply hiring a tailor to sew new Islamic fashions for the dolls. She named the refurbished dolls Salma and marketed them as respectable dolls, wearing respectable clothes and head scarves.[15] Thus, Barbie became Salma, whose clothing choices alone made her suitable for and worthy of being placed in the hands of Muslim children.

Certain questions deserve consideration: Why, how, and by whom have playthings become associated with religious duty, observance, and practice? When marketers shamelessly assign the religious label "Islamic" to a plastic man-made object, another question comes into play: How might a doll created by the hand of man become a symbol of Islam and piety?[16] According to the first principle of Islam, all that Allah has created in the universe, including human beings, may be considered "Muslim" in the greater sense because they are all created by and therefore obedient to God. Man-made toys or other man-made objects cannot be considered either Islamic or Muslim. That is, God cannot have any partner, since Allah is the sole creator. Acknowledgment of the oneness (*tawhid*) of God is the essential core of Muslim belief. The toy that is purely the creation of man cannot be Muslim because a toy does not follow a religion. In other words, a Muslim is a person who is obedient to Allah and also follows the religion of Islam. A doll is not in the same category as humans; thus the man-made doll cannot be a Muslim.

In the Beginning Were Sara and Dara

Nevertheless, the demand for—or, more aptly put, the craze for—decently dressed toys started with dolls manufactured in and by the Islamic Republic of Iran. The dolls, female and male, were named Sara and Dara. The dolls were clearly and purposefully identified as sister and brother rather than girlfriend and boyfriend, which meant that it would be halal, acceptable, for them to keep each other's company. These dolls constituted, then, the Islamic world's first anti–Barbie and Ken campaign. This project began with clear intention to create a pair of national Iranian dolls dressed in folk costumes, not what is commonly known as Islamic dress, from various regions of the country that would divert the attention of young Iranian girls away from the American Barbie. For the Islamic Republic of Iran, Barbie represents Western decadence and immorality. In the Iranian Muslim psyche and culture, Barbie's scanty clothing and nude body are indecent, her lifestyle with Ken as her boyfriend and companion and not her legitimate husband unacceptable, and her unmarried female friend Midge, who is pregnant, scandalous. All these aspects seemed sufficient to condemn the Barbie phenomenon.[17] The first Barbie ban came from Iran's religious rulers in 1996, at which time the doll was not only declared un-Islamic but also deemed destructive to the very social and cultural fabric of Iran.

A number of other cultural dolls were launched for different reasons, such the Bosnian Dolls that were developed to educate the public about various religious groups in the Balkans. The Bosnian Dolls are dressed in costumes representing four groups of people: Mara in a Bosnian Orthodox costume, Emina in a Bosnian Muslim costume, Ana in a Bosnian Catholic costume, and Hana in a Bosnian Jewish costume. In this sense the dolls are meant to represent the main cultures and religious orders in Bosnia. Another example of a doll that is not produced on a mass scale but still represents a culture is Mastana, the Afghan burqa dolls made by hand and packaged as a collector's item.[18]

Barbie is not alone on Iran's list of banned toys—dolls from the TV series *The Simpsons* are also blacklisted. According to a Global Post news report in 2012, "Officials would not explain what was problematic about the Simpsons dolls, other than to say that toys in Iran cannot have distinguishable human genitals, be based on adults or blare Western music."[19] Curiously, the Simpsons toys do not have human genitals. An article in an Israeli news source reported that the ban on Simpsons toys resulted from concerns about Western culture, although "Superman and Spiderman were allowed, because they helped the 'oppressed.'"[20] The same article indicates that in 2011, Iran imported $57 million worth of toys. Officials estimated that some $20 million more worth of toys were smuggled across the border the same year. Reference to the oppressed (*moztasaf*) is a reminder of the Islamic Republic's establishment and the end of the shah's reign. Ayatollah Khomeini made ample use of the word *moztasaf* to reinforce one of the primary objectives for bringing down the monarchy. It is worth noting how, decades after the Iranian Islamic Revolution, the same political terminology is consistently inserted into all aspects of daily life, even extending to the toy industry.

Like Iran, Turkey is fast becoming a thriving market for Islamic toys. In 2010 the *Hürriyet Daily News* reported on a new series of dolls

Bosnian dolls. The *Sarajevska Tribina* (Sarajevo Tribune) offered a set of four Bosnian Dolls—Orthodox, Muslim, Catholic, and Jewish—with a music CD and a book as a way "to educate about peace and tolerance." The image of these three is from a *Doll World* article that the *Sarajevska Tribina* posted to its website, http://www.sarajevskatribina.info/.

Afghan doll with burqa. Zarina's, an online traditional clothing and goods store, described the doll as "a one of a kind, handmade collector's item or toy." Image from Zarina's, http://www.zarinas.com.

named Elif that was registered at the Turkish patent office. The doll was created with the financial support of twelve national institutes through-out Turkey. The article explains, "Turkish children now have their own 'traditional Turkish doll,' Elif, thanks to the efforts of the country's Education Ministry, according to the principal of an Eskişehir vocational institute for girls."[21] A blog post titled "Barbie Is Out, Elif Is In—in Turkey" calls attention to media coverage of the new doll:

> Mainstream Turkish daily *Aksam*'s frontpage report says that a new Islamic doll Elif has replaced the Barbie dolls in Turkey's toy market. Elif doll kneels and performs namaz (Islamic prayer). When its hands, feet and chest are pressed Elif recites various sura from the Koran in Arabic, and chants Islamic prayers in Turkish too. Accessories to Elif doll, such as a toy laptop, teach toddler to six-year-old girls about Islamic rules and namaz rituals.[22]

The writer uses *sura*, meaning chapter, but I believe the report intended to say *aya*, meaning verse.

Depending on which agency was reporting the news, Elif was promoted differently. One agency reported that the doll was created solely as an effort to promote Turkey's cultural heritage, similar to the Dara and Sara dolls of Iran, and to preserve its long-standing tradition of handicrafts, which contribute to the local economy by employing women. Other news agencies reported that Elif was developed in direct competition with the American Barbie doll.[23] Printed in the Turkish language, the following text appears on each Elif box and clearly provides direction as to how to use the doll:

> When you squeeze Baby Elif's left hand, she recites the Subhaneke prayer.
> When you squeeze her right hand, she recites Sura Ikhlas.
> When you squeeze her right foot, she sings a Turkish spiritual song.
> When you press on her chest, she recites Sura al-Fatiha.
> When you squeeze her left foot, she says a prayer in Turkish.[24]

In 2007, many tourists visiting Yemen noticed and purchased veiled dolls for sale in the marketplace. Anne Menely, exploring this phenomenon, referred to the dolls as Chador Barbie, a local production and obvious imitation of the Barbie doll. Unlike dolls in Iran and Turkey, the Chador Barbie doll is in no way linked to decency and modesty, nor does it represent any attempt to symbolize the observant Muslim woman in her *hijab*. Rather, the marketability of such dolls to foreign consumers is based solely on their dollar value as souvenirs. After all, who wouldn't want to take home Chador Barbie as a reminder of Yemen's exotic culture? Why not let Westerners reinforce their misperception of all Muslim women as subservient to men? The local Muslim salesmen hawking these *hijabi* dolls very well understand how to commodify and profit from such a product. Yemeni businessmen are only too happy to maximize profits while exploiting the West's fascination with the veiling of Muslim woman. Thus, they are intentionally using what Anne Menely has described as "the concept of strategic marketing, by misrepresentation of the Yemeni cultural dynamic."[25]

In contrast, a veiled doll produced solely for the Muslim market is the Fulla doll, created by a UAE manufacturer from Dubai called New-Boy FZCO. Fulla does not have a male companion and is dressed in modest clothes covering her knees and shoulders. The Economist reported that "over 1.5m dolls have been sold since 2003, plus a range of spin-offs including hand wash and chewing gum."[26]

An Afghani addition to the doll line-up is Shola, a little girl from Kabul—designed and manufactured in Hong Kong by Playmates Toys. The average list price for Shola, available at Toys "R" Us and Target, is $28. The consumer immediately notices on the packaging a clever marketing gimmick. That is, when one buys this doll, $1 of the purchase price ostensibly goes to World Vision to help children worldwide.[27] The Playmates Toys Hearts for Hearts Girls doll series includes Shola and carries a mission statement:

> We invite all girls to become agents of change—to improve the lives of girls in their communities, across their country, and around the world. We promise to deliver meaningful products and experiences and to tell all girls, "You can help."

Furthermore, Farsi (Persian) script appears in disjointed letters on the box's interior, a script that translates to "Changing the World One Heart at a Time." Since Shola hails from Afghanistan, the script is necessarily Persian and not Arabic. To the best of my knowledge, this doll would never be sold in Afghanistan or at least among Pashto language speakers because Pashto is the predominant language of the Taliban, which promotes the extreme form of dress (burqa) for all girls and women. According to Pashtun custom, Shola would not qualify as a properly attired Afghan female.

Shola Afghan doll. This doll, dressed in blue and fuchsia, is from the author's personal collection.

Shola's story. Text on the packaging says Shola is a ten-year-old girl in Kabul. On the upper left corner of the box for the doll, text reads, "$1 of the purchase price goes to World Vision to help children worldwide." The doll is one of Playmates Toys' Hearts for Hearts Girls, "changing the world one [heart] at a time"; http://www.playmatestoys.com/.

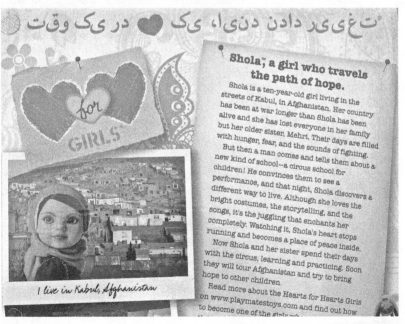

I live in Kabul, Afghanistan

Shola, a girl who travels the path of hope.

Shola is a ten-year-old girl living in the streets of Kabul, in Afghanistan. Her country has been at war longer than Shola has been alive and she has lost everyone in her family but her older sister, Mehri. Their days are filled with hunger, fear, and the sounds of fighting. But then a man comes and tells them about a new kind of school—a circus school for children! He convinces them to see a performance, and that night, Shola discovers a different way to live. Although she loves the bright costumes, the storytelling, and the songs, it's the juggling that enchants her completely. Watching it, Shola's heart stops running and becomes a place of peace inside.

Now Shola and her sister spend their days with the circus, learning and practicing. Soon they will tour Afghanistan and try to bring hope to other children.

Read more about the Hearts for Hearts Girls on www.playmatestoys.com and find out how to become one of the girls

Finally, one can only hope that the cash donation actually goes to children in need, as advertised on the packaging. The considerable efforts to represent Shola through a lens of social activism is impressive, though one wonders if this is not just another clever strategy to sell a product.

Exploiting Children through Advertising

Symbolic interaction theory asserts the importance of play in a child's development and future life. The symbolic interaction theorists such as Gregory Stone, Donald Ball, Norman Denzin, and Gary Alan Fine all emphasize the importance of play in developing the self and in developing competence as a social actor.[28] While role play is a normal aspect of a child's growth, then, sociologists nevertheless worry about the impact of some toys that are used by children to mimic society's troubling features and issues. Certain toys, especially those cleverly advertised to capture a young child's attention, may create undesirable mental impressions.

All children, particularly those below the age of eight, are highly vulnerable to the chicanery and inducements of commercial advertisement. Children tend to emulate their parents, so a young child may adopt a consumer obsession if one or both parents tend to embrace this type of behavior. The act of obtaining a variety of consumer goods, including those classified as nonessential such as toys or certain brands of cereals, can become inordinately important in a child's world and can even sabotage his or her mental health.

Joel Best addresses another key point, suggested by researchers as well as activists, implicating certain kinds of toys as damaging to young children—including toys that could be labeled hazardous, sexist, racist, war-related, and (allow me to add to that list) religiously motivated. These are toys with the potential of altering a young child's psychological perspectives and well-being, toys that may teach the innocent mind to become permanently opposed to and afraid of other religions. Conservative Muslims may worry about the scantily dressed Barbie as a harmful example for their daughters. And Best suggests, "Conservative Christians worry about *occult toys* based on some of the very ideas namely witchcraft, idolatry, emulations, and murders, that God warns against."[29]

Agencies such as the Federal Trade Commission, an independent agency of the US government, have conducted revelatory studies regarding the general effects of advertising on young children.[30] Anup Shah, in the article "Children as Consumers," reports that these outcomes may be psychologically damaging. In 1991 the Swedish government implemented a ban on all advertisements during prime-time television, a decision based on research findings "that children under 10 are incapable of telling the difference between a commercial and a program, and cannot understand the purpose of a commercial until the age of 12."[31]

The American Psychological Association has conducted similar research studies. The APA Task Force on Advertising and Children, chaired by Professor Brian Wilcox, underscores in a 2004 press release that "because younger children do not understand persuasive intent in advertising, they are easy targets for commercial persuasion." The report concludes that

> children under the age of eight are unable to critically comprehend televised advertising messages and are prone to accept advertiser messages as truthful, accurate and unbiased. This can lead to unhealthy eating habits as evidenced by today's youth obesity epidemic.[32]

Parents are left having to remain vigilant of the intense barrage of advertising and its impact on their children's daily lives and well-being. Marketing moguls pay big bucks to oppose progressive politicians and social activists seeking to regulate child-advertising standards. Marketers are quick to point to the concept of individual choice and, at every turn, oppose government regulation or interference.

Whether in Dubai or Ojai, conscientious parents try to teach their children to be prudent consumers. Providing guidelines regarding the value of money ultimately supports a child in becoming a financially independent adult. However, obsessive consumerism in contemporary societies is changing the roadmap of childhood development. The role of children as consumers in American society, for example, has changed dramatically over the past forty years.[33] They now rival adult consumers in terms of conspicuous consumption and compulsive buying.

The ways in which products are advertised and marketed inarguably influence unwanted behaviors in children. Mark Crispin Miller, then director of the Project on Media Ownership in New York, pointed out in a *Christian Science Monitor* article in 2000 that "advertisements not only encourage kids to demand toys from their parents, but they encourage boys to celebrate violence and girls to consider their self-worth by how they look."[34]

Enormous amounts of money are being generated in the youth marketplace.[35] In a 2008 *Future of Children* journal article Sandra Calvert observes, "Youths now have influence over billions of dollars in spending each year. In 2002, US four- to twelve-year-olds spent $30 billion."[36]

In terms of national and international economic gains, youth culture is crucially important given that children influence and shape the buying patterns of their families in many areas such as vacation choices, meal selection, and even larger-ticket items such as automobiles. The 2000 *Christian Science Monitor* reported that in the United States "children are influencing the purchase of everything from new cars to frozen pizza—up to $500 billion a year in family buying."[37]

Toy Entrepreneurism and Advertising Online

Not all businesses that advertise play objects for children as Islamic begin with sophisticated mechanisms of research and development. Some entrepreneurial efforts emerge quite simply from supply and demand. Apparently this is the case with business websites such as Muslim Kids TV, which highlights "videos and crafts for Muslim children."[38] An explanation posted at the website says its creator, who goes by the name Merve, is a practicing Muslim and engineer in New York. With a love for arts and crafts, she wanted to teach her son about nature, manual skills, and Islam. Unable to locate books for Muslim children, Merve created her own website, one that offers Islamically sanctioned games and activities in which parents can participate. Merve writes that she created the website for the sake of God: "I hope [it] is useful to our Ummah [Muslim community] with educational activities, Islamic teachings, original Muslim stories." This website has a panoply of crafts, Muslim etiquette, cartoons, and even children's *nasheeds*, songs in praise of Allah and the Prophet Mohammad.[39]

Upon closer reading, one discovers that the Muslimkidstv.com programs are not strictly Merve's unique creation. Indeed, the website states, "Some of the videos on this site come from various websites including but not limited to muslimkidstv.com itself and our sister sites. We use the method to 'embed' videos from various sites on the net that offer this method as a way of sharing videos on social networking pages, websites and blogs."[40] Merve is like many other astute Muslim and non-

Muslim entrepreneurs who have seized the moment to create businesses that offer products not necessarily new or innovative but rather that have been modified for a new market. Merve, like Indonesian engineer Sukmawati Suryaman, also re-dresses regular dolls to become *hijabi* dolls and does the same with existing board games, cleverly modifying them to satisfy Muslim consumer criteria.

When parents support and remain loyal to certain manufacturers of toys, games, videos, cartoons, and so forth, then, needless to say, the marketers and producers of such items emerge the real winners. Hooking devout Muslim parents into the net of religiously oriented children's products is more than worth entrepreneurial time and effort. One such businessperson seized on a relatively simple idea and as a result, *The Economist* reports, created a profitable enterprise:

> Fehmida Shah set up Smart Ark, a London-based online firm that sells Islamic books, toys and gifts, mainly for children. "HSBC [a bank] was doing Islamic bonds and religious books were selling well, so I thought why not tap into the niche but growing market?" she says. Customers from Britain to Singapore have bought her products. They include a pricier Fairtrade range that includes stickers of mosques around the world and a book on why Muslims should recycle.[41]

As demonstrated by Ms. Shah, it only takes a stretch of the imagination to commodify Islamic goods. Recycling is now part and parcel of contemporary life and, from an ecological standpoint, makes perfect sense for everyone regardless of religious belief. However, creating a link between recycling and religion in order to sell books to children is something altogether new. This is the angle that Fehmida Shah understood and exploited, turning her vision into a lucrative business.

The emergence of a savvy Muslim marketplace is reflected across the Internet, with numerous sites that tout Muslim toys and games, such as Muslim Heroes: "Today, Little Big Kids is the first US brand to offer parents a wide range of culturally inspired products for kids of all backgrounds. Our goal is to incorporate beautiful Arabic and Islamically inspired themes into common products that are an everyday part of your child's life."[42]

Because today's youth and children are well adapted to technology, marketing professionals have explored various ways to access and influence this giant segment of global consumers. Marketers can reach children not only through television but also on cell phones, iPods, game platforms, and other digital devices. Banner ads that resemble traditional billboard ads but market a product across the top of an Internet page appear on most web pages. And "advergames" integrate products such as cereal and candy into online video games to sell products to youth.[43]

In addition to standard advertising techniques targeting young children during their favorite television programs, cartoons, music videos, and films, advertisers have engaged new techniques, namely "stealth advertising, in which marketers attempt to conceal the intent of an ad . . . [and] blur the line between the advertisement and the content."[44] To the consumer, the effect of a concealed advertisement is much greater than an unconcealed one. The theory behind stealth techniques is that advertising is most effective when consumers do not recognize it as advertising.

Viral marketing and product placement that traverse many types of media are newer marketing strategies being used more commonly to reach consumers. Commercial and noncommercial content are becoming more indistinguishable, sophisticated, and blended, presenting a special challenge given the limited capacity of younger children to process these messages cognitively.[45]

Stealth forms of advertising are only permitted on Internet venues, in contrast to children's television, where clear markers must separate commercial content and program content. Such newer forms of marketing can be run with significantly smaller budgets than traditional print, radio, and TV ads. Sandra Calvert points out the potential for profit in her 2008 article:

> [O]nline venues can reap large returns for relatively small investments. For example, Wild Planet Toys spent $50,000 for a four-month online promotion that was associated with a doubling of Wild Planet's yearly revenues. A comparable buy for a television advertising campaign would have cost $2 million. And a recent Nabisco World game and puzzle website designed to increase awareness of Nabisco's cookies and crackers cost only 1 percent of the company's advertising and marketing budget. Advertising on online games was expected to grow from $77 million to about $230 million between 2002 and 2007.[46]

Competition in the children's toy and game market remains fierce. Thus, the craze continues to spin off "new and improved" items and/or to develop increasingly innovative product strategies. At the same time, new toys and game products run certain risks in the market based on global political and cultural differences. That is, toys may be subject to harsh criticism if they seem even slightly irreverent or sacrilegious—and for a variety of other reasons as well.

Toys: Sacrilege, Mockery, and Islamophobia

Soon after Fulla and other *hijabi* dolls showed up in the marketplace, waves of criticism issued forth from Western media. Islamophobic blogs offered opinions such as this on the Atlas Shrugs blog from a commenter who identifies as Dutch Wolf: "Do you believe this one? Where will Islamization of Europe stop? This is obviously a new idea of the [Muslim] ideology to suppress their women."[47] Dutch Wolf and other commenters accord more power to a plastic doll dressed in a costume than it deserves. Ironically, the importance given to Barbie bears a close resemblance. Government officials in Iran and Saudi Arabia, afraid of the power of Barbie to corrupt the Islamic and traditional culture, have banned the sale of Barbie. They are, in imposing the bans, revealing the same mentality demonstrated by bloggers likewise afraid of losing cultural and heritage identities because of two dolls, one fully covered and the other half-naked. The plaything is assumed to be invested with political power. Recently the makers of Barbie have felt competing market pressure from the *hijabi* dolls that are emerging fast and finding a place in the children's doll market. Mattel, the maker of the Barbie, decided to create a special *hijab*-wearing Barbie doll. Obviously, in the global marketplace, Mattel could not lose the opportunity to miss out on the profits afforded by veiled dolls, and so, in 2009, Barbie in a burqa was introduced. So many debates and discussion have been generated over these veiled dolls that sometimes the real value of the dolls is lost. The ultimate value of these dolls may be mostly in the dollar sign and not in the cultural heritages they are supposed to reflect.

Some blog posts reflect an awareness of the role that corporate greed plays in the creation of a halal/haram toy industry. Interestingly, one finds similar levels of suspicion regarding toy products and their manufacturers among Muslims and non-Muslims alike. An attitude of distrust and vigilance creates wary consumers in the marketplace. Non-Muslim parents voice concern when toy products or games threaten to push their children into Islamic conversion. Fisher-Price's baby doll marketed as Little Mommy makes cooing and babbling noises when picked up. A games blogger on Yahoo raises the issue of a hidden agenda: "Unlike many baby dolls, though, this one reportedly hid subliminal religious messages: parents claimed to hear the doll saying: 'Islam is the light' and 'Satan is king.'"[48] Although Fisher-Price adamantly claimed that the gibberish contained no mysterious messages but was exclusively due to the toy's cheap speaker system, in 2010 the toy manufacturer felt sufficiently pressured to remove the voice chip from further production. This controversy around Little Mommy, with its purported hidden Islamic messages, revealed concerns about a bigger plot, as expressed by a commenter on Yahoo:

> This is a plan by those evil enemies of America to tear her apart from the inside. But how far does it go? Beyond mass-producing little jihadists in our very homes, what other diabolical schemes have they concocted to bring our beloved country to its knees? Perhaps this is only just the beginning. Perhaps even our new President, Barack Obama, is involved? After all, he is a Muslim, isn't he? . . .
> I will tell you where he who is all that is not us hides, poised and waiting to strike on our unwitting and innocent youth. *In their toys.*[49]

This comment exemplifies paranoia on the part of non-Muslims that Islam intends to take over the world and destroy American freedoms. Comments such as this plant seeds of fear and dread and contribute to a certain level of hysteria regarding the threat of toy-based secret agendas. In this particular case, the irrationality of such accusations is underscored by the fact that Little Mommy is made in the United States by a non-Muslim company.

A short message on a YouTube clip of News 10 Indiana describes an electronic game by Nintendo called Nintendo-DS Baby Pals in which the following statement is supposedly heard: "Islam is the light." The Nintendo Company has insisted that a third party manufactured this game, which apparently is not true, as the patent and label on the toy states differently, and that the company is not responsible for it.[50]

In another example, one observes, somewhat incredulously, Muslim paranoia vis à vis toys in Catholic-dominated Spain. In a one-minute YouTube clip, Egyptian cleric Salem Abu al-Futuh, on Al-Nas TV, laments the situation in Spain, "where little Muslim children have their toys taken from them."[51] The unedited English subtitles to the cleric's words in Arabic read,

> They [Spanish Catholics] are doing all kinds of things. So people keep suffering. They send Christian Missionaries in the form of doctors and nurses. Who caress and embrace the child like they do in the West.

They give him a very beautiful toy. And all of the sudden they snatch it away from him. When the child screams: "where is my toy?" They say to him Muhammad stole it from you. Thus, from infancy, they make the child to hate Muhammad. That's what they do in Spain.

This video clip, reflecting a delusional state of mind, suggests that toys are being used as objects of Christian propaganda. The clip provides no further information beyond what is stated above.

Suspicion about toys with subliminal messages and malevolent agendas is seen on the Muslim side toward toys that "mock Islam," as a June 2012 article reports:

> The United Arab Emirates Federal National Council (FNC) has issued a recommendation to the Cabinet to pass legislation on children's toys that "mock Islam." Mohammad Msallam Bin Ham, FNC member, called on the government to issue a legislation to tighten controls on imports of toys that are against Islam. "This is the responsibility of the ministry of economy, which should be in charge of securing the country's borders and gateways through enhancing inspection on imported products."[52]

Bin Ham urged authorities to be vigilant at all land, air, and sea entries regarding the inspection of such toys.

An item posted on the website Inquistr referred to an incident at one of the best-known fast-food restaurants in the world, McDonald's. It all started with the McDonald's Happy Meal: "The people of Saudi Arabia are furious with the McDonald's fast food chain for a toy which they say desecrates the name of Muhammed, the prophet of Islam."[53] The plastic action toy, part of the Happy Meal, steps out on top of Muhammed's name from the base of the toy where the name is written in a circle. A few days after the toy was distributed, the problem of the Prophet's name was discovered. Several public campaigns clamoring in protest included Help your Prophet and Together in Support of the Prophet. When angry religious sentiments gained momentum, McDonald's moved quickly. The news story continues, "Saudi McDonald's has taken the toy out of circulation at all of its restaurants stating it was important, 'to safeguard against any accusations or misunderstandings.'"[54] McDonald's decision to pull the toy from circulation was inarguably the best business strategy, thereby avoiding huge losses of revenue in the Saudi market.

On November 30, 2012, the BBC reported an incident from Sudan involving a toy and an insult to the Prophet Muhammad's name. Gillian Gibbons, a British citizen and schoolteacher in Sudan, was sentenced to fifteen days in jail by a court of law in Khartoum. Her crime? The children in her classroom had named a teddy bear Muhammad. This single naïve act triggered waves of demonstration. Protestors took to the streets in Khartoum demanding that Gibbons be shot to death. Many of the marchers chanted, "Shame, shame on the UK."[55] This extreme response to what was perceived as a toy mocking Islam exemplifies the highly defensive, hair-trigger mentality that some Muslims have angrily adopted toward non-Muslims, perhaps as a holdover of resentment from generations of colonialism.

Nazlida Muhamad Hashim and Dick Mizerski note that Muslims and Muslim consumers are affected and informed by numerous fatwas issued by various sources in different parts of the world. However, the authors contend, "it is more likely that devout consumers seek out information for fatwas that are controversial by searching the less formal sources for accuracy of such rulings. Some consumers are also only searching for sources of fatwas that are only associated with a certain product category."[56]

On the heels of the school teacher's case in Sudan, a concerned Muslim parent wrote to Sheikh Muhammad Salim 'Abd al-Wadud asking for advice.[57] The question and answer are posted by the Islamic Research Foundation International. The parent explained that his young daughter watched *Adam's World*,[58] a puppet series for Muslim children, and asked the sheikh,

> Is it right or wrong to name plush toys and puppets with the names of prophets? If not, should I dispose of these videos? Also, my daughter has named her plush toys with different names. She has a toy horse named Ahmed, a toy cat named Aisha, and a toy rabbit named Muhammad—these are the names of her uncles and her aunt. Is this alright? Am I sinning by letting her keep these names for her toys?[59]

The answer given by Sheikh Muhammad Salim 'Abd al-Wadud is detailed and lengthy but informative and insightful in terms of examining a question from multiple aspects before arriving at a conclusion:

> If the person who did so was a small child, then there is certainly no sin involved, since a small child is not legally accountable.
> If the person is an adult, then the question of sinfulness rests with

the person's intention. If the person intended by giving the character or toy a certain name as a means to insult or belittle one of the prophets, then the person has committed a sin. Deliberately insulting any of the prophets is a serious sin. It does not matter which of the prophets it is, since we as Muslims do not differentiate between the prophets in their right to be accorded our respect.

If the person did not intend any insult by doing so, then the person incurs no sin.

Now, we shall turn our attention to the appropriateness of naming cartoon characters or toy characters by the names of the prophets.

It is certainly wrong to make any inappropriate representation of any of the prophets. If a person presents a cartoon character, a puppet, or an animal character as representing one of the prophets, then the person is doing something wrong. The person might have a good intention behind doing so, but the act itself is incorrect. If the person does so in ignorance and without any bad intention, the person will not be sinning. However the person should be informed of the mistake and should cease doing so as soon as his or her attention is drawn to the matter . . . As for naming cartoon characters and toy animals by these names as simple names for the characters, there is nothing inherently wrong with this. . . . Cartoon animal characters and toy animal characters—since they are characters in a story or are used for imaginative play—are naturally given names and personalities that are customarily associated with people. Therefore, names that people customarily have can be given to fanciful characters in the same context. . . . Therefore, we see nothing wrong with these shows as long as their content is wholesome, and we see no objection to your allowing your daughter to give her toys the names of her aunts and uncles. However, we still need to pay heed to both general sensibilities and cultural norms.

For instance, it would certainly be wrong to give a cartoon or toy animal that is seen as unclean in Islam—like a pig—the name of a prophet, regardless of the context in which it is presented, since this is inherently injurious to Muslim sensibilities. Also, with respect to any toy or cartoon character, the various sensibilities of the local communities—which differ from country to country—should be respected. A Muslim should never knowingly and unnecessarily insult or offend other people. And Allah knows best.[60]

Reading the detailed, carefully considered explanation of Sheikh Muhammad Salim 'Abd al-Wadud, one questions the hasty conclusion reached by judges in the case of the classroom teddy bear named Muhammad. After all, the teacher's intention was not to mock the Prophet. Furthermore, millions of men are named Muhammad, and yet we know with certainty that although they share the same name with the Prophet of Islam, they are not sharing his personhood or sharing the prophecy with him.

The commotion over sacrilegious children's toys is not limited to the Prophet Mohammad but, on occasion, also involves the Prophet's favorite wife, A'isha. A 2012 Lebanese incident centered on a toy gun that allegedly insults the Prophet Mohammad's wife A'isha. One report made the claim regarding the plastic toy M16 rifle that "when the trigger is pulled, an audio recording says, 'Hit Aisha,' referring to Aisha Bint Abu Bakr, known in history as the favorite wife of the Muslim Prophet Mohammad."[61] This toy gun stirred controversy and provoked accusations toward Shi'is who may have tampered with the original English audio recording, "Go, go and take the hostages." If this is indeed the case, then it is Shi'is—and not non-Muslims—responsible for the mockery and for creating sectarian tensions in Lebanon, already affected by the neighboring Syrian civil war. Lebanon's highest Sunni authority, Dar al-Fatwa and the General Security, have both rejected such accusations.

There are those who would claim that Muslims are overly sensitive, even paranoid, about the possibility of children's toys being used to signal disrespect toward Islam and the Prophet. But a closer look at this intensely vigilant behavior reveals a deeper, more complex issue: long years of East/West conflict that are indelibly fixed in a people's memory—domination, colonialism, and perceived insult within the general Muslim psyche. Profound political issues, therefore, may lie just beneath the surface of ongoing tensions and controversy regarding dolls and toys.

Marketing to Muslim Youth: A Future Vision

Beyond the mainstream marketplace, savvy advertisers are increasingly targeting consumers with special needs. As we have seen, some of the most successful marketers direct their efforts toward individuals with specific religious requirements. Fifty years ago, who could have predicted that the teachings and practices of world religions such as Islam would have an impact on product development and demand? Nevertheless, in today's Muslim youth consumer culture, Pamela Nilan finds that religiously devout young people "may engage with Muslim media and cultural products not only because these things are *halal* (permitted within the faith) but also because they bestow 'blessings.'"[62] Marketers target this consumer group, taking maximum advantage of religious piety.

Nilan observes that devout Muslim Indonesian youth have selectively chosen certain beneficial aspects of Western culture while consciously marginalizing what is deemed offensive. Such selectivity must be taken into account when marketing to this segment of Indonesian society, Nilan suggests: "It is very crucial to understand how young people are able to navigate between the external western influences and their own internal cultural norms which is inclusive of devoutness to Islam."[63] Although it is natural that Muslim youth would choose to incorporate only what appear to be wholesome aspects of Western culture, the outcome is unique and a kind of hybrid. Urbanized children, especially, live and grow up in highly sophisticated marketing environments that affect and influence their behaviors and preferences for material goods. One can assume that generational identities are delocalized, and in this way, hybrid cultures of contemporary youth are formed. It can be assumed that all youth are connected to some extent to the networked global society and are affected by global events, even though at the same time youth cultures remain localized and shaped by their personal environments inclusive of ethnicity, language, gender, class, and religion. The youth create a culture that has not existed before and is different from that of their parents.

Predicting how this hybrid youth dynamic will affect future buying patterns and coming up with viable marketing strategies to attract the contemporary—and variable—young Muslims is key to successfully competing in the market. After researching halal and Islamically sanctioned toy products, I have my own predictions to make about possible future scenarios: Imagine that it is Saturday morning. Muslim children gather around the TV waiting for their favorite Islamic cartoon to begin and open a box of halal sugar-coated cereal, hoping to find a cheap, plastic prize (perhaps a small halal coloring book) hidden inside. A few halal board games for boys are spread out on the floor, while the little girls adjust veils on their dolls. The kids in this scenario intently watch a religious cartoon production that provides solid moral advice at the end. The children are bombarded with commercials selling halal games, toys, and various packaged snacks. This scenario is not farfetched. In fact, conceivably, it is already happening in one form or another in various parts of the world.

Both Muslims and non-Muslims share concerns about toy industry methods, including adverse effects of advertising on children. Many understand that market greed and detrimental influences threaten to undermine the mental and physical well-being of children. Tainting this shared concern, however, is finger pointing and ongoing paranoia that often to a ludicrous degree arises between religious groups. Regardless of religious, ethnic, or national affiliation, children's best interests must come first. If adults can reach a common ground of mutual respect and compromise, children will undoubtedly be the beneficiaries.

CHAPTER 5

Halal Cosmetics and Skin Care:
The Islamic Way to Beauty

Regardless of religious or ethnic background, women are the primary consumers of beauty supplies. It is often the female of our species who is most interested in maximizing her natural beauty. Brand Islam is only too happy to accommodate these consumers. Indeed, Muslim women, even those covered by *abaya*, an outerwear garment that is typically black and drapes from the head or shoulders down to the feet, are enthusiastic consumers of cosmetic lines. Saudi Arabia and the United Arab Emirates represent the fastest-growing cosmetics markets in the world and top the list in the Persian Gulf region in terms of purchasing organic and natural beauty products.[1] As a bonus, Brand Islam cosmetic labels are also attractive to non-Muslim women and men looking for products that are environmentally friendly, that do not use animal testing, and that do not contain substances derived from animals.

Today's enthusiastic trend toward healthful foods and body care products signals good news for the natural cosmetics market. The future of natural or organic hygiene and toiletry items is secure; markets are expanding. Consumers are turning away from harmful chemicals, additives, colorings, and animal ingredients, especially when purchasing products that may be absorbed into the bloodstream. Educated consumers tend to read labels carefully, although many consumers are still fooled by clever marketing and attention-getting advertisements. Pretty packaging may contain harmful products, but who is the wiser? When making purchasing decisions, the consumer's concern about physical appearance must be balanced with good judgment and a conscientious attempt to question fraudulent or deceptive practices.

Specific to Muslim consumers, the marketing of harmful or adulterated non-halal products packaged as halal often exploits the average

Cosmetics company reassurances. In this image Amara Cosmetics addresses potential customers' concerns about violating Islamic teachings by wearing makeup with alcohol or animal products in it. The company website also says Amara cosmetics have no paraben preservatives, gluten, petrochemicals, or raw materials tested on animals and are vegan-friendly as well as halal-certified. Image from Amara Cosmetics, http://www.amaracosmetics.com/.

consumer's inability to discern reality from appearance. What specific ingredients are listed? What are their sources? Is the labeling language purposefully obfuscatory? Wording such as "environmentally friendly products" and "all natural ingredients" does not necessarily translate to "halal."

Although halal cosmetics are fairly new to the global marketplace, expanding numbers of companies are manufacturing halal cosmetics and personal hygiene products with great gusto in anticipation of profits.

On the general market, alcohol and animal fats are often used in soaps, shampoos, body lotions, hairsprays, perfumes, shaving creams, lipsticks, and nail polish. Most consumers evidently do not care. However, religious groups and vegan and vegetarian consumers require more precise information about products to discern whether the ingredients align with their lifestyles. Several companies not only manufacture halal products but also further gear their products toward specific groups such as veiled women. In this category we have shampoos for *hijabi* women. A toothpaste brand has the Arabic word *meswak* in its name to link the product to Islam and even pre-Islamic Arabic cultures.

Here I explore various aspects of cosmetic and toiletry products, particularly those labeled halal. The roles of religion and politics figure into the discussion, as does the economic potential of halal cosmetics and toiletries in this growing industry's future.

Shampoo and conditioner marketed to women who wear *hijab*. The British company Medina, named after the city of the Prophet of Islam in Saudi Arabia, labels the products as halal as well as vegan and sells them online. Image from Muslimah Beauty, http://muslimahbeauty.com/.

Sunsilk shampoo for *hijabi* women. The advertisement in Urdu says, "Keeping hair covered all day releases sweat and sebum that creates itchy scalp dandruff. So world-class dermatologist and scalp expert Dr. Francesca Fusco has created this shampoo with lime extract, which controls these symptoms so that you too can be lively and fresh!" Translation by Tanweer Aslam and Fawzia Afzal Khan. Image from Jawa Report, http://mypetjawa.mu.nu/.

Toothpaste ad in the Bengali language. The Dabur company's ad begins, "Smile Bangladesh—September 12, 2012—World Oral Health Day." The word *meswak* or *miswak* in Arabic, Persian, and Urdu means toothbrush, not toothpaste. The toothpaste contains extract of *Salvadore persica*, the "toothbrush tree" used since pre-Islamic times as a chewing stick to keep teeth white and shiny. Mohammad is quoted in referring to *meswak*'s qualities. Perhaps the name Meswak is a strategic choice for a product manufactured and distributed in Bangladesh, a country with a 90 percent Muslim population. Translation by Dipshikha Mitra. Image from dabur.com.

Criteria for Halal Cosmetics and Toiletries

Fewer than fifty years ago, no one voiced particular concern or gave much consideration to halal products. In Muslim-majority nations, the average Muslim looked upon the concepts of halal and haram as primarily pertaining to food, such as pork and its derivatives, and alcoholic beverages. The devout Muslim would likely avoid alcohol, if possible, in toiletries and perfumes. Certainly most would not have imagined what a thriving, profitable business halal products and services would become. Few Muslim consumers could have predicted the necessity of reading label ingredients on virtually every processed food or cosmetic item purchased at the market. In fact, at the time they dealt minimally with such issues because fifty years ago most of their groceries and food items were not sealed in packages or cans. Consumer saws firsthand exactly what they were purchasing. A limited number of cosmetics and processed foods were available; therefore, choices were simple compared to those today. Local vendors familiar with the culture and customs provided most commodities, and these vendors were often members of the communities they served.

At that time, very few Muslim consumers, whether Middle Eastern or Asian, had access to imported goods. Such products would have been prohibitively expensive for the average consumer. Today's Internet world, of course, has changed all of that. Products are instantly visible and immediately accessible. Online marketing abounds in every consumer category. Entrepreneurs grab each and every opportunity to capture product sectors. The relatively new sector of halal cosmetics is beginning to catch on with global cosmetic corporations, although the Muslim Village website cites a news item about Revlon having halal-certified products since the late 1990s: "Halal cosmetics . . . are making more waves now with eco-conscious consumers. Revlon, the American cosmetic company, has had at least two hair color products—Colorsilk and Colorsilk Luminista—certified halal for more than a decade."[2]

Products such as breathable nail polish qualify as halal. The late Wojciech Inglot, a Polish chemist and founder of Inglot Cosmetics, worked for four years to formulate a polish allowing passage of air and water or moisture when applied to the nail surface. The problem with conventional nail polish is that lacquer prevents water from being absorbed into the nails when washing one's hands, an issue for religious ablution (*wudhu, wudu*) performed by Muslims five times a day before praying. As part of the ablution process, both arms from the elbows to the tips of the fingers must be rinsed with clean water. Thus, breathable nail polish makes sense for devout Muslim women who previously would have avoided nail polish entirely.

Inglot's invention, which he called O2M and began selling in 2013, was the first of its kind. A Yahoo News article reports, as might be expected, "A craze built up around it with Muslim women . . . after an Islamic scholar in the United States tested its permeability and published an article saying that, in his view, it [complied] with Muslim law."[3] Thus a new halal cosmetic product was born. After the media reported this religious ruling, Inglot found that his company was unable to fill the massive influx of orders.

With advances and innovations in the area of cosmetic technology, more cosmetic ingredients have become available to manufacturers. Some ingredients are derived from animal sources, a key area of halal concern. These sources may be derived from haram, or forbidden, animals such as pigs and dogs or from improperly slaughtered halal animals such as cattle, sheep, and chickens.

Some Sharia-dominated governments, including Malaysia's, are going to great lengths to protect Muslim consumers, as Puziah Hashim observes in proceedings from a 2009 symposium:

> According to the Malaysian Standard MS 2200 (3), the definition of halal cosmetic and personal care products are products permitted under the Islamic Law and meet the followings conditions for the ingredients: do not contain raw material from human parts or ingredients derived from thereof; do not contain any parts or substances derived from animals forbidden to Muslims by Shariah Law; do not use halal animals which are not slaughtered according to Shariah Law; do not contain any materials or genetically modified organism (GMO) which are decreed as najs [religiously impure]; and do not harm the user. Materials for cosmetic and personal care produced synthetically are halal except those that are hazardous and or mixed with materials that are decreed as najs. Najs according to Shariah law are things and animals that are themselves not permissible such as dog and pig and all its derivatives, blood and carrion.[4]

As with halal slaughter and halal foods, halal criteria require adherence to regulations in production, packaging, transportation, and storage. A respected and trustworthy agency must certify halal-advertised cosmetics and toiletries in the same way as food and drink items and assume the responsibility of revealing ingredients clearly and with credibility on the products' packaging.

Halal manufacturers now claim that plants and plant extracts can be used as viable substitutes for haram ingredients. In a Cosmetics Design article, Ahlam Momein, owner of Shifa Cosmetics, a certified halal company, says that plant ingredients are as good as animal-derived ingredients.[5] Many companies worldwide are pursuing a share of this market, and consumers increasingly want natural, green, and halal products. Others pose the question of whether natural cosmetics are indeed healthier for the skin. A Web MD article indicates that they are not:

> "The perception is that natural ingredients are more pure and kinder to skin than something made in the lab, but nothing could be farther from the truth," says dermatologist Joel Schlessinger, MD, past president of the American Society of Cosmetic Dermatology and Aesthetic Surgery. In fact, he says, if you're buying natural products to avoid breakouts or allergic reactions, you might be disappointed; they won't necessarily be a better option.[6]

The notion that a product labeled "natural" is harmless is erroneous, Schlessinger says. He warns the consumer to read labels carefully and to watch out for "parabens (which are used as preservatives); petrochemicals and their byproducts (often found in skin creams, foundations, and lip balms); mercury (in mascara and eye drops); lead (in lipsticks); dioxane (in shampoos, soaps and body washes); and phthalates in nail polishes and hair sprays."[7] Most of the ingredients he lists are not considered haram. Thus, the challenge is to be a competent consumer who can wisely navigate the maze of marketing advertisements, labels, and spokespersons promoting their products.

Natural Ingredients: Safe or Hazardous?

Animal ingredients found in cosmetics can include collagen, hyaluronic acid, sperm, glycerin, and carmine sodium. Among the most common natural ingredients used in the production of cosmetics are human and animal placentas. These are often found as extracts in pharmaceuticals, hair care and food products, and health tonic ingredients. From cow brains and human placenta to cryogenics and leeches, human vanity often ignores processes, ingredients, and sources in the search for the elixir of youth. The potential hazards inherent in using questionable

products—to us and to our children—may not be immediately apparent. As early as 1998, a *Clinical Pediatrics* article reported on hormonal
effects of placenta extracts on young girls:

> The FDA maintains that placenta extract may be potentially hazard-
> ous and its use is subject to restrictions and requirements of warnings in
> at least some products. In one study, four girls between one and eight
> years of age developed breasts or pubic hair two to 24 months after
> starting the use of estrogen- or placenta-containing hair products. Their
> breasts and pubic hair regressed when they stopped using the products.
> No other cause for early sexual development was found. Discontinuing
> the use of the hair products resulted in regression of the breast or pu-
> bic hair.[8]

One ingredient in high-end cosmetic creams and used in scientific
testing is derived from the foreskin of circumcised infants. The company SkinMedica manufactures a face cream using this derivative; the
company advertises anti-aging and various skin care products. One can
purchase what is advertised as "TNS Essential Serum. The all-in-one rejuvenating product for $260.0 an Oz." The product description says,
"Specialty ingredients provide immediate visual smoothing."[9] This special ingredient, foreskin, is carefully obscured, revealed neither on the
company's website nor on the product packaging. Another little-known
ingredient in anti-aging remedies that is not yet as popular as placenta
and foreskin is human sperm. An Internet posting at Plasmetic in 2009
titled "Anti-Aging Property of Human Sperm" provides information
from a company that sells it:

> The quest for youth has seen many products coming into the mar-
> ket. From toxins to natural products, people have tried out many dif-
> ferent things to attain a youthful skin. Now Norwegian company Bio-
> forskning has said that spermine, found in human sperm, can make the
> skin look beautiful, soft and supple.
>
> HIGHLIGHTS OF SPERMINE
> a. This is a powerful antioxidant.
> b. It is found in human sperm.
> c. It can apparently diminish wrinkles and make the skin smooth.
> d. Bioforskning has already synthesized the substance in laboratories
>   and is now selling it.

COST AND AVAILABILITY
Around $125 to $250 per spermine facial, two spas in NY offering
these facials are Townhouse Spa and Graceful Services.[10]

Zoe Ruderman, in a 2009 article for *Cosmopolitan*, writes about her
experience of receiving a "sperm facial" now gaining popularity in the
United States. Ruderman received her treatment at the swanky Townhouse Spa in New York City. She comments: "My skin felt very smooth
and moisturized immediately. And a few days later I noticed it was
clearer. And if nothing else, at least I have a great addition for when my
friends and I [are] playing "Never have I ever."[11]

Unconventional ingredients abound in salon-based cosmetic products; a 2009 post in *Newsvine* touts ingredients such as "bull sperm
combined with the roots of a plant named Katera which is very rich in
protein. Treatment starts with hair shampoo then massaging the hair
with the conditioning treatment. Hair is put under a steamer then blow
dried."[12] Hari's, the top hair salon in London, now offers clients a conditioning treatment made of bull's semen. This treatment is also known as
"Viagra for hair," which in 2013 was priced at $138 per treatment.[13] An
article in a 2001 issue of the *Journal of the American Chemical Society*
concludes that cholic acid and spermine are important for facial hydrophilicity and that spermine substantially increases facial hydrophilicity.[14]

Placental ingredients, too, are playing an increasingly significant
role in anti-aging serums, lotions, and day and night creams. Recently
dermatologists discovered that the prolonged use of Retin A cream,
suggested for acne treatment, also reduces wrinkles around the eyes.
Basically, Retin A is a placental cream derived from sheep. Many international cosmetic companies use placenta, among them the Korean
company 3WClinic, which sells a Premium Placenta Age Repair Kit and
an Authentic Mosbeau Placenta Body Scrub. Because the sale and use
of human placenta as a raw material is also freely allowed under Russian law, one can easily find Russian-made skin creams containing human placenta. The Russian company Plazan promotes its products as a
merger between medicine and cosmetics:

Plazan has worked in the market of cosmetics and medicine since 1991
and is a group of highly skilled experts. They are doctors and candidates of medical, pharmacological, and biological sciences.
    The Russian Academy of Sciences [awarded] Plazan a grant for inno-
vative activity for research of biologically active placental cell extracts,

and in 1991 the placental cell preparations developed by the company were entered into clinical tests by the health authorities. Since 1998 Plazan is the only company officially recognized as the developer of placental cell preparations by the Ministry of Health for Russia.

The company has its own research laboratory, which is engaged in a system of allocation for the stabilization of placental components. It creates new medicinal forms that act as a base for the Plazan cosmetic range.[15]

The Plazan website is dense with detailed information about the company's use of natural products and openness to divulging all ingredients. It even includes information about the function of each ingredient found in the products and states that "the active ingredients undergo rigorous quality testing from source to product in full compliance with the requirements of the World Health Organization and the Ministry of Health."[16]

In Japan, the use of human placenta for cosmetic purposes is also sanctioned and openly advertised. One example is the website of the Dr. Makise Supplement Clinic, which advertises "rejuvenation by human placenta":[17]

The main treatment consists of injections of extract of human placenta. Human placenta is not permitted in Europe and the United States. So, even at the world famous rejuvenation clinics in Switzerland, you cannot get it. In Japan it can be officially administered since more than 50 years ago. Two Japanese companies produce it, and export to Korea and Malaysia. Japanese made human placenta extract is very safe. The donor of placenta is thoroughly checked. She should be free from syphilis, gonorrhea, tuberculosis, HBV, HCV, HIV, HTLV (adult T cell leukemia), HPV/B19 (slap cheek). And she should have been in only Japanese hospitals. This is to ensure that the strict standards have been adhered to. And 300 capsules of oral human placenta extract are offered to continue the effectiveness, too. It is approximately for 3-month-use at home. It is recommendable to take it with vitamin E to improve the absorption.[18]

What are the risks of receiving placenta by direct injection or by oral supplement? Apparently no one knows. In Japan, people who receive placental injections are not allowed to donate blood, given the risk of passing on blood-borne pathogens. The US response to the use of human placenta for manufactured products such as cosmetics is not clear and on occasion is contradictory. In 2009 the *Washington Times* reported, "A San Francisco cosmetics company [Neocutis Cosmetics] ignited an outcry among pro-lifers for including an unexpected ingredient in its anti-aging creams: skin-cell proteins from an aborted fetus."[19] By law, European cosmetic and skin producers are limited to animal rather than human placenta. Those who feel that the foreskin or placenta of human beings is objectionable as an ingredient in body creams and rejuvenating serums may be scandalized to learn that a cosmetics company in China uses executed convicts' skin to develop beauty products for the European market, the *World Tribune* reported in 2006.[20] The unidentified company is developing collagen for lip and wrinkle treatments from the harvested skins of Chinese prisoners who were executed by shooting:

> The agent [for the Chinese cosmetic company] said some of the company's products have been exported to Britain, and that the use of skin from condemned convicts was "traditional" and nothing to "make such a big fuss about," the Guardian reported.[21]

According to Amnesty International, China also harvests human organs from convicted prisoners, claiming prior permission from the individuals or their family members, almost immediately after execution. A 2005 *Guardian* article reported on this practice and the potential for a lack of regulation to put consumers at risk: "Doctors and politicians say the discovery highlights the dangers faced by the increasing number of Britons seeking to improve their looks. Apart from the ethical concerns, there is also the potential risk of infection."[22]

As consumers become more educated, they are looking "for products that align with their beliefs—whether it's being halal for religious reasons or to avoid cruelty to animals,"[23] Susan Dewhirst, spokesperson for halal cosmetics company Samina Pure Mineral Makeup, told a reporter for Muslim Village. The company is owned by a Muslim woman and based in Birmingham, England. *Cosmetics and Toiletries* reported in 2012 on the halal sector of this market:

> International sales of halal-certified beauty and personal care products are upward of $5 billion, and a growing number of beauty and cosmetic ingredient firms are taking up halal certification in Asia. The highest adoption rates are in Muslim countries where multinationals that in-

clude Colgate-Palmolive and Avon have launched halal-certified products. Also, international chemical firms like BASF and CP Kelco are developing ingredients certified for such markets.[24]

Few global cosmetic corporations have gone for double certification of their cosmetic products, that is, certifying products as both organic and halal. *Cosmetics Design* cites a complication in attaining dual certification:

> According to Organic Monitor, some companies have started to formulate natural/organic cosmetics with Halal certification as they realize that Halal products, while increasingly popular, often fall short in terms of their ecological credentials as the formulations are similar to conventional cosmetics.[25]

To certify a product as both organic and halal can be prohibitively costly. In addition to monitoring the use of halal ingredients, attention must be given to the processing facility and packaging method and materials as well as to all tools and utensils used in manufacturing. By contrast, the most important factors in the production of natural and organic cosmetics are simply the ingredients. The Cosmetics Design article explains that "natural & organic cosmetics cannot have potentially harmful synthetic chemicals like parabens, phthalates, SLS, etc. . . . [while] halal cosmetics allow such ingredients, but forbid gelatin, collagen and other livestock ingredients not from halal sources."[26]

Halal Cosmetics: A Global Market Makeover

Historically, women have gone to great lengths to beautify; both men and women have used a mystifying array of dermabrasion techniques to resurface and encourage radiant skin. This process has been performed for thousands of years with different agents, including salt, pumice, ground grains, bone, and horn.[27] In today's market, one of the most popular skin rejuvenation remedies is a drink named Gold Collagen.[28] But according to Memphis plastic surgeon Peter A. Aldea, Gold Collagen is nothing more than a scam:

> Collagen is just another protein chain which when eaten is digested by the stomach acids and the upper small bowel into its particular amino

acid subunits. As long as the source of protein is high in amino acids (instead of fat, etc.), any one source of eaten protein is not better than another. Don't waste your money.[29]

With online technology at their fingertips, today's consumers—and particularly those with money to burn—spend a huge amount of cash every day by placing body and skin care products in their virtual shopping carts. This global Internet culture is in no way limited to a single religious affiliation. Indeed, one finds unbridled enthusiasm and interest in beauty and skin care products among a wide swath of consumers, and Muslims are no different. Now and in the future, Muslim women, both young and mature, will be obvious candidates for rejuvenating products designed for the halal lifestyle.

In 2013 a published research article cited a series of variables to be noted by those who select halal cosmetics, however: "Purity has been identified as the main factor that influences the intention to purchase halal cosmetics products."[30] Few doubt the potential market for halal cosmetics and halal toiletries, even for very conservative, *niqabi* (also spelled *nighabi*), or veiled-face women, followers of Salafi Islam.[31] Entrepreneur Bunda Alifa of Indonesia operates an online business, the House of Bunda, that sells alcohol-free halal beauty and health products in compliance with Salafi Islam principles. She emphasizes the sexy and feminine side of her halal cosmetic products in addition to their health and beauty aspects. The House of Bunda offers products, as described in an *International Journal of Cultural Studies* article in 2013, such as "Breast Care Spa, V Whitening Lotion, V-spa and Beauty Buster, and even a product for men called Natural Oil Enlargement."[32] Bunda contends that women must look attractive and sexy to their husbands. When queried as to why she had chosen to carry this particular line of products, she replied,

> "Hahaha . . . it must be like that, sister, because I want my husband's eyes to be focused only on me." She wanted other Muslim women to have the same experience. Thus, *cadari* [face veiled] are not immune to the demands of the beauty culture, but they try to adjust these demands to suit their Salafi lifestyles by using halal products. The justification for the use of these products is in line with Islamic teaching: to provide pleasure for the husband's gaze.[33]

In the cosmetics industry, exploiting halal as a desirable concept has become strategic to guaranteeing a share of the profits among Muslim consumers. Malaysia has taken the lead in this initiative. The first international conference on halal cosmetics and toiletries was held in Kuala Lumpur in 2010.[34] Panel discussions included strategic management of the Department of Standards Malaysia, an entity that developed the Malaysian and halal standard for toiletries and cosmetics. The conference addressed halal standards for the production of fragrances, product formulation, branding, and marketing.[35] Reports on the event indicated that this relatively new industry of halal cosmetics and toiletries held enormous financial promise corresponding with the Muslim population growth globally. Global sales for halal-certified personal care products are rapidly growing, more than $50 billion per annum, which means an average increase per year of 20 percent in the global market.[36]

After the 2010 Kuala Lumpur conference, various cosmetics manufacturers experimented with developing and promoting the halal concept. This turned out to be more challenging than imagined, even in a Sharia-dominant country like Malaysia, as researchers observe in a 2012 journal article:

> Even though Halal cosmetics have been well established in Malaysia, it still hasn't captured the eye of the consumers and gained high market share in the country. This has proven that there is still lack of interest and urge in Muslims in Malaysia on Halal cosmetics. One of the factors is the Halal lifestyle. The slow development of the Halal lifestyle category, in comparison to the food category, can be attributed to two factors. First, albeit important, it does not have the same urgency as food. Second, both Muslims and multinationals learned late that as Halal actually extends beyond food, normal day activities can also be Islamized and classified as Halal, and thus special Islamic-compliant lifestyle-related products began to be developed to meet the needs of this market and to, at the same time, capitalize on the opportunity it provides.[37]

New players in cosmetic and toiletry industries are attempting to profit from Brand Islam or "Islamic-compliant lifestyle-related products." This includes manufacturers outside of Muslim-majority regions. Tom's of Maine, an American producer of body and oral care products, announced on its website in 2006 that it was now halal-certified:

> Tom's of Maine now has the opportunity to serve a whole new community of people who make buying decisions based on their values. We're excited by this news and believe when you create products with clear

values in mind, you end up with higher quality ingredients and more effective products.

A cross-functional team of Tom's of Maine employees worked with IFANCA to obtain certification. Tom's products also have kosher certification. It is very easy to understand why Tom's of Maine products can easily be qualified for halal and kosher certification. Reading the ingredients on every product makes it clear that this company only uses simple, natural substances derived from minerals and plants only. The company also strives for eco friendly philosophy [and adheres] to the policy of no testing on animals. Tom's of Maine products—toothpaste, mouthwash, floss, deodorant, and soap—do not contain artificial sweeteners, preservatives, colors, flavors, or animal ingredients.[38]

Colgate, another American-based company, received halal certification, enabling the corporation to market its products in Malaysia and other Asian countries where sizable numbers of Muslim citizens reside. The company website cites a statement from JAKIM, the Department of Islamic Development Malaysia, regarding Colgate toothpaste:

JAKIM acknowledges that Colgate Toothpaste is certified Halal by Islamic Bodies recognized by JAKIM as follows: Central Islamic Committee of Thailand, The Islamic Community of Ho Chi Minh City (Vietnam), China Islamic Association (China) and Federation of Muslims Associations of Brazil (Brazil).[39]

IFANCA, an Islamic organization and halal certification entity, provides information on its website detailing which companies have been halal certified and each certification's expiration date. Not only is IFANCA fastidious about maintaining its credible reputation, but the organization is also strongly invested, and for good reason, in certification revenues. No doubt IFANCA is discovering lucrative certification territory in India, where Muslims comprise more than 14 percent of the population. In addition to its domestic Muslim market, India has begun to export personal care and cosmetics to the UAE, Malaysia, Saudi Arabia, Bangladesh, and Turkey. All of these countries have Muslim majorities that are embracing halal lifestyle products.

In India particularly, the certification entity Halal India reports, "The potential is great for [the] halal cosmetics market for Indian Muslims as current demand of Halal certified women beauty products in India could be doubled . . . during the year 2019–2020. More than 19.6 million Muslim women . . . between 20 to 40 years could be a huge market to introduce cosmetics products." It notes that for now, "given the price-sensitivity of the Indian consumer who does not normally prefer to fork out a large sum at one time, many cosmetic and toiletries companies launched their products in smaller pack sizes to make them more affordable."[40]

A significant number of homegrown Indian halal products, produced with sensitivity to Muslim religious requirements, are already available on the market. For example, CavinKare and Amrutanjan Healthcare have been seeking halal certification to shore up their marketing opportunities in Singapore, Malaysia, and the Gulf Cooperation Council (GCC), an alliance of six Middle Eastern countries that was established in 1981. The *Indian Muslim Observer* cites R. S Vijay Kumar, general manager of international business at the personal care company CavinKare, based in Chennai, India, on advantages of recognition: "The certification is a reason-to-belief for customers on quality parameters. The certification will also give an edge over our competitors."[41] The potential for Halal India certification is great, says its CEO Mohamed Jinna in the 2012 Halal India article: "With many brands embracing halal, Indian brands may look at an export market opportunity of about $200 billion in the next ten years."[42]

Some manufacturers actually exploit the Muslim *hijab* to market shampoo and other hair cleansing and styling products. Sunsilk is a haircare label from the Unilever group, acknowledged as a premier global corporation and the world's second-largest manufacturer of shampoo products after Procter and Gamble.[43] A Sunsilk shampoo ad in Pakistan targets women who wear the *hijab*, translated here from Urdu to English:

Keeping hair covered all day releases sweat and sebum that creates itchy scalp dandruff. So world-class dermatologist and scalp expert Dr. Francesca Fusco has created this shampoo with lime extract, which controls these symptoms so that you too can be lively and fresh![44]

This ad refers to a medical authority—and, therefore, surely an expert—whom Muslim women can trust to understand the perils of wearing the *hijab* every day. Dr. Fusco has predicted an unhealthy scalp for *hijab* wearers, and he knows how to fix this problem. The ad also indicates that although *hijabi* ladies do not want to expose their hair and publicly expose their natural beauty to everyone, nevertheless they possess a hidden beauty requiring special care. (See the images on page 115.)

Noor al-Qasimi, author and formerly a postdoctoral fellow at the

Centre for Cultural Media and Creative Industries at Kings College, London, examined how advertisers of various shampoo products circumvent issues around the veil in order to successfully compete in the Saudi market. In her study al-Qasimi looked at nine shampoo ads, including ads for Pantene, Pert Plus, and Head and Shoulders. Ironically, these ads, while not specifically focusing on product ingredients as halal, attempt to target all female Saudi consumers. Although the advertisements for the Pakistani Sunsilk and the various Saudi shampoos enjoy similarities, their differences reflect distinct marketing approaches. They make *hijabi* women the primary focus of their advertisements, while the more generic multinational companies purposefully avoid portraying *hijabi* women in their ads for hair care products. Neither kind of ad targets the halal concept or references any halal shampoo ingredients.

In Pakistan the marketing of shampoo products is handled slightly differently. Pakistani advertisements tend to show women from the front in stylish veils, all wearing makeup, but with no hair visible, while adjacent to the woman's image an expert opinion reminds us that wearing the *hijab* may possibly cause scalp problems. In contrast, the Saudi shampoo advertisements directly focus on the beautiful, long, shiny, and healthy hair of the model. The photographs are angled from the back of the model's head so her face is never showing. Thus, Pakistani and Saudi manufacturers and marketers of shampoo deal with the issues of *hijab* and modesty in their own unique ways. One takes advantage of the veil, attracting consumer attention to shampoos specifically formulated for the *hijab*-wearing woman and focusing on the prevention of dermatological problems, while the other ad promotes the product by showcasing the healthy condition of the model's hair. However, in neither of the ads is the word "halal" mentioned. That is, not yet.

In 2004, shampoo manufacturers advertising on Saudi Television (SATV) faced a series of challenges. Due to the Saudi social norm of females covering their heads and following the modesty code, advertisers had to be unusually innovative and creative about promoting a commodity involving hair care. How they did it, Noor al-Qasimi reveals in a 2012 *Camera Obscura* article, is that "a woman is initially shown turned away from the camera with her hair in evidence. In a second frame, her damaged hair is represented in isolation, while in a third her face appears in hair-free close-up."[45] This type of censorship has been tested and implemented since 1981, when the Islamic Republic of Iran set new rules and regulations for the manner in which Iranian cinema could depict women on screen. Sometimes the regulations made the scenes unrealistic, forcing directors to come up with highly creative solutions in terms of how they angled the shots and engaged in the editing process.[46]

Surprisingly, indicators suggest that it will not be Saudi Arabia, Iran, or any Middle Eastern nations blazing the trail of interest in halal cosmetics and toiletries; rather, it will likely be Asian countries. Brunei, on Borneo's north coast in Southeast Asia, promotes halal-certified cosmetics. Tenji Takahashi of Japan, deputy general manager for research and development at Reinhalt Corporation and an expert in halal cosmetics science and technology in Brunei, told Halal Focus that Brunei has the potential to develop its own halal cosmetics industry: "Brunei is an ideal place for such an endeavour in Halal cosmetics as the nation makes it a national project to certify and thus guarantee that certain products are indeed Halal. It is accepted not only by Bruneians but also Muslims from other countries."[47] Despite enticements in ads and assurances on labels, consumers everywhere still can face uncertainty about even natural or "halal" products and their safety.

Toxins and Fraud: Not a Pretty Sight

Natural News reported on results of a 2009 study that highlight the toxic load in everyday beauty and personal care products: "The average woman applies 515 chemicals to her face a day. Makeup, perfumes, lotions, mascara, and other beauty products all contribute to the toxic brew that is causing health problems for many women. . . . Aside from aluminum, many of these products contain other harmful ingredients like synthetic dyes, fragrances, and parabens. When applied continually, the many beauty products are exposing women to a wide range of carcinogens."[48] In 2006 the Environmental Working Group (EWG) reported that the majority of the cosmetic ingredients responsible for hormonal disruption also cause immune dysfunction as well as developmental problems and may be affecting younger people as a result of excessive use.[49]

Indeed not every natural ingredient can be assumed to be safe. The eye cosmetic kohl, which has been used since ancient times, is a good example. Made by grinding lead sulfide, also called galena, and other ingredients, kohl is commonly used in South Asia, the Middle East, and North Africa. Kohl is also known by other names, such as *kajal* in Urdu, *pinaari* in Bengali, *surma* in Persian and Turkish, and *kol, kehal,* or *ko-hal* in Arabic. Women in many parts of the world apply kohl on a daily basis to darken their eyebrows and eyelids. A study published in 2001 about the lead content in traditional Moroccan cosmetics and remedies targeted kohl and natural henna, both substances frequently used by women on their bodies and on the skin of children and infants. The study suggested that kohl could be a dangerous substance, especially when mixed and blended with a host of other harmful ingredients.[50]

Noteworthy information surfaced in the 2001 study about henna, a traditional Moroccan product used in rituals such as weddings, births, and religious ceremonies. As a cosmetic and a natural dye for hand-woven carpets, henna has been a popular choice for centuries. Customarily, other ingredients such as herbs, oils, lemon juice, and freshly beaten eggs have been added to henna to increase its color, to bolster hair treatments, or to decorate the skin. The study indicated that

> concentrations of lead found in non-elaborate (henna only) samples of henna were low. However, when henna was mixed with other products (elaborate henna), these concentrations increased. Lead concentrations in kohl were very high, however. Unlike henna, [lead concentrations] were lower in mixed kohl as mixing with other products diluted the concentration of lead. Nevertheless, in both types of kohl, lead concentrations were very high and consequently constitute a risk for public health, particularly for children.[51]

In a 1998 study, researchers examined a total of forty-seven kohl samples from eye cosmetics commonly used in Oman and found that ingredients in the samples were mostly toxic and harmful. Their findings applied to the eighteen samples of kohl produced in Oman as well as the rest, which were produced in other countries.[52] Such studies should give these cosmetics' consumers pause for thought. Most traditional eye cosmetics are not quality-controlled. Labels may be false and misleading. Such products usually contain toxic metals, and the consumer needs to be informed about the contaminants. Authors of a 2002 *Journal of Ethnopharmacology* article found that lead-contaminated cosmetics and similar products "can cause a significant increase in the blood lead levels which in turn could lead to sub-clinical lead poisoning."[53] The authors of a 1991 *Environmental Health Perspectives* article regarding kohl eyeliner sold in Great Britain and North America likewise warns of potential hazards:

Those kohls that contained lead were sold in violation of laws on lead in cosmetics in both of these nations. Third-world physicians and health care workers appear to be unaware of possible lead uptake from unsuspected traditionally used items. Physicians in developed nations with patients from Asia, the Middle East, and North Africa need to factor in the possibility of past or present lead intake from unorthodox sources such as kohl.[54]

Some of the dangers inherent in unregulated makeup or body-modification ingredients include blood-borne diseases such as hepatitis C, hepatitis B, tetanus, and tuberculosis. Furthermore, delivery equipment may be contaminated, allergic reactions could occur from injected dyes, scarring is possible, and redness and swelling may be caused by local bacterial infections. Additionally, removal of the makeup is a painstaking process requiring several costly treatments, and the skin may likely be scarred by the procedure. In terms of the halal or haram aspect of permanent makeup or tattoos, the following is narrated in the al-Sahihin hadith of the Prophet, compiled by Muhammad bin 'Abdullah Abu 'Abdullah al-Hakim al-Nisaburi:

'Abd-Allaah ibn Mas'ood (may Allaah be pleased with him) said: "May Allaah curse the women who do tattoos and those for whom tattoos are done, those who pluck their eyebrows and those who file their teeth for the purpose of beautification and alter the creation of Allaah." (al-Bukhaari, al-Libaas [section], 5587; Muslim, al-Libaas [section], 5538)

A related hadith, by al-Bukhari, also comments on tattoos and the permissibility of permanent makeup, according to the Prophet Mohammad. Cited by Mufti Suhail Tarmahomed, the hadith is contained in the answer to a question, both posted online by Jamiatul Ulama of KwaZulu of Natal, South Africa:

Question: Is permanent makeup permissible for females? Fatwa Department Jamiatul Ulama (KZN), Council of Muslim Theologians, Jamiatul Ulama of KwaZulu-Natal, South Africa
Answer: Permanent makeup is not permissible as it entails tattooing. This is why it is also known as cosmetic tattooing. The Prophet of Allah (Sallallahu Alaihi Wasallam)[may blessing of God be upon him] forbade tattooing and cursed the tattooist and the tattooed. The prohibition behind this is that a tattoo entails changing the colour of one's

skin. "May Allah curse those who tattoo, those who have (their bodies) tattooed, those who have their eyebrows plucked and those who create gaps between their teeth. They are changing what Allah has created. Why should I not curse those whom Nabi (Sallallahu Alaihi Wasallam) has cursed whilst it has been recorded in the Qur'an?" (Sahih al-Bukhari, Hadith #: 5943)[55]

This hadith leaves no doubt that, according to the Prophet Mohammad, both tattoo and permanent makeup are considered haram—and, therefore, a taboo direction for any pious Muslim to follow.

In order for a product and brand name to thrive in the marketplace, consumer confidence and trust in the manufacturer's integrity must be secured. The satisfied customer becomes a marketing agent for the product, given the value of word-of-mouth testimony. In the long run, a company or corporation only damages itself by selling fraudulent or toxic products. Doing so leaves the door wide open for lawsuits and onerous fines; equally important is that consumers resent being bamboozled by false advertising. Regardless of whether the customers are restricted by health or religious considerations, they will tell their friends and family members and may even become more vocal in terms of consumer advocacy.

Cosmetics Design posted an article about a 2007 report by the Environmental Working Group indicating that 323 of the cosmetics products in the US market were banned in other nations because of harmful ingredients. The EWG later offered "its conclusion in a web-published protest letter to the FDA, claim[ing] that nearly one in 30 cosmetics sold in the US fails to meet one or more industry or governmental cosmetics safety standards."[56] Jane Houlihan, a spokesperson for EWG, elaborated: "Cosmetics do not have to be approved as safe by the FDA before they are sold. As a result, they too often contain dangerous ingredients banned in Europe and Japan, or chemicals deemed unsafe for specific uses by their own industry scientists."[57] This statement is revelatory; essentially, consumers may be exposing themselves to materials already banned in other parts of the world. As might be expected, cosmetics company representatives responded angrily to the report, calling the EWG's findings baseless and insisting on the safety of their products: "Cosmetics continue to be one of the safest categories of products used by Americans each day."[58]

That same year, 2007, the EWG published another report on the danger of commonly used petroleum-based cosmetics, also described in Cosmetics Design: EWG "suggests that a significant number of cosmetic and toiletry products with petroleum-base may contain a cancer-causing impurity called 1,4-dioxane." The cancer-causing chemical was found in other items such as soaps and hair products marketed for children and infants. The report also indicated that "80 per cent of cosmetic and personal care products sold in the country contain one or more of around 24 known impurities that have been linked to cancer."[59] The EWG issued a public warning that consumers should choose products free of these carcinogenic impurities and, above all, carefully read ingredients listed on the label. Two years prior, in 2005, state legislators in California introduced a bill requiring cosmetics manufacturers to disclose which of their products sold in the state contained potentially harmful chemicals or toxins. Brands such as Avon, Grecian Formula, and wet n wild were targeted. This bill faced serious opposition by the cosmetics industry, which described it as "anti-cosmetics legislation."[60] Opposition groups worried that trade secrets and formulas that had required years of product research and development would be exposed. Nevertheless, on October 8, 2005, California's governor Arnold Schwarzenegger signed the Safe Cosmetics Bill, legislation that a Safe Cosmetics website article calls "the nation's first state law on chemicals in cosmetics":

> Companies . . . now have to notify the state when they use chemicals linked to cancer and birth defects. . . . The decision caps a two-year campaign by Breast Cancer Action, the Breast Cancer Fund, and the National Environmental Trust to bring additional scrutiny to an industry accustomed to only minimal oversight.[61]

Since 2005, other state legislators, individually and collectively, have introduced and worked toward policy to assure consumer safety in terms of cosmetics and personal body care products, Safe Cosmetics reports:

> Rep. Jan Schakowsky, D-Ill., and Rep. Ed Markey, D-Mass., introduced the Safe Cosmetics and Personal Care Products Act of 2013, which [gave] the Food and Drug Administration authority to ensure that all personal care products are free of harmful ingredients. Existing law, which [had] not been significantly updated since 1938, [had] loopholes that [allowed] chemicals linked to cancer, birth defects, learning disabilities and other illnesses in products we use on our bodies every day.[62]

Consumer advocates in the United States continue to challenge cosmetics companies resisting the switch from toxic chemicals to safer alternatives. Consumer groups cite a list of chemicals known to be linked to cancer and other diseases, including formaldehyde in soap and shampoo, lead in lipsticks, and mercury in skin creams.[63] Thanks to California's trailblazing legislative efforts, some of these chemicals have indeed been banned in the United States.

Strangely, those harmful chemicals may still be considered halal. Thus, the halal consumer must be intently vigilant and aware of the chemical composition of any given cosmetic, skin care, or hair care product—and at the same time remain informed about possible haram ingredients that, while not overtly toxic or harmful, still compromise the religious principles upon which a halal lifestyle is based.

Necessity for Regulation: Halal and Beyond

The cosmetics industry, much like the food industry, must face the demands of regulatory standards. Government safeguards must be firmly set in place to assure the safety of any cosmetic or body care product. Consumers must demand truth in advertising as well as a comprehensive and comprehensible listing of ingredients. Various new and expanded laboratory processes have been developed globally, particularly in Malaysia, to test and identify the purity of cosmetics and toiletries for halal requirements. The Malaysian government is once again taking the lead in protecting its Muslim citizens by strongly supporting university research efforts to refine halal testing methods.

The use of cod liver oil demonstrates the importance of such testing. Cod liver oil is a common ingredient used in many skin care and fragrance products and in first aid as an occlusive, or air- and water-tight, trauma dressing. The US Food and Drug Administration permits the use of cod liver oil as an active ingredient in over-the-counter skin care products. The industry-funded Cosmetics Ingredient Review board has deferred evaluation of this ingredient because the FDA assessed the product and assured the public that cod liver oil is safe.[64]

One characteristic of cod liver oil is to slow water loss from the skin by forming a barrier on the skin's surface. It also temporarily protects injured or exposed skin from harmful or irritating stimuli and may provide relief. Cosmetics Info notes, "Cod liver oil that complies with European regulations on animal by-products, may be used in cosmetics and personal care products marketed in Europe according to the general provisions of the Cosmetics Directive of the European Union."[65]

Aside from cod liver oil, an article in 2002 reported that one of the world's largest producers of the oil, the Norwegian company Maritext, also had produced seven tons of processed cod sperm for the international makeup market. Frank Hansen, a biotech engineer at the company, commented on the product's qualities: "It neither smells nor tastes of anything." He predicted that the company would be the leader of cod sperm for cosmetics purposes. Cod sperm extract boasts medicinal uses, can serve as a breast milk substitute, and was "being used in chocolate and to treat salmon according to the fishery research in Tromsø [Norway]."[66]

In a 2009 issue of the *Journal of the American Oil Chemists' Society*, researchers Abdul Rohman and Yaakob B. Che Man reported on their testing for adulteration in cod liver oil. The aim of their study was to determine if other, cheaper oils from animal fats had been used in products claiming to contain only cod liver oil. The study used FTIR, Fourier transform infrared spectroscopy, "a nondestructive and fast technique for the determination of adulterants in cod liver oil. Attenuated total reflectance measurements were made on pure cod liver oil and cod liver oil adulterated with different concentrations of lard."[67] Lard greatly resembles cod liver oil in chemical composition. Interest in cod liver oil has risen because of its nutritional advantages, its healing quality, its texture, and even as alternative source for losing weight. The authors of the report emphasize that because of cod liver oil's therapeutic properties and uses it is "important to have reliable methods either for its identification or for the detection of potential adulterants. . . . FTIR is one of the most popular methods used for authentication analysis, especially in fats and oils."[68]

The same authors, Rohman and Che Man, this time in a 2011 *Middle-East Journal of Scientific Research* article, turned to cream cosmetic formulations. Their focus? Detecting the presence of lard, using the same FTIR technique. At issue was—and still is—the permissibility of including lard in cosmetics products given that its use is not sanctioned by certain religions such as Islam and Judaism. The technique of combining FTIR with two other analytic approaches "was developed for the quantification and classification of LD [lard] in cream formulation."[69] The researchers conclude, "The results can be extended to various types of topical cosmetic preparations using oils as a base in their formulations. The tedious time and chemical consuming reagents and solvents can be avoided; therefore this technique can be considered as a 'green analytical technique.'"[70] In short, the process of combining these various detection methods may find multiple applications, especially in situations where oil adulteration is suspected. It is interesting to note that the authors link their type of analysis with the word "green." Using this particular word may have been a deliberate effort to connect the concept of halal with processes and products that Muslim consumers value as being environmentally friendly.

As halal-conscious consumers become more interested in eco-sustainable lifestyles and more aware of ingredients in their toiletries and cosmetics, no doubt halal products will grow in popularity. In a report published by Cosmeticsdesign.com (2008), Katie Bird writes: "The Muslim market presents significant opportunities for cosmetics and fashion brand, according to management consultancy firm A T Kearney."[71] This report reveals the huge market potential for halal cosmetics, given a burgeoning Muslim population worldwide. Because few products or companies are halal-certified at present, the market is ripe for development. Entrepreneur Mah Hussain-Gambles, founder of the British halal-certified company Pure Skincare, is literally banking on this idea.[72] It is obvious that the craze is about using products that not only are aligned with Muslim principles of halal but also can accommodate vegans, vegetarians, and Jewish consumers.

In theory, wearing cosmetics, according to some Muslims, is haram, forbidden, but in practice a significant proportion of the younger Muslim female generation is wearing cosmetics and prefers to use halal-certified products. The Body Shop is an excellent example of a mainstream, non-halal-certified company with products extremely popular in the Middle East. Rather than depending on packaging alone to lure consumers, multinationals like the Body Shop have been successful in the Persian Gulf market by focusing strongly on ecological and health awareness concerns. The company is a successful retailer with a "strong stance against animal testing and using a number of natural ingredients in their products."[73] Even so, a halal-conscious consumer may prefer to spend her or his money with companies other than the Body Shop if those companies' products are labeled with halal certification logos.

The consumer of halal cosmetics is often concerned about the use of fatty substances, with lard from pigs being one of the most common fats in cosmetics processing. Any type of solid or liquid vegetable oil may be substituted for lard in order to accommodate halal requirements. Scientific collaborations are well under way to determine the optimum type of oil to use in halal cosmetics. In a study entitled "Special Oils for Halal Cosmetics," three nonconventional oils were extracted, analyzed, and tested for toxicity and their possible safe use in halal cosmetics production.[74] The three oils selected for this experiment were date palm kernel, mango kernel, and rambutan seed. All with stable qualities, these oils "melt at skin temperature, have good lubricity and are great sources of essential fatty acids; they could be used as highly moisturizing, cleansing and nourishing oils because of high oleic acid content."[75] This study suggests that relatively unknown and infrequently used extracts like these will be finding new niches in the market as they are introduced into halal skin care products such as massage oils, hair care products, shampoos, soaps, body washes—and vaginal lubricants.

Among body care and hygiene products being marketed as halal and targeting Muslim women, vaginal lubricants are not at the top of the list—at least not yet. But surely some ingenious entrepreneur in some part of the world is giving serious thought to the development and marketing of this product—especially because, according to Islam, sex between married men and women is not only halal but is also meant to be pleasurable. In other words, sexual satisfaction for both sexes is Islamically sanctioned. The purpose of sex, according to Islamic dictates, is not only for procreation but also for personal pleasure. Muslim marriage counselor Wedad Lootah bases her sex advice firmly on the teachings of the Qur'an and says that "sex is an important part of marriage, that's in the Quran." She continues:

> My advice for married women is to buy lots of dresses. Look beautiful. Be clean. Use the perfume. . . . I give the same advice to men: be like what you want your wife to be like. Brush your teeth.[76]

Above all, she says, when it comes to the bedroom, couples should remember variety is the spice of life. Wedad Lootah says in a 2009 article in *Jezebel* that the objective of her book, *Top Secret: Sexual Guidance for Married Couples*, is to "guide people about how to satisfy each other. . . . We're talking about Islam. We're not talking about sex."[77] Because of the increasingly open discussion of sex within the context of Islam, there is new interest in using products that enhance sexual pleasure between husband and wife—products such as those offered by Abdelaziz Aouragh's online shop Al-Asira (also El Asira), which addresses

Muslim couples from an Islamic perspective, that is, one that promotes sexual well-being with halal and Sharia-compliant advice and products. An article about the company offers some background:

> There are different entrances to the site for men and women. Mr. Aou-ragh even consulted a Muslim scholar before putting the website online to make sure every detail was permissible according to Islam. He hes-itates to call the website 'halal' but says that as a Muslim he wouldn't put anything on sale that he wasn't allowed to use himself.[78]

The website posts photos of bottled lubricants and oils and jars of what are claimed to be powerful aphrodisiacs, again all halal-compliant according to the online information. Here is a commercial site offering products that "boost the customer's libido . . . [with] quality aphrodi-siacs . . . [like] Pure Power capsules which heighten male performance, desire and pleasure."[79] Desire-enhancing capsules for women will soon be available from the Al-Asira shop as well as sensual stimulators for both partners and special halal lubricants based on cocoa butter, water, or silicon. Aouragh explains that his products contain specific herbs that have been in use for centuries and that he has altered to intensify plea-sure and function.[80]

Shopping online at websites catering to the Islamic consumer, spe-cifically sites that offer halal sex-related products, means that one's pas-sions can be enhanced privately without violating religious law. The website Sex Toys Islam operates out of Atlanta, Georgia.[81] From a de-sign perspective, this website is cleverly presented—making full use of images that signal all things Islamic and halal. The home page cites Qur'an verse 7:189:

> It is He who created you from a single soul,
> And made its mate of like nature
> in order that you might dwell with her in love.

Among the noteworthy products offered by Sex Toys Islam are "Mak-ing Whoopie Arousal Cream-Orange Passion," "Touch of Honey Edible Body Dust-Passion Berry," "Guilty Pleasure Arousal Cream-Strawberry Malt," and "Vanilla Foaming Lubrication."

Another website, Nikah Shop (*nikah* in Arabic translates to "mar-riage"), advertises "Provestra women halal enhancer." This online site makes open reference to a woman's sexual desire and strongly supports her right to achieve orgasm:

Every woman deserves a passionate sex life, filled with intense desire, uninhibited pleasure, exquisite sensations, and easily achieved orgasms. No matter what your age! That's why our team of sexual health experts has formulated Provestra™: It's the 100% safe, doctor-endorsed daily supplement, created to dramatically increase a woman's desire for sex . . .

How Does It Work?

Provestra™ is a proprietary blend of the highest quality herbs, nutrients, and aphrodisiacs making it halal, all proven to help balance the hormones and nutrients associated with all aspects of the female reproductive system.[82]

There are numerous Internet sites hawking sexually related products as halal or Islamically approved. One need only use one's imagination to envision the next generation of halal-labeled personal care products, from lubricants to arousal creams. Internet entrepreneurs are proving particularly clever; their sites offer products that basically are already available on the general market. However, through the use of carefully crafted language and Islamically oriented images, they are discovering successful, albeit manipulative, strategies with strong appeal to the Muslim consumer.

Beauty and the Beast of Profit

The manufacture and marketing of cosmetics and personal care products continues to be a thriving, lucrative business. For some manufacturers, quality and customer satisfaction rank as top criteria. For others, the bottom line is profit. Unfortunately, like mainstream cosmetic products, the halal cosmetics and toiletries market will continue to be exploited by fraudulent practices. While government regulations are meant to protect consumers, there is little doubt that fraudulent labeling as well as price-gouging will continue. The process of authentic halal certification, based on scientific methods and research, may ultimately eradicate these practices—particularly as halal-minded consumers increase in numbers and begin to strengthen their advocacy efforts. Growing numbers of Muslims, and Muslim youth in particular, will pay higher prices for quality cosmetics and skin care products guaranteed by the halal-certified logo. Reliance on the religious purity of the products will become an increasingly significant factor in Muslim consumer choices. Universal access to online shops and the speed of Internet delivery will also contribute to skyrocketing sales in the global marketplace of halal cosmetics and toiletries.

Meanwhile, established corporations and budding entrepreneurs continue to invest time, effort, and money in targeting and catering to niche consumers with special needs—including halal-minded consumers. Paul Temporal, founder and managing director of Temporal Brand Consulting, contends that managers can benefit from learning about other cultures. Cited in *Indian Muslim Observer*, Temporal says managers must also develop keen awareness regarding differences in market value systems:

> If you look at Islamic values, most of them are emotional and this makes for good branding and marketing. A more careful look reveals that a lot of these values do not just suit Islamic audiences, but are of a universally appealing nature. The issue or challenge is to find where these people are and to reach them with suitable products.[83]

On the Islam in Europe blog, Mohammed Cheppih, a Muslim professor at Al-Kauthar Institute,[84] is befuddled by the fuss about halal cosmetics:

> If you look at it from a theological perspective, the usage of shampoo and such products is not 'consuming'. According to Islam you may use alcohol in some cases, for example, also as a medicine. The danger is that those who don't have any knowledge will think in terms of allowed and not allowed.[85]

Cheppih further states that those who are obsessed with the "haramness" of cosmetics and other personal care products may be using the banner of religion, as well as the concepts of halal and haram, simply to make a sale.[86] The truth is that Islam is merging into commodity marketing, promoting capitalist consumerism by appealing to Islamist sentiments.

The craze of buying and selling halal-labeled body care items is fast becoming a multibillion-dollar business. Religious, economic, and political factors have merged to produce this outcome. The reality is that even the ulama cannot agree about the halal/*haram* issue where cosmetics are concerned, and therefore, their fatwas have differed significantly and, on occasion, contradicted each other.

While religious precepts and government policies can make or break

حجاب
زیباست
زیبایی
نیست

تنها مواظب باشند این راه مبارک انقلاب را گم نکنند
امروز، سرگرم شدن به زر و زیور
برای زن مسلمان ایرانی انقلابی عیب است
امروز، پر کردن سر و سینه و دست از زیورآلات
و بت قرار دادن زیور و آرایش و مُد و لباس
برای زن انقلابی مسلمان ایرانی ننگ است
آن کسی که در پی این گونه چیزهاست، ارزشش پایین است
مُد، برای زن ارزش آفرین نیست
بی‌اعتنایی نسبت به مُدهای دام‌گونه‌ی ساخته و پرداخته‌ی دشمنان
برای زن ارزش است

A warning about makeup, jewelry, and fashion. It advises Iranian women to remain
on "the joyful path" instead: "It is shameful for the Iranian Islamic Revolutionary
woman to wear layers of jewelry on her body. . . . Fashion does not create a
higher status for any woman. What brings worth for a woman is to ignore all
the fashionable traps that are created by the enemies." Image from PersianGig,
http://reyhancg.persiangig.com.

Lipstick as enemy weapon. The poster reads, in Persian and Arabic, "No-Fire Zone" equating tubes of lipstick with rifle bullets. The image is from the Iranian website Hijab Poster that promotes chastity and the veil, http://www.hijab-poster.ir.

Lipstick bomb. This poster reads, "One-second bomb. Each second = 22 bombs. Every second 22 lipsticks are sold around the world." The ticking bomb in this case is the morally destructive explosive capability of women wearing makeup. Image from Hijab Poster, http://www.hijab-poster.ir.

Consumers kill innocents. This is a clear message about purchasing L'Oreal products as direct support for Israel. The Star of David on the lipstick lid underscores the English text. Image from Hijab Poster, http://www.hijab-poster.ir.

Worldly nail polish. The saying on the label, "Be aware that the world does not color you," tells women not to let the material world engulf them. Image from Hijab Poster, http://www.hijab-poster.ir.

an industry, it is useful to understand how any goods including cosmetics can serve as propaganda. The Islamic Republic of Iran publicly displays posters that convey strongly disparaging messages, hidden and overt, that rage against the West. Targeting women's consumer goods as a vehicle for political sentiments and as a strategy for keeping a society under control seems somewhat desperate. Nevertheless, after the 1979 Islamic Revolution, makeup was banned. Once this new rule was imposed, women started pushing back against these restrictions. Some Iranian women purposely wore heavy makeup, signaling resistance and opposition to the Islamic regime. Religious authorities continued to clamor and complain: Iranian women were modeling themselves after Western women. How else had they developed the habit of using such heavy cosmetics and adorning themselves? What a ludicrous notion! In various parts of Iran, archaeological evidence dating back at least three thousand years points to the cultural richness of women's interest in jewelry and makeup. Iranian women's decision to "paint" (a term preferred by religious authorities) themselves, to take great personal care in the act of beautification, is as ancient as the Persian Empire.[87]

I have examined and included posters here from an online campaign based in Iran. These posters focus on lipstick and rant about the sinfulness of cosmetic use in general and the evils of nail polish. The nail polish poster warns women not to be painted, varnished, covered, or coated by surface color. Basically, the message is twofold: women should not be fooled and distracted by the beauty of colors, and a made-up face is not a true representation of the natural state of a woman. This attitude reflects the stance toward lipstick and cosmetics originally adopted by the Islamic Republic of Iran and put forward by ideologues such as Ali Shariati (1933–1977), a highly respected intellectual educated in France with a doctorate in sociology from the Sorbonne who juxtaposed the Westernized Iranian woman with "the painted Western doll."[88]

Lipstick, especially bright-red lipstick, has enjoyed a controversial, provocative history and has been linked in many different cultures to the archetypes of temptress and prostitute. The official party line in Iran toward makeup, particularly lipstick, has not changed since the early days of the revolution. The fact that government posters equate lipstick with a weapon of destruction, assign it Zionist stature, and claim that it is more harmful than a missile boggles the mind. Clearly one should never underestimate the power of religious authority to manipulate and exploit the most mundane practices in order to achieve political agendas—even if it means delving into a woman's makeup kit.

CHAPTER 6

Islamic Dress and the Muslim Fashion Industry: Halal Fashion

It is commonly assumed, particularly in the West, that Muslim women are indifferent to fashion. Given that many wear *hijab*, surely this must reflect an obsession, a need to cover their bodies in shapeless, simple black cloth. Nothing could be further from the truth! Although Islamic clothing is indeed designed with modesty in mind, Muslim women pay as much attention to beautiful presentation as women in the West do and are highly attuned to style and fashion.[1]

Nevertheless, when marketing and design gurus research what is called Islamic fashion, the *hijab* is a logical starting point. Furthermore, using Islam as a portal for selling modest yet highly stylish attire has proven a shrewd business decision. In fact, Brand Islam has initiated marketing campaigns in the realm of women's fashion that capitalize on the very core of Islamic precepts: Sharia. One needs to look no further than companies such as Malaysia's Kivitz, a company that uses the phrase "Syar'i and Stylish"—a clever partnering of fashion and religious law.

In exploring the innovative, and often political, statements that Muslim and non-Muslim designers are making, I focus here primarily on the status of Islamic clothing for women in Turkey, Indonesia, and Iran and, to a lesser extent, the United Arab Emirates.

In 2010 the Turkish newspaper *Milliyet* estimated the global Islamic clothing market to be worth around $2.9 billion. To fully grasp the importance of this rapidly growing market, one must examine the historical evolution of Islamic commodities sold in the West. The marketing of Islamic commodities began as a simple idea generated by a few importers. Some of these individuals began simply by importing modest clothing and ethnic groceries to cities in Western Europe and the

KIVITZ
Syar'i & Stylish

t:@_KIVITZ_
e:www.kivitz.blogspot.com
f:www.facebook.com/KivitzShop

Sharia style. Models pose in Kivitz designs of polkadot and floral prints, pitched in Malay in the ad as Shariʿa and stylish at the same time. Image from Kivitz, http://kivitz.blogspot.com/.

United States where sizable Muslim populations resided. What started as a small endeavor ultimately morphed into a competitive and lucrative industry, including clothing for women. Over time, national and international designers became involved in the production and sale of chic Islamic fashions, arranging regular fashion venues during which professional models showed off trendy styles. Many clothing designers began to use the term "Islamic" as a desirable descriptor, creating controversial discussions about what types of apparel fit that category and whether defining clothing as "Islamic" is halal, or even appropriate.

I examine the commodification of Islamic dress, including its political, historical, and economic considerations. What strategies do designers use to target Muslim consumers? How is the growing phenomenon of Islamic apparel affecting the fashion industry? What enterprises are emerging to profit from this phenomenon? What role, if any, does the history of veiling play in this dress evolution? What are the design criteria or restrictions behind fashions created for Muslim women who live in different regions, hail from different socioeconomic backgrounds, and adhere to varying levels of Islamic piety?

Dress Defined: A Brief History of the *Hijab*

A variety of fashion terms are applicable in this discussion, among them "clothing," "garments," "apparel," and "adornments." However, I will use the term "dress" as a general referent. Mary Ellen Roach-Higgins and Joanne B. Eicher, social scientists as well as textile and clothing scholars, offer a broad definition:

> Dress . . . includes a long list of possible direct modification of the body such as coiffed hair, colored skin, pierced ears, and scented breath, as well as an equally long list of garments, jewelry, accessories, and other categories of items added to the body as supplements.[2]

Dress obviously provides many functions, including communicating one's identity. Research by Stone, Goffman, and Stryker has confirmed the apparent link between a person's dress and his or her identity.[3] The veil, or *hijab*, is defined by *The Oxford Dictionary of English* as "a head covering worn in public by some Muslim women." The concept of modesty in dress and behavior is encouraged by Islamic tradition both for women and men. Nevertheless, few would argue that one of the most visible signs of Muslim identity and religious piety is a woman wearing a *hijab* or other forms of clothing associated with Islamic dress. One step beyond is the face veil, or *niqab*, a far more conservative type of attire.

The cultural environment of a society, both past and present, dictates the type of dress to be worn and the meanings of that dress. Cultures are not fixed but rather evolving over time so that the meaning and function of dress will also change and may even stand in contradiction to earlier times. In terms of veiling, Reza Shah Pahlavi (1878–1944), the first Pahlavi Shah of Iran, implemented a series of policies to Westernize Iranian society, including making veiling unlawful. In 1933, the shah ordered authorities to remove women's veils—if necessary, by force—in order to "emancipate" women and encourage them to be more like Europeans. Many Iranians considered this new look superficial in that women enjoyed no new privileges or rights as a result. In Iranian history, this era is referred to as *kashf e hejab*, the unveiling period. Almost a half century later, in 1979, Iranian women were forced to veil to fit yet another male vision, that of the Ayatollah Khomeini, of the emancipated woman.

Prior to 1933, forced unveiling had already taken place in Turkey under President Kemal Ataturk. Reza Shah of Iran had simply followed suit. One can say, then, that during the earlier part of the twentieth century, from a progressive standpoint, wearing the veil was viewed as ignorant and backward. In contemporary times the connotation of the veil, assuming it is adopted voluntarily, has changed, especially for many young urban Muslim women. Because donning the veil is voluntary in Turkey and elsewhere, one can no longer make assumptions about the wearer. She may be progressive and highly educated as well as a devout Muslim, and her veil is not an indication of her old-fashioned attitude or limited education.

Contemporary Muslim youth have unlimited access to online information and are thus exposed to a wide variety of advertisements and products, including clothing and popular fashion. Thus, even in Iran, where women are restricted by an imposed *hijab* and Islamic dress code, they still exercise creativity in their color choices and styles. The only exception is that all female school employees and government workers must wear uniforms designed by the government. As for the remaining female population, the Iranian government requires that women wear a head covering, long sleeves, long pants worn under long tunics, or a long garment covering the legs entirely. No close-fitting clothes, no cinched belts, and no tightly fitting bodices framing a woman's bosom are allowed. Except for the hands and face, no skin must be shown. Despite this strict dress code, Iranian women continue to experiment with a variety of design interpretations. The various interpretations that young Iranian women apply to the required *hijab* create ongoing tensions between the authorities and the women following the fashion

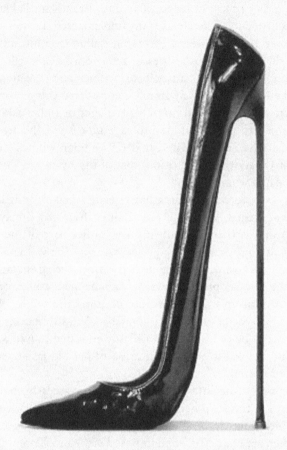

A woman's stature. Text below the image says, "In choosing a wife, consider a woman who ranks one step below your status, and when choosing a friend consider those above your own status." Image from Hijab Poster, http://www.hijab-poster.ir.

Hijab campaign psychology. The contrasting images of women in the poster are explained in text: "Psychologists believe that those who like to wear too much makeup and improper clothes are suffering from low self-esteem." Image from a 2010 blog post by Dutch nonprofit CrethiPlethi, http://www.crethiplethi.com.

Fashion as weakness. The poster title is "Following Fashion," and the text reads, "Those with low self-esteem, with no personal opinion or much intelligence, try to cover up their shortcomings by wearing fashionable clothes in public so they can show off and be praised by people to hide their own weakness." Image from Hijab Poster, http://www.hijab-poster.ir.

Hijab or harassment. The poster from the Iranian hijab and chastity campaign reads, "We [women] are responsible for creation of street harassment. The women who do not have a proper form of clothing and do not look appropriate will be targeted for street harassment and physical abuse." Image from CrethiPlethi, http://www.crethiplethi.com/.

No to skirt, yes to hijab. Beneath "ILUVIslam.Com" is the slogan "Discover the Beauty of Islam." Image from Hijab Poster, http://www.hijab-poster.ir.

Hijab as banner. The text accompanying this image says, "Hijab is a struggle. Hijab is the flag of struggle against the cultural invasion." Image from Hijab Poster, http://www.hijab-poster.ir.

trends. Many anti-Western fashion posters are published and distributed by agents authorized by the Iranian government such as the cyber group promoting chastity and the veil that use various images and texts, sometimes quite insulting, to fight against women's fashionable *hijab* and gowns in public.[4]

This daily battle in Iran between the conservative authorities and young women who love to display their fashionable selves is also evident by other styles of posters created by the cyber group promoting chastity and the veil, such as signs in public restrooms and posters openly stating that the *hijab* is part of a battle or struggle against cultural invasion.

Generally speaking, whenever Islamic dress and *hijab* are discussed, the conversation lends itself to moral viewpoints. Goffman refers to the juxtaposition of moral standards and dress as it relates to "sexuality, social rank, and beliefs about the body as an object for display versus a residence for mind of spirit."[5] Moral judgments vary from culture to culture. In Mali, urban Muslim women demonstrate an attitude that being a devout believer does not sabotage their ability to enjoy fashion, while women belonging to extremist Islamist groups such as Pakistan's Jamaat-e-Islami preserve traditional values at all costs, demonstrating the notion that attention to fashion undermines religious piety, female modesty, and appropriate submissiveness.[6]

Among certain conservative communities advocating Islamic values in India and Pakistan, veiling translates to seclusion. This practice, *purdah-nashin*, means "one who is observing seclusion." Muslim women living in this type of environment are restricted in order to "maintain social order," to prevent *fitna* (chaos).

In this context, the veil serves as a portable seclusion mechanism, ensuring a woman's modesty wherever she goes. Much has been written on the subject of veiling and from numerous perspectives, including social science and anthropology. These academic fields particularly have contributed to our understanding of the history, value, and in some instances justification of *hijab* in Muslim-majority nations and in the West.[7] Academic research has revealed that the veil connotes different things to different people in different times and places, as I have noted elsewhere:

> On the one hand, the veil is a simple garment, one which millions of women deal with in their daily lives as a matter of habit, without a second thought. They are raised to wear it; it is just another article of clothing. On the other hand, the veil is an enormously important sym-

bol, as it carries thousands of years of religious, sexual, social, and political significance within its folds. Its original purpose, to separate respectable women from slaves, prostitutes, and women with low social
status, has been blurred to a point at which it has different meanings to
different people in different cultures, and even in the same culture.[8]

A quick Internet search of *hijab*- and veil-related topics yields numerous published articles and sources. The growing curiosity in the West
around veiling specifically and Muslim culture and religion in general
are no doubt linked to the ongoing tragic episodes of terrorist bomb-
ings and rise of political Islam. Unfortunately, this increased attention has led to stereotyping by Western media that frequently portrays
the veiled Muslim woman as a victim, cruelly repressed by the yoke of
patriarchy.

What is little known and even less publicized is that for some Muslim women, the act of veiling is considered a strong feminist statement.
After colonization of the Middle East in the nineteenth century, the
veiling issue divided into two camps: anti- and pro-feminist. The pro-
feminist veiling camp argued that hiding one's body from the lustful
gaze of men allows women to be dealt with as individuals, to be independent, with their own values and intelligence, rather than being
judged solely on physical appearance. Conversely, according to the anti-
feminist veiling camp, covering one's body in order to divert the unwanted gaze of men is onerous. Why can't men behave appropriately, re-
spectfully, and control their hormonal urges? Why do women have to
take all the responsibility for *fitna* (chaos, temptation)? Both groups offer valid arguments.

During the 1970s and 1980s, a movement emerged among Islamic
revivalists eschewing Western fashion. This movement encouraged Muslim women to wear garments associated with Islamic conservatism, to
dress in ways that unmistakably communicated modesty. The Islamic
dress adopted by many Muslim female college students at this time was
easily recognizable: dress and sleeves were both extremely long and
loosely fitting, sometimes worn with long pants or concealing overcoats,
and a large scarf, usually black, wrapped around the neck and head. Colors reverted to a somber, muted palette. Visually, this style of Islamic
dress resembled a uniform and was easily recognizable in public spaces.

Not surprisingly, the individual responsible for launching this Islamic
dress "revolution" was Iran's Ayatollah Khomeini. His religious leadership spearheaded a new spirit of conservatism and influenced Muslim

nations far beyond Iran's borders. Even after his death, Khomeini maintained a kind of a charismatic hold over Iran's Shi'i masses and other Shi'i global communities. His familiar motto "Na sharghi na gharbi, Jomhoriy e Islami" (Neither Eastern nor Western, [only] the Islamic Republic) encouraged many women to begin wearing Islamic dress.

Many Muslim women adopting this garment were well educated and from middle- and upper-middle-class families. Because their families were directly affected by changing economic conditions, governmental policies, and tax increases, these young women became political activists, especially at the grassroots level. In terms of dress, this movement rapidly morphed in the 1990s toward more fashionable trends, reflecting increased interest in consumerism as well as an interest in making one's Islamic piety visible.

Although many of the young Muslim women of the 1970s and 1980s had patterned their politics after basic tenets of Islam, which suggests equality for all, they purposefully eschewed extreme Islamic clothing choices; that is, they chose not to wear the *burqa* veiling that entirely covers the face. Norah Vincent refers to this article of clothing as "a powerful symbol misused by Islamists and Western feminists alike."[9] For many Muslim women, even today the *burqa* remains a choice and a right and represents alignment with the most rigid, conservative Qur'anic interpretations. These women may be members of extreme Islamist groups in Saudi Arabia, in Yemen, among the Taliban in Afghanistan, and in other parts of the Muslim world, or they may be just conservative individuals. It should be noted, however, that among many of the Arab and some non-Arab indigenous cultures, the *niqab* existed before Islam. The tradition of wearing the *niqab*—which, unlike the *burqa*, does not cover the eyes—was carried over to lands conquered by Muslim armies and therefore came to be understood as an Islamic obligation.

A quick glance at Muslim communities around the world reveals that women adopt Islamic dress for very different reasons. Caroline Osella and Filippo Osella have found that among Muslims living in southern India,

concerns with *decency* are always negotiated within desires for *fashion*. Kerala's Muslim community is more [affluent on average] and Muslims are especially interested in dressing well and participating in worlds of fashion, which may be vernacular *ishtyle* (Indian film-driven) or global (brands).[10]

Generally speaking, Islamic fashion is moving away from the sobriety of black and leaning toward colorful choices. Indeed, the commodification of fashionable Islamic dress has proven so successful that innovative styles continually emerge to satisfy the trendy Muslim consumer. As I have noted, given that Muslims live in such different cultures globally, one would expect their modes of dress to vary. The *abaya* robe or cloak traditionally belongs to the Arab world and is worn by men and women across North Africa as well as in Saudi Arabia, Iraq, the UAE, and other Persian Gulf countries. Women pull *abayas* over their heads in Saudi Arabia, Kuwait, and Iraq, for example, while men drape them over the shoulders. Annelies Moors notes, "In the Gulf States some started to transform the abaya from a non-distinct, shapeless, all-enveloping black gown into something more akin to a fashion item, with seasonally changing cuts and models, materials and decorations."[11] Muslims including non-Arab women are following this trend with highly expressive, colorful *abaya* fashions emerging in regions far beyond the Gulf States.

Fashionable *Hijab*: Halal or Haram

How does the Qur'an approach the issue of *hijab*? Should a Muslim woman wear *hijab*, chador, burqa, or *niqab*? Pierre Tristam asserts that while "the Quran has no requirement that women cover their faces with a veil, or cover their bodies with the full-body burqa or chador, as in Iran and Afghanistan, [it] does address the matter of veiling in such a way that it has been interpreted historically, if not necessarily correctly, by Muslim clerics as applying to women."[12]

Certainly there are verses relating to veiling and *hijab* in the Qur'an, in Surah 24 (al-Noor), verse 31, and Surah 33 (al-Ahzab), verse 59. These are cited as evidence that wearing the veil is obligatory for Muslim women. Ironically, even those who press this issue of required veiling conveniently avoid quoting verse 60 in Surah al-Noor concerning the position of elderly women:

And women of post-menstrual age who have no desire for marriage—there is no blame upon them for putting aside their outer garments [but] not displaying adornment. But to modestly refrain [from that] is better for them. And Allah is Hearing and Knowing.[13]

Dress requirements, then, appear to shift for a woman as she advances in age. Presumably, menopausal and postmenopausal women are less attractive, less seductive, and therefore less likely to incite *fitna*. This level of discrepancy confuses the veiling rules and points to the real likelihood that one tends to read Qur'anic verses selectively in order to further personal agendas and interpretations.

Islamic authorities tend to offer their own private and occasionally contradictory opinions. Muhammad Abdul Bari, leader of the Muslim Council of Britain, advises, "No one should be compelled to wear either the *hijab* (headscarf), the *niqab* (face veil) or the *burqa* (full body covering). [But] Islam calls upon both men and women to dress modestly."[14] While a number of religious and/or political Muslim leaders do not say "that the *niqab* is an Islamic requirement, two leading Saudi religious scholars, Shaikhs Ibn Uthaimin and Ibn Jibreen, have issued fatwas proclaiming that it is mandatory for women to wear the *niqab*."[15]

On occasion news reports record the issuance of bizarre fatwas such as one in Al Arabiya in 2013: "A Saudi cleric has called for all female babies to be fully covered by wearing the face veil, commonly known as the *burka*, citing reports of little girls being sexually molested."[16] Sheikh Abdullah Daoud's baby burqa policy did not go unnoticed. In response, "Sheikh Mohammad al-Jzlana, former judge at the Saudi Board of Grievances, told *Al Arabiya* that Dauod's ruling was denigrating to Islam and Shariah and made Islam look bad."[17] This example underscores the contradictions inherent in various authoritative interpretations of acceptable dress, even within the same nation and religious sect. Islamic dress and the subject of *hijab* have generated numerous fatwas issued by credible Muslim scholars and by "wannabe" mullahs and ayatollahs. Therefore, one should be aware that not every fatwa posted on the Internet regarding appropriate dress for Muslim women is based on religious scholarship or comes from a bona fide religious authority.

Several fatwas have related specifically to Islamic fashion. In 2012 the prominent Islamic seminary Darul Ulum Deoband in Lucknow, India, issued a fatwa regarding the production, sale, and purchase of any designer *burqas*. A news site explains, "Not only this, the seminary has said that selling designer burqas amounts to promotion of fashion which is against Islam and promotes sin."[18] This well-known Islamic authoritarian group did not provide details elucidating how designer fashion promotes sin, especially if the fashion in question completely covers the body. Such pronouncements appear increasingly arbitrary and reflect interpretations that make a thinking person stop and ponder.

The Darul Ulum Deoband also proclaimed that modeling is an unIslamic career and that "exhibiting bodies by Muslim women while modelling is against the Shariat law."[19] Yet another of these authorities' fatwas was issued against women working in beauty salons. This decree stated that running a beauty parlor "is unIslamic and a violation of Sharia law" and "against the norms of parda," or Islamic veiling.[20]

Fashion shows highlighting *hijab* or Islamic dress have led to online questions by pious Muslims seeking advice on whether these events are halal:

> As-salamu alaykum. Is it OK for hijab to look pretty (colorful, artistic)? And is it OK to hold Islamic fashion shows that display beautiful hijab clothing on models or to promote those.[21]

The religious authorities answered on this blog about fatwas:

> As far as Islamic Shari'ah is concerned, there is nothing wrong for hijab to be colorful and artistic as long as it is not unusually attractive. One of the objectives of hijab is modesty and bashfulness. A Muslim woman is obliged to wear hijab, which is part of the beauty and ornament that cannot be concealed. In his response to your question, Sheikh Mohamed El-Moctar El-Shinqiti, director of the Islamic Center of South Plains, Lubbock, Texas, states, Almighty Allah says, They (women) should not display their beauty and ornaments except what (must ordinarily) appear thereof (An-Nur 24:31). Hijab is part of the beauty and ornament that cannot be concealed, and should not be concealed. There is nothing wrong for hijab to be colorful or artistic unless it is unusually attractive and flashy. As for Islamic fashions and using models, they go against the objective of hijab, which is modesty and bashfulness. Therefore, I do not think it is permissible.

The specific fashion show in question was organized in 2005 as a girls school event in conjunction with an annual gathering, or *jalsah*; it caused heated controversy. The *Voice of Islam*, an online publication created by a branch of Darul Ulum Deoband in Port Elizabeth, South Africa, presented an undated question-and-answer session on the issue.

The original question is prohibitively lengthy to be cited here in its entirety; this is an edited version:

> Among the girls were baaligh [mature] ones. They modelled eastern outfits—shararas, gararas and punjabis. The girls had make-up on and their hair was hanging loose, and uncovered. Although men were not allowed to view the fashion show, they could hear the description given of the clothing these girls were modelling. A wedding gown was also modelled. Various Hadiths were quoted to justify the fashion show. One was from Bukhaari Shareef [collection of Al Bukhari's hadiths] which states that Hadhrat [honorable] Aishah (radhiyallahu anha) [may Allah be pleased with her] loaned a beautiful dress to someone to wear on her wedding day since one has to look the best on one's wedding day. Qur'aanic aayats [verses] were also recited to support the fashion show. Another proof was that a woman can [could] dress up in front of her mahrams [those men who are not haram to her, such as son, uncle, husband and father] and ladies. Is this all acceptable in the Shariah? This event has caused our community to split into two. The female teachers have resigned. Please comment and advise us on this issue.[22]

The answer, again too lengthy to reproduce here—eight pages—begins with an expression of sorrow that the fashion event took place on the Muslim holy day of Friday:

> We can lament with certitude that on the Friday which followed this evil and haraam fashion parade of Jaahiliyyah, when the Malaaikah presented the deeds of the Ummah to Rasulullah (sallallahu alayhi wasallam), his mubaarak heart must have bled profusely. Every Friday the deeds of the Ummah are presented to Rasulullah (sallallahu alayhi wasallam). Most assuredly, Nabi-e-Kareem in Aalam-e-Barzakh must be viewing with total revulsion the evil which learned people are in this day perpetrating in the name of the very Qur'aan and Sunnah which Rasulullah (sallallahu alayhi wasallam) delivered and taught to destroy kufr and all vestiges of immorality and Jaahiliyyah which applies to the haraam modelling show or fashion parade. No Muslim requires knowledge to understand the evil and prohibition of this fashion show. It is absolutely revolting that Qur'aanic aayaat and Ahaadith were presented in substantiation of a haraam fashion show in which baalighah girls

were so callously misused to parade their haya [innocence] for the haraam pleasure of the audience. The all-women audience makes absolutely no difference.[23]

The excessively harsh tone of this response continues with an attack on those who organized, produced, and agreed to the "evil fashion parade":

The very concept of a fashion show is immoral in the Shariah. Islam
teaches its womenfolk to conceal themselves, not expose and express
themselves. . . . Men listening to the description of the dresses, which
the girls modelled. This is zina [sexual unlawful intercourse] of the
ears. It incites lust in the diseased hearts of men. And, only men with
diseased hearts will venture into proximity of such a mal-oon [wicked
and detestable], and mabghudh [disrespectful?], haraam modelling parade. . . . Allowing the girls to parade bare-headed with their hair all
loose, and painted up like gay coons with haraam cosmetics, aggravates
the evil. . . . It was indeed utterly shameless for the organizers and the
girls to have appeared in public (even if only in front of women) with
their heads uncovered. They have to cover their heads for even Allah
Ta'ala when performing Salaat, in fact, when they are not even performing Salaat. The natural haya of a Mu'minah [believer] dictates that she
keeps her head covered out of shame for even Allah Azza Wa Jal. . . .
The modelling show was in total conflict and negation of the Islamic
concept of Hijaab with its emphasis on female concealment. This evil
fashion parade is in violent conflict with the whole corpus of Akhlaaq-
e-Hameedah (The Beautiful attributes of excellence). . . . Show, parad-
ing, fashioning and modelling are all elements of riya [hypocrisy] and
lewdness. These are acts of the kuffaar [non-Muslims]. Fashion shows
are integral constituents of the kuffaar, more specifically western, idea
of pleasure and recreation.[24]

These judgments leave little room for doubt—the fashion show is inarguably haram.
The ulama again unleashes vitriol at those responsible:

Modelling the wedding dress was an aggravated factor of evil. What
must have been going through the mind of the young girl when she
donned the wedding dress projecting herself as a married woman? A
wedding dress has no place in Muslim society. It is a customary prac-

tice of non-Muslims. Muslim society is a society of the Sunnah, not a society which has enslaved itself to the norms and styles of westernism. A wedding is associated with a relationship in the making with a male. The young girl was schooled in the idea of zina [fornication] of the mind. She was simulating a relationship with some imaginary man. Her seniors are guilty of having polluted her mind and heart. . . . There is no Qur'aanic verse nor any Hadith from which substantiation could be drawn for this haraam fashion show.[25]

Woven throughout the responses is a unifying theme: Muslim women should not display themselves on stage or allow themselves to be the center of attention. Even though women organized this event for women only and no men were allowed to attend, all was considered haram, according to the ulama's interpretation. One can only imagine how these same religious *mulanas* (similar to ulama) would respond to professional Islamic fashion shows with Muslim models sporting innovative and colorful *hijab*-inspired clothing—attended by a multitude of spectators and with many more watching on TV.

Muslim Fashionistas: Agencies of Change

Regardless of fundamentalist jargon, new enterprises are emerging that reflect shifting attitudes toward Islamic dress—including professional "Muslim" modeling agencies. Indeed, Islamic fashion designers are now recruiting highly trained models from all over the world. Mohammed Shariff, a New York–based fashion and entertainment lawyer who works with models and modeling agencies, sees growing opportunities for Muslim women who want to be models and for those who want to employ models. Yet he also voices concern about seeing "Muslims in modeling agencies who suffer from the assignments; they feel that they compromise who they are for it."[26] While Muslim girls love the idea of a modeling career, of working in the fashion industry, few want to take anything off. Rather, they want to stay within their faith.

Nominally Muslim professional modeling agencies continue to pop up in the most surprising places and—along with Islamic fashion shows—are establishing bases in Russia and other countries where Islam is the second most widely practiced religion. The Pew Forum on Religion and Public Life reports that the Muslim population in Russia will expand to approximately 18.6 million by 2030. This means "an increase from 11.7 percent in 2010 to 14.4 percent in 2030."[27] With the blessing of the official Muslim authority in Russia, the Muftis Council, Islamic fashion shows are finding their way to Russian venues. On the Halal Expo Moscow website is an announcement for an Islamic fashion show held in Moscow June 13–16, 2013:

> The world tendency to combine ethics and fashion, the Sharia norms and modern trends to show that one can be stylish and at the same time distinguish religion through appearance has proven successful. The demand for individual Muslim image[s] . . . [has resulted in] a number of talented designers. Such recognized world fashion houses as Yves Saint Laurent, Jean Paul Gaultier, Dolce & Gabbana more and more include Islamic style in their collections. And authoritative fashion experts claim that the world fashion industry would take inspiration from the Muslim countries. Islamic Style International Festival unites designers from various parts of the world and Russia. Many Festival participants have [already] won the hearts of consumers. Others are only on their way to success.[28]

News regarding this Islamic fashion show also appears on the Russian Muftis Council website. The council's public relations effort regarding this event is surprisingly positive. The Russian muftis encourage attendance at the Islamic fashion show; their position toward the event is clearly halal, and they praise the goal of inviting public attention to Islamic dress code in order to transform the stereotypical image of Muslim women. These muftis applaud the event's objectives to spread "right understanding of Islamic culture in relation to clothing, aid the development of costumes of traditional Muslim peoples of Russia, and help build the brands of Russian fashion designers and Muslim clothing manufacturers."[29]

That Islamic religious authorities should be so eager to educate the public about the relationship between religion and clothing gives one pause for thought. The average consumer cannot help but wonder if, sandwiched between their words of enthusiastic appreciation, another hidden agenda is being nurtured, if not paid for, by Russian clothing manufacturers.

Given that the buying and selling of Islamic dress is rapidly developing as a global phenomenon, the fashion industry has begun to invest serious money in modeling agencies. These agencies prepare young women for runway and photographic modeling of the latest Islamic styles. It would be an understatement to say that the business of train-

ing professional female models, many of whom are Muslim, has resulted
in an avalanche of fatwas.

Nevertheless, on February 11, 2012, *The National*, a government-
owned English-language newspaper published in Abu Dhabi, reported
the opening of the world's first Muslim modeling agency in New York
City. The agency, Underwraps, is Muslim owned and operated by the
daring entrepreneur Nailah Lymus. *Arabian Business* reported that
Lymus established Underwraps with the express intent of specializ-
ing in Muslim female models and was "looking to set up partnerships
with agencies in the Middle East and welcomes applicants from wannabe models in the Gulf."[30] Lymus, an American-born Muslim, holds
some radical ideas about fashion modeling, including recruiting Muslim
women who, although religiously observant, are excited about entering
this competitive industry. The *Female Daily* blog explains, "The agency
will assist Muslim women working with mainstream designers, but still
observe religious requirements (that clothes be loose enough not to reveal their shape, and that only face, hands, and feet can be exposed)."[31]
Lymus reportedly was intent on creating a positive link between modesty and fashion.

CNN reported in 2015 that H&M, a retail chain store for clothing
and shoes, hired a Muslim female model wearing a *hijab* in a video clip
to promote recycling clothes and to present Muslim women modeling
fashionable clothes. The model, Maria Hidrissi, said some people might
think modeling fashion conflicts with the principles of Islam. However,
she said, "as long as I'm dressed correctly, according to Islam, then
there's no problem. It's just promoting the hijab, in a way. If anything,
it's good."[32] It is understood that H&M is getting publicity out of this
clip and is credited with promoting diversity. But most importantly, a
Muslim woman is given a break by being portrayed in a favorable way.
The blog *MuslimGirl* is quoted in *Glamour* magazine about the H&M
model: "Maria Hidrissi didn't just model for an ad campaign, she awak-
ened the people. In a simple and quiet way she made others look at a
Muslim woman without fear or contempt but with a healthy curiosity.
Maria opened a conversation that has always been strained."[33]

In January 2013, HijUp Model Look (HML) was launched in Indonesia to search for new models interested in working in the Muslim
fashion industry. Public relations around this event described specific
objectives, as reported in *Aquila Style*:

> Fifteen chosen finalists will be enrolled in acting and modelling classes,
> as well as becoming a part of Zaura Models, a Muslimah modelling

agency. They will also have the opportunity to be cast in a hijab-themed movie directed by Hanung Bramantyo, a notable Indonesian director who previously directed the box-office movie Ayat-Ayat Cinta (Verses of Love). Five finalists will also be awarded exclusive contracts as HijUp .com models. Judges for the modelling contest include one of the first hijab-wearing movie stars in Indonesia, Zaskia Adya Mecca, and fashion photographer Vicky Astro.[34]

Indonesia: Commanding the Runway

Indonesia is poised to become one of the top Islamic fashion power-houses, with well-known Islamic fashion designers including Lulu El-hasbu, Dian Pleangi (DP), Itang Yunaz, Ida Royani, and Ria Miranda—all of whom have created their own brand names. Indonesia is already renowned for showcasing new as well as more established Islamic fashions and fashion accessories. The *Jakarta Globe* reports that Dendy Oktariady "is the director of Fame Management, which consists of a modeling agency, stylist and casting divisions . . . related to the serious business of fashion."[35] While many of the young women working in Dendy's agency come from Brazil, Russia, Poland, Holland, Germany, and the Philippines, the majority of models are Indonesian—and Muslim.

Fifty years ago, few envisioned a day when Islamic fashions, including the *burqa*, would be hot items on haute couture runways. Not only at Jakarta's annual Fashion Week but also across a wide swath of the Middle East, many designers are being invited to participate in Islamic fashion shows. Without missing a beat, the Indonesian government has forged ahead in promoting its national fashion industry and "is aiming to become the trendsetter of the Muslim fashion world . . . [and] the capital of the Muslim fashion world by 2020."[36] As a result, new global markets are opening, such as South Africa, now one of the "top export destinations for Indonesian fashion products."[37] Internet technology is also playing a key role, in that individuals can quickly obtain information about trends in Muslim apparel and order commodities online with little effort. It should also be noted that Indonesia is comprised of multiple regional cultures, each contributing to a rich array of fabrics and designs. Furthermore, in Indonesia, "the Ministry of Tourism and Creative Economy is responsible for developing the creative economy sector, which includes creation of new fashion designs."[38]

Perhaps the innovativeness of Indonesian fashion designers and pro-liferation of "Muslimwear" relates to the fact that in Indonesia, Islamic

Poster advertising the Indonesia Islamic Fashion Fair 2013. The event held at the Jakarta Convention Centre was billed as the biggest of its kind. Image from the (now defunct) blog What I Wear, http://blog .whatiwear.com.

Hijab and makeup tutorials poster. The Kivitz founder-designer co-sponsored and co-taught the classes at UI Fashion Week 2012. At the bottom left corner the United Integrated Nation of Creation is identified. Image from Kivitz, http://kivitz .blogspot.com.

garb is seen as a choice and not a compulsion. This is in stark contrast to other Sharia-dominated countries including Saudi Arabia and the Islamic Republic of Iran where women are forced to wear *hijab*. In short, creativity flourishes in the absence of censorship and in environments where policing activities by governmental authorities are not a high priority. Indonesia is an excellent example of clothing designers remaining faithful to Islam while exercising their own outrageous creative visions.

In contrast to Indonesia's imaginative and, on occasion, flamboyant Muslim fashion industry, Iran's government-sanctioned design program directors have tried unsuccessfully to promote an uninspired brand of Islamic fashion. The strategy of handpicking and hiring state-controlled designers to generate lucrative profits for the government has fallen flat. The clothing designs have almost always been a variation on the basic chador theme, in black or somber colors. Despite concerted efforts, the Iranian government has been unable to pique the general public's interest, even with "fashion festivals" primarily targeting the youth population. The *Tehran Times* describes the preparations and intent of the debut event:

> The first Fajr Fashion Festival, offering a variety of Islamic-Iranian new designs, will be opening in March [2012] in Tehran's Hejab Hall. The festival has been arranged to organize fashion in the country and maximize the use of the artistic potentials of the designers, Deputy Culture Minister for Artistic Affairs Hamid Shahabadi said at the press conference. . . . Encouraging the ladies to put on nicer Islamic outfits and promoting hijab are among the goals of the festival. . . . Shahabadi, who is also the director of the committee for organizing costume and fashion, continued that the best designs will be selected and awarded at the end of the festival, adding that the top researcher and the top article submitted to the secretariat will also be presented with awards. "We have a young society and the youth are very fashion conscious, so we aim to provide the means for them to gain access to new designs more easily," he said.[39]

A closer reading of this announcement reveals government supervision of "the artistic potentials of the designers," which translates to restriction on design and constriction of originality. Secondly, Mr. Hamid Shahabadi's statement is problematic: "Encouraging the ladies to put on nicer Islamic outfits and promoting hijab are among the goals of the festival." What he actually means is that Iranian women had better not follow Western fashion if they know what's good for them. Long story short, the male-dominated government knows best, has the cheek to limit designs on women's clothing, and intends to earn commensurate revenues by controlling Iran's fashion industry.

Regardless of these restrictions, fashion is a thriving business in Iran for those who can afford it—elegant attire that in no way resembles the rigid, government-authorized *hijab*. This underground fashion scene, thriving mostly in large urban areas, is held in secret locations and attended by élite, trusted clientele. In some ways, this phenomenon parallels the Iranian youth subculture that promotes and supports its own genres of jazz and pop music. The sale and copy of such music is dangerous, but the risk has not reduced the young generation's love for and avid interest in such alternative music.[40]

The underground fashion scene locations are publicized only by word of mouth, and to the very last minute, few know the exact location. There is always the threat of being discovered. Many home-grown Iranian fashion designers have developed an impressive following for their daring designs—fashions that are never seen in the public but rather are reserved for private parties. In 2007 Borzou Daragahi, a staff writer for the *Los Angeles Times*, wrote an article describing an upscale underground fashion show he attended in Tehran:

> Putting on a clandestine fashion show in Iran requires stealth, careful planning, imported models and designs that are just fabulous.
>
> The guests slide out of dark overcoats to unsheathe daringly low-cut dresses and open-slit gowns, form-fitting sweaters and go-go boots, skin-tight T-shirts and acid-washed jeans. Skinny, long-legged models giggle as they slip into outfits of satin and silk. A red carpet serves as a runway. A clandestine Tehran fashion show glitters gloriously to life. "Everyone is putting on a show," declares Azita, a 46-year-old designer attending the show with her 20-year-old daughter, giddily taking in the swirl of lights, music, perfume and colored fabrics. "All the ladies have gotten into the fashion business. We love it so much because the clerics hate it." She and others taking part and watching the show asked that their family names not be published for fear of retribution.[41]

It should be noted that fashion catalogs published in Iran omit designer names for fear of government persecution. No one is officially allowed to create fashion that runs counter to the government's strict dress code.[42] Iranian authorities equate Western fashion with all things haram. It is hard to imagine the level of intimidation that religious authorities must experience around female fashion, condemning any woman daring to prefer Western dress styles, as *Newsweek* has reported:

> Lacking the manpower to crack down on this barrage of Western clothing, authorities have zeroed in on local designers—especially female ones—whom they consider a greater threat to the values of the theocratic regime than racy imports like Victoria's Secret lingerie or Manolo Blahnik pumps.[43]

Numerous government-sponsored posters mock Western fashion, invoke images of demons, and warn Iranian women against becoming slaves to the world of fashion and wasting their time. Worst of all, these posters insinuate that fashionable women shamelessly provoke men by appearing immodestly in public.

As everywhere, young people in Iran are drawn to style and interested in expressing their generation's individuality. Beyond government-produced fashion shows, which are propaganda events, no opportunity for individual creativity exists. Thus young Iranians who are passionate about design can only experiment underground with their hybrid and often highly talented styles of fashion.

Common sense would suggest that by following Indonesia's lead, the Iranian government could realize significant economic benefits. Instead, its rigid restrictions actually drive many young Iranian women away from Islamic dress toward Western styles. Since 1979 the Islamic Republic of Iran has had a difficult time enforcing a public dress code. The Islamic government of Iran has consistently had a scorecard type of mentality; that is, the more shapeless, dreary, and somber one's clothing, the higher one's religious piety score.

Ongoing resistance by Iranian women to government-mandated clothing signals a failed outcome. In the long run, only by the most extreme means can authority coerce a citizenry toward symbolic piety. Furthermore, spending a sizable proportion of the national budget to hire tens of thousands of moral police, all working the streets to enforce regulations around hairstyle, hem lengths, looseness or tightness of garments, shoes and accessories, makeup, and style is a waste of Iran's financial resources. Still, reports on crackdowns are not unusual, with women and sometimes men arrested and taken away by police for ignoring dress codes.

Satanic steps. The hijab and chastity campaign text says, "Women should not stomp
their feet on the ground when walking in order to not expose what is hidden as
jewelry or draw attention to their anklets." Image from Hijab Poster, http://www
.hijab-poster.ir.

Thousands of Iranian women have been cautioned over their poor Islamic dress this week and several hundred arrested in the capital Tehran in the most fierce crackdown on what's known as "bad hijab" for more than a decade. It is the talk of the town.[44]

In Iran, when political factions clash or become mired in controversy, women and their *hijab* become convenient scapegoats, deflecting attention from real issues and from authoritative shortcomings. A *Washington Post* article in 2011 tracks "the annual crackdown" that primarily happens during the hot summer months:

> [T]he issue of how women wear the veil—and what the government does about it—has become part of an intensifying rift between President Mahmoud Ahmadinejad and powerful Shiite clerics. . . . Ahmadinejad's critics charge that his inner circle of advisers is plotting to undermine their influence on the Islamic Republic. They accuse the president and his men of advocating more personal freedoms to widen their popular base. . . . Clerics say the practice protects the purity of women. But the law is imprecise and, with more and more women wearing tight fitting coats and loosely fitted scarves, clerics complain that Iranian cities increasingly resemble Western metropolises where women roam the streets "practically naked."[45]

Perhaps the most important point here is that, unlike Iran, Indonesia—the largest Islamic nation on earth—has no problem with an evolving, thriving fashion industry. Why? Because religious authorities in Indonesia are busy with more important matters than restraining fashion-designer talent or monitoring women's adherence to dress codes. From an economic standpoint, they see prosperity on the horizon and are aware that the fashion industry "will bring benefits to all Indonesians, regardless of their religion or fashion tastes. According to Aries Mufti, an economic expert from the Indonesian Sharia Council, the Muslim fashion sector already contributed $7.5 billion to the Indonesian economy in 2011."[46]

The manufacture and sale of Islamic dress is also thriving in Turkey and the United Arab Emirates, although the end products vary. The UAE is renowned for beautiful *abaya* designs. By contrast, Turkey produces chic Islamic women's clothing consisting of a fashionable long outer gown with matching sets of pants, all accessorized by stylish large scarves. Turkish designers tend to be in sync with global fashion seasons

Banner on a Hijabik.com page. The online Islamic fashion site describes the *hijab* selection as "made by Neva Style, a Turkish Islamic fashion brand on the forefront of style and trends producing stunning silk Turkish designs and manufacturing." Image from Hijabik, http://hijabik.com/.

and European clothing styles. There are a number of Islamic fashion houses that maintain an online presence with trendy designs and innovative styles in Turkey and UAE region.

Since 2006 Turkey has played a major role in presenting veil fashions in haute couture fashion shows. Such events have drawn controversy from secular populations and devout Muslims. Banu Gökariksel and Anna Secor have noted, "Veiling fashion crystallizes a series of issues about Islamic identity, the transnational linkages of both producers and consumers, and the shifting boundaries between Islamic ethics and the imperatives of neoliberal capitalism."[47] In the case of Turkey, veiling has had a checkered history given that along with the separation of church and state, Kemal Ataturk (1881–1938) included unveiling in reform efforts to model the Ottoman Empire after a secular and modern Europe. Indeed, the head scarf remains one of Turkey's most divisive clothing issues, as most conservative Muslims regard Islamic fashions unfavorably. They perceive it as a mode of exploiting religion as a commodity, that is, as a damaging kind of Islamic capitalism. Turkey's popular Islamist Justice and Development Party operates, a National Defense Institute paper asserts, "within a framework of strict secularism [that] has generated controversies over the boundaries between secularity and religion in the public sphere—tensions that were brought to a head over the selection of the new president and that led to parliamentary elections, along with a new mandate for the party, in July 2007."[48] At the same time, Turkish secularists express objections to haute couture Islamic fashion as a pretentious way of demonstrating Islamic piety. Some ask why a woman has to wear modesty literally on her sleeve.

Interestingly, one of the first Turkish Islamic fashion manufacturers chose the name Tekbir (Greatness of Allah, or God is great) for its label. Using the brand name Tekbir was a well-considered strategy, directly linking the designer to Islam. Alexandra Hudson elaborates:

Mustafa Karaduman, founder of Islamic fashion house Tekbir . . . nicknamed "Allah's Tailor" in the Turkish media, sees the changes in society and is hopeful [for] further growth. "Our work was quite amateur in the first decade. Then in 1992 we organised the very first headscarf fashion show, which brought us global attention. Now Islamic style clothes are on the agenda everywhere around the world," [he said].[49]

The 1980s brought surprising fashion changes to parts of the Muslim world. In Turkey, homemade, shapeless outer gowns became popular among young urban women. They wore the shapeless gowns with large scarves in public to symbolize their support for Islamic tradition. Prior to that time, urban Turkish women had followed European-style fashions and associated the veil with a regressive way of life.

Initially the 1980s movement was meant to be a silent protest against the imposition of forced unveiling. As the number of protestors grew, both men and women, fashion designers and the apparel industry recognized an untapped potential: the marketing and commodification of Islamic dress. Today Turkish Islamic fashion (*tesettiir*) is thriving, in part because, a *Fashion Theory* article reports, "the new generation of covered women who demand fashionable, trendy, comfortable yet religiously appropriate clothes and the increasing number of female *tesettiir* designers compel manufacturers to update their collections."[50] Thus it is consumer demand along with effective marketing and advertising that dictate the direction of Turkey's Islamic fashions. Also influential, paradoxically, is the twenty-first-century anti-*niqab*/anti-*hijab* sentiment coursing through Western Europe. As a sort of backlash, increasing numbers of Turkish women are choosing Islamic garb to signal solidarity with Muslim women seeking freedom of expression in European nations like France, Britain, and the Netherlands.

Islamic Fashion by Designing Women

As contemporary clothing designers quietly launch their collections of Islamic wear, the predictably traditional *hijab* styles are falling away, and exciting, somewhat experimental fashions are taking their place. Although relatively new to fashion runways, Islamic fashion design is fast developing popularity among well-heeled clients so that Muslim and non-Muslim designers alike are participating enthusiastically and preparing for a vibrant, prosperous future.

Their goal is to marry modest, reserved fashion with design concepts that are beautiful and chic, no easy feat. Some designers understand this challenge firsthand since they themselves are Muslim. British designer Sophia Kara explains in a BBC News story what it means to be female, Muslim, and in love with style:

> After her marriage, when she decided to adopt dressing modestly as part of her life, she began designing her own garments that appealed to her aesthetic nature. "I thought, oh my god I cannot wear this because this is not me. It just was not my identity at all. . . . That is why I started designing—something that suited me, that I was more confident in. . . . I brought the jilbab [*hijab*] into the new era."[51]

Another newcomer to Muslim clothing design is Nzinga Knight, an American living in New York City. Knight has said she sees herself as a devout Muslim and is convinced that one can be stylish and well dressed in apparel that is also modest. "The look of my work is sensual, mysterious, innovative," she said, describing her target as "a woman who's happy to be a woman."[52] Nailah Lymus, the Brooklyn-based creator of Underwraps, is an aspiring fashion designer who uses bright colors and patterns in her dresses. Her clothing line, Amirah Creations, targets all women, not just Muslims. In an interview she stated, "I like colors and I like flowers, and I like head pieces with feathers coming off of them, and all I do is just put it on top of my hijab instead of putting it on my hair. . . . I am a woman—I am attracted to those things, so I really want to break down that stereotype."[53] Not all Muslim women are enthusiastic about Amirah Creations; many criticize these fashions for revealing bare arms and the upper torso. A reporter notes, "Although Ms. Lymus says she wants to design for women who are Muslim and those who are not, she can't wear many of the pieces in her own collection because they show shoulders and arms. Her solution is to 'Islamify' her looks" by simply adding a blazer or sweater over the shoulders.[54]

An impressive number of *abaya* designers are women from the Persian Gulf states who are using embellishments with marked originality. In addition, established fashion houses of Europe are now designing *abayas* and participating in catwalk shows with Islamic fashions—including basic *abaya* designs that have been manipulated to provide a fresh look, a sense of newness. Some of these highly individualized *abaya* styles are created by women who also own private salons.[55] One such entrepreneur, Al-Jassim, of Saudi Arabia, has had exceptional suc-

cess in the Gulf region and in the West despite having to deal with challenges and obstacles faced by career women in Saudi Arabia. Many of
her creations are awe-inspiring, beautiful variations on the traditional
abaya design. She has also designed women's ready-to-wear clothing, all
sold at Alkhobar-based Dar Breesam Couture Establishment, which Al-
Jassim privately owns.[56]

What's in an Islamic Brand Name?

The commodification of Islamic dress is being achieved in a variety of
ways, including branding. Following the practice of mainstream designers, some Islamic fashion houses are promoting their own success as
well as sending forth messages of faith, by stamping, painting, or em-
broidering their brand names on *hijab* and related apparel. This is a sure
indicator that Muslim fashion designers are coming of age. Since their
designs are being featured on the catwalks of Paris, Belgium, and Britain, they find it increasingly reasonable—and profitable—to juxtapose
terms such as "faith" and "style" in order to situate their products, as in
this ad slogan:

> Faith, Modesty, Style & Inspiration. Promote your *faith*, uphold you[r]
> *modesty*, define your *style* & be an *inspiration* to others.[57]

This is the slogan of Sisters Couture, an enterprise created by sisters
Mona and Nadine (last names withheld), who are only too happy to advertise online that their twin loves are fashion and Islam.

Paris-based Karima Saouli, founder of La Maison Saouli, creates her
fashionable Muslim designs for export to Arab nations in the Gulf region. Some Islamic designers, such as London-based Lamee, only manufacture head covers (*shelas*) and *abayas*. Marketing strategies employed
by these emerging fashion salons know no limits; some offer assorted
scents and accessories that, combined with their design creations, comprise a more packaged effect. These entrepreneurs may be new to the
game of fashion, but they are fast learners. One is Hibah's Couture Islamic Fashion:

> Hibah's collection consists of high quality one-off Abayas, Jilbabs, Hi-
> jabs and Saris. Swarovski Pins & Brooches and Oudh by Ajmal are also
> offerd by Hibah as the perfect accessory for the perfect outfit.[58]

Designer websites tend to refrain from using "Islamic" or halal labeling when advertising *abayas*. Rather, marketing language is more focused on the importance of tradition, loyalty to nation or region, and
on occasion, the unity of Arab culture and identity. A 2008 Lombok Island blog post notes, "In fact as the oil-rich Saudis, Qataris and Dubai
dwellers have become increasingly brand-conscious over the years (just
check out their malls), it's become no contradiction to demand the finest
in designer wear."[59] Balqees is one brand name for fashion *abayas* sold
in the United Arab Emirates. The Balqees website states that among its
key objectives is "bringing back Royalty and Elegance."[60] The company
website associates the fashion brand with an exhaustive historical nar-
rative concerning Queen Balqees (alternatively named Queen of Yemen
and Queen of Sheba) and provides the reader a distinctively Muslim-
oriented account of Sheba and Solomon. With its rich tapestry of graph-
ics, photos, and paintings, the website intentionally links Balqees's "innovative" *abayas* with the region's cultural history rather than with
Islam or with any notion of halal or haram.

Revenues generated by oil-rich Arab nations have fueled the demand
for exquisite Muslim clothing, propelling numerous world-class design
houses such as Yves Saint Laurent, Jean Paul Gaultier, and Dolce and
Gabbana to incorporate distinctly modest clothing in their collections
inspired by the lucrative promise of Islamic fashion commodification.

Muslim women across the globe are challenging restrictions on Islamic dress and in some instances questioning the arbitrary rulings of
religious authorities. In brief, they are pushing Islamically acceptable
boundaries when it comes to fashion. Annelies Moors and Emma Tarlo
caution in a 2007 issue of *Fashion Theory*,

> It is important to distinguish between what Muslims wear and what has
> come to be defined in the literature and the market place as "Islamic
> fashion." What counts as Islamic or not is a matter of considerable de-
> bate amongst Muslims. Whilst many consider modesty an important Is-
> lamic virtue, how this translates into particular styles of dress is highly
> variable.[61]

The widely held belief that religion and modesty remain driving forces
behind Islamic fashion is now being challenged. Some suggest that at
least in part, the dynamic growth of the Islamic fashion industry may
be the result of a grassroots movement among young Muslims who be-

lieve that faith and modernity are complementary. Others see increased prosperity—in the Gulf region, for example—and higher levels of education as possible catalysts.

Because Islam is practiced across vast geographical areas with diverse cultures, languages, and histories, styles of clothing reflecting Islamic culture must and do vary significantly. Consequently, a question arises of whether there can be an appropriate, universal standard for Islamic fashion. From the historical *abaya*, popular in the United Arab Emirates and occupying a fashion category of its own, to Iran's somber chador, instantly recognizable as a state symbol, the commodification of Islamic dress is here to stay as a multibillion-dollar business. With young Muslim women designers rising in the ranks to support increasingly innovative styles, Islamic fashion is maturing as a hot commodity and entering a new entrepreneurial phase.

In response to these developments, ulama, ayatollahs, *mulanas*, and sheikhs continue to exert pressure by imposing fatwas and denouncing contemporary Islamic fashion as haram. Predictably, women in fundamentalist Islamic societies will continue to feel this tightening grip most intensely. Islamic dress, in one form or another, has historically served as a political and social place holder, either accommodating or resisting authoritative dictates. Today is no different except that as an economic force, the Islamic fashion industry is gaining momentum with Muslim consumers across multiple socioeconomic levels.

As this industry prospers, becoming more organized and sophisticated, related enterprises such as Islamic fashion magazines and Muslim modeling agencies will benefit. In sportswear, intimate wear, and the seemingly limitless kinds of clothing accessories, designers and manufacturers are creating a host of spin-off ventures, focusing on modesty and exploiting halal/haram concepts to the fullest degree. After all, fueling consumer demand and attracting new customers willing to pay elevated prices for goods that conform to religious values is what makes the business of Islamic fashion so attractive.

CHAPTER 7

Sportswear, Lingerie, and Accessories— the Islamic Way

Only recently have devout Muslim women been able to participate fully in athletic competitions. This is largely because they now have access to Islamically sanctioned sportswear. Designed and marketed to ensure modesty as well as performance, this halal attire includes bathing suits, track suits, and various other sports-related outfits deemed both practical and Islamically correct. New materials and innovative designs are attracting Muslim female athletes whose religious and moral values demand a modest presentation.

Similarly, well-educated young professional Muslim women are buying into the notion of sexy halal lingerie and other intimate apparel for enjoyment in the privacy of their homes. As one might imagine, this segment of Islamic commodification, intimate apparel, is enjoying particular success. When it comes to sexy yet religiously approved underwear, there can be no underestimating interest and demand.

Finally, to put finishing touches on the Islamic fashions discussion, the halal-conscious consumer is paying impressively high prices for fashionably chic handbags, leather belts, and footwear.

Of these clothing and accessory categories, the one that actually supports Muslim women's success and creates equality between Muslim female athletes and their non-Muslim peers is sportswear. We have seen plentiful examples of the Brand Islam label exploiting Muslim female consumers either by implying or directly stating a relation between fashion and Sharia. By contrast, here I discuss how manufacturers are finally making it possible for Muslim women and girls to participate in national and international sports events—including Olympic games. Without the development of a Brand Islam sportswear market for women, these inspiring and enthusiastic female athletes would be relegated to the passive role of spectator.

The discussion encompasses halal-approved sports apparel for Muslim women, the marketing and sale of Islamically acceptable intimate wear, halal accessories produced for the devout yet discerning consumer, halal/haram debates concerning the marketing of these goods, and challenges merchants face in advertising and displaying such goods, especially in conservative Islamic environments.

Dressing for Athletic Success

Throughout history, Muslim women have shown themselves to be enthusiastic and capable athletes. In patriarchal societies, they have had to push back in the face of discrimination and against immense obstacles placed in their way to thwart athletic development and participation. Religious authorities have often limited and not infrequently forbidden women from entering the sports arena. Historically, across diverse Muslim cultures, one finds women's participation in games and sports activities fairly limited, although today's trend points toward increased interest and access. From the Ottoman Empire to the 2012 Olympics, the history of Muslim women in sports has been continually shifting and changing. During the Ottoman era, participation in sports was limited to a privileged few, including the wealthy élite, high-ranking military officers, and those in the sultan's court.[1]

In the 2012 Olympics, however, a record number of Muslim female athletes participated and, for the first time, Brunei, Qatar, and Saudi Arabia sent women athletes to the games.[2] As might be expected, the Muslim athletes wearing *hijab* received significant media attention, most obviously because the *hijab* set them apart from other Olympic athletes and not because of their remarkable achievements.

In a similar way, many school-age Muslim girls whose immigrant families live in the West also feel set apart and often the center of unwanted attention. These are girls who may not participate in school-sponsored sports events or physical education classes that require them to remove head scarves, to wear shorts, or to show up in figure-hugging jerseys or uniforms, especially in co-ed environments.

The imposition of Western sportswear and the prohibition of *hijab* in schools have stirred heated political debate, primarily in Europe. Muslim girls living in France and other European nations where the *hijab* is banned on campus may not participate in mandatory sports classes. This in turn affects a student's grade point average (GPA). After years of social and political activism, schools and some international sports federations are beginning to accommodate certain types of head wear specially designed for Muslim girls. In their study of Muslim girls and physical education, Manal Hamzeh and Kimberly Oliver assert that physical educators should promote healthful and active life practices with Muslim students, particularly girls, and recognize "the diversity of Muslim youth in schools and their varied ways of interpreting the *hijab* discourse and their [M]uslimness."[3] The authors also call upon "educators and researchers to deracialize and deculturalize the conceptualization of physical education studies and pedagogies and invite all participants to an engaging dialogue across differences."[4]

In 2009 a Swiss court ruled against exempting Muslim students from compulsory, mixed swimming classes, finding that equality between sexes and the integration process should have priority over religious considerations. The ruling sparked debate over the rights of minorities to follow their religious beliefs. The 2009 decision contradicts a 1993 court ruling that allowed the exemption of a Muslim schoolgirl from attending mixed swimming lessons that violated the tenets of her religion.[5]

Sarah Murray, director of Women Win, an international, Amsterdam-based humanitarian organization aimed at equipping adolescent girls to exercise their rights through sport, covers stories about women's empowerment through physical activity. Murray argues in an article posted in 2003 on the Women's Sports Foundation website,

> To promote truly global growth of female athleticism, we must sow and nurture the seeds of recognition, empowerment and equality in Muslim countries as we do at home. . . . We [American women] have struggled for decades to provide women with equal opportunity in sport and have overcome both the prejudices and extremist discrimination that keep Muslim women's sports unexposed and underdeveloped today. For the sake of unity and humanity, it's time to unveil the myths and truly celebrate the glorious participation of all women in sports.[6]

Fundamentalist Islamic authorities, firmly rooted in their biased interpretations of religious texts, continue to forbid women from participating publicly in virtually every genre of performance art and sports. As a result, in global events such as the Olympic games, Muslim women continue to be underrepresented. In some Sharia-controlled countries, women have absolutely no opportunity to participate in any athletic competitions and therefore can never dream of rising to Olympic levels. Muslim female athletes have traditionally faced this type of discouragement not only from authoritative Islamic figures but also often from their own families and communities. In 1996 Algeria's Hassiba Boulmerka won the Olympic gold medal in the 1,500-meter race. She wore running shorts like her peers. The victory worked against Boulmerka because an Algerian Muslim religious authority condemned women "daring their nudity before the whole world."[7] Death threats followed. Boulmerka became an outcast. Instead of receiving a hero's welcome, she was forced into exile, unable to return home due to fears for her physical safety.

Sania Mirza likewise faced Muslim fundamentalist opposition to women in sports. BBC News reported that in 2004 a fatwa was issued against Mirza, a Muslim Indian tennis champion, for "standing half-naked on the tennis court while playing, which is against Islam." The Jamiat-Ulema-I-Hind, an Islamic scholarly group in India,[8] stated that it found "female tennis players' dress code objectionable."[9] In 2004 an Egyptian theologian, Shaikh Yusuf al-Qaradawi, stated that female sport is exploited as a means of undermining "divine morality." In the same year Ayatollah Emami Kashani, one of Iran's ruling mullahs, went even further by sermonizing that encouraging women to compete in the Olympics was a "sign of voyeurism" on the part of male organizers.[10] In these examples one begins to understand the patriarchal obsession with Muslim women's bodies.

Saudi Arabia's policies toward women and athletics are perhaps the most rigid. Even though Saudi women competed for the first time in the 2012 Olympics, Saudi girls are effectively barred from playing sports in public schools, even in gender-segregated schools. A *Jerusalem Post* article in 2012 reports that "neither of the two Saudi women athletes at the Olympics—Wujdan Shahrkhani in judo and Sarah Attar in track and field—live or train in Saudi Arabia."[11] Given that Saudi religious leaders frequently express opposition to women's participation in sports, Shahrkhani and Attar would never have been able to attain athletic mastery in the kingdom, as the article underscores:

Grand Mufti Abdul Aziz ibn Abdullah Aal as-Shaikh told the country's Saudi's al-Iqtisadeh TV channel . . . that women had no need to play sports, and that their role was to be housewives. The negative attitude toward Saudi women in sports spilled over onto social media, after Saudi Twitter user Sultan al-Halali began a campaign against Olympians Shahrkhani and Attar by using the site to encourage others to criticize the women, by posting tweets with an Arabic hashtag (keyword) that translates as "Olympic whores."[12]

I would like to state clearly, once again, that it is not the religion of Islam that mandates exclusion of women from developing strong and healthy bodies or forbids them from participating in athletic games and sport activities. Rather, it is fundamentalist men whose arbitrary Qur'anic interpretations keep women at the mercy of repressive governments and patriarchal supremacy. A healthy body contributes to a healthy mind, longevity, and productivity. What good can come of rigid regulations that effectively ban women from pursuing physical well-being—women who are the backbone of their cultures and who comprise half of the global population?

Although no other Muslim nation restricts women's sports activities quite as extremely as Saudi Arabia does, there are, nevertheless, unfavorable if not insurmountable obstacles to overcome in other Islamic countries. In Iran young Muslim women interested in public sports participation have had to struggle for decades in the face of religious and authoritative pronouncements. Remarkably, through the power of persistence, dedication, and love for their sports, they are pushing the boundaries to benefit future generations of female athletes. The *Jerusalem Post* article points out that "despite the difficulties they face, Iranian women are determined to play and compete in a wide variety of sports, including soccer, polo and even rugby, which is a controversial sport even for women in the West."[13]

One of the most vocal Iranian activists has been Faezeh Hashemi-Rafsanjani, daughter of the first president of the Islamic Republic of Iran.[14] Hashemi-Rafsanjani successfully campaigned in 1990 for Iranian women to compete in Olympic events, even if it meant doing so in Islamic dress. Hashemi-Rafsanjani served as president of the Islamic Countries' Sport Solidarity Council, vice president of Iran's National Olympic Committee, and a member of the Islamic Republic's High Council for Women's Sport.[15] Openly criticizing discriminatory laws hindering women's rights, she spent six months in jail in 2012. In March 2013 she was released on condition that she be barred from political participation for five years. Although Hashemi-Rafsanjani herself wears a traditional Iranian chador, she insists that wearing *hijab* must be optional and not forced. In an opening speech at the Second Islamic Countries Women Sports Games, Hashemi-Rafsanjani describes an issue the athletes face:

> [I]t has always been by and through the efforts of women themselves that their rights and legitimate wishes were respected. In order to prove our rightfulness and with regard to our participation in social and sports activities, we Muslim women have no intention whatsoever to resemble men. We practice sports because it guarantees our health and grants us joy and strength, but not at the cost of damaging reverence and sanctities.[16]

As in all categories of activity, Iranian officials keep a close watch on Muslim female athletes, monitoring how they behave and how they dress, whether at home or abroad. During Olympic events, if a male referee should come into physical contact with an Iranian female athlete, she must automatically forfeit her right to participate in that event. This type of physical contact is considered haram and Islamically improper, according to Iranian authorities. Furthermore, no Iranian female may compete in Olympic swimming events because Iran's government forbids women to wear the basic Olympic regulation swimsuit. For this reason, female Iranian athletes often sacrifice their passion for swimming and switch to rowing. In this way, they can at least compete in a water-related sport that does not require skin-revealing suits.

Soccer *Hijab* and the Female Footballer

Although female athletes in the Middle East face familial, political, cultural, and religious pressures, there are encouraging signs on the horizon. In Morocco, Turkey, Kuwait, and elsewhere, soccer associations are now campaigning to promote women's right to play the game. A Huffington Post article in January 2013 notes, however, that a Muslim "woman's right to play and pursue an athletic career remains controversial and at a time at which political Islam is on the rise."[17]

Geoff Harkness and Samira Islam have studied how the revival of wearing the *hijab* and the love for sport among Muslim girls and young women "has created a contested space: their heads."[18] Ongoing controversy concerning what Muslim female athletes may and may not wear is creating tension and uncertainty among those wanting to take a greater part in sports activities. In some Muslim societies progress is evident. In 1998 Morocco created its first national women's soccer team. Four years later, the Moroccan Football Federation (Fédération Royale Marocaine de Football) for women was established. Nowadays, many more Moroccan girls play the game, and more than ever, Moroccan families are willing to let their daughters participate. Despite these progressive steps, though, professional soccer leagues still remain very male-oriented. Harkness and Islam have found, "Social pressure pushes young girls into more 'feminine' sports, the formal infrastructure suffers from a lack of will and financial support, and there is still no national championship. In this way, football reflects the push and pull of a society and its contradictions, which exist in all cultures when new ideas confront old ones."[19]

Personal testimonials from female footballers in Morocco reveal the extent to which players face social backlash. A former player, Sadia Salah, recalls traumatic incidents and disrespect:

> The boys would follow us throwing stones, when we would enter the field, they would climb the walls and throw rocks and we would stop playing. Then women wearing traditional clothing, they would peek over the wall and they would say, "come look come look," they would call each other and just stare at us. We got embarrassed so we stopped. It was like they were kicking us out by just staring. Today many of the girls practicing here play in head scarves—wrapped extra tight, for sport. A group of boys huddles outside the fence, watching and criticizing almost every touch the girls make.[20]

While many Moroccan families are accustomed to seeing their young daughters running around and playing soccer with neighborhood boys, Nicole Matsuka finds that these liberal attitudes generally change as the girls grow up:

> It is no longer as acceptable for 18- or 19-year-old girls to still be playing football, especially in rural areas or smaller cities and towns. Girls are often discouraged from playing sports. Instead, they are pushed towards schools or starting families—persuaded that football and adult life are an impossible combination. . . . [T]he girls must give importance for their study because the sport now is without salary and not [a]

job, you can practice sport only for your health and your feeling, not for a job. . . . [A]s girls get older, more of them are pressured to leave the game by their families and society.[21]

Required *Hijab*: Female Footballers and FIFA

July 2012 marked the end of a year of negotiations with soccer's international regulating body, FIFA (Fédération Internationale de Football Association), during which time policies regarding Muslim female athletes wearing *hijab* at Olympic soccer matches was reconsidered. After these lengthy negotiations, an agreement was finally reached. Interestingly, the decision was based on the FIFA medical committee's conclusion that a *hijab* does not endanger the player—providing that the design conforms to one of two models that were being considered for adoption. Fortunately for female Muslim athletes, FIFA required a *hijab* sports design that prevented strangulation. Many suspect that FIFA's decision was the result of efforts by Prince Ali of Jordan, a FIFA vice president. Additionally, Wilfried Kemke, the UN special adviser on sports, submitted a letter to FIFA president Sepp Blatter supporting safe head scarves saying, in part, "As the governing body of the world's most popular sport, I believe FIFA has the responsibility to ensure that everyone has an equal chance to participate in football, without any barriers and regardless of gender, race, ability, age, culture or religious beliefs."[22] The approved designs incorporate quick-release Velcro fasteners and magnets.

Two companies submitted designs for the footballers' *hijab*: Capsters and ResportOn. Capsters, headquartered in the Netherlands since 2001, offers a variety of *hijab* alternative sportswear designed for female athletes that may be used during activities such as aerobics, track, soccer, surfing, and swimming. Dutch designer Cindy van den Bremen created Capsters as a graduation project. An excerpt from the Capsters website emphasizes freedom in one's choice of apparel:

> We at Capsters believe the choice to cover yourself should be yours, and yours only. Whether you want to cover your head because of religious convictions, due to problems of hair loss, or just because you want to keep warm or express your identity, it is all up to you! Still today Capsters believes the hijab should not limit girls and women to practice

sports wherever, whenever. We believe in the empowerment of women through sports. Our business is built along the lines of trust and integrity and we hope that reflects in our communication with our wearers and fans.[23]

IQO Design, which manufactures ResportOn, is the other company to have submitted a FIFA-sanctioned *hijab* design. CTV News Montreal reports that ResportOn, conceived by Elham Seyed Javad, an Iranian-born Canadian citizen, "is made of a lightweight, elastic fabric called Cool Max. The scarf is secured in place with magnets and comes off safely with the slightest tug. If pulled off, another cap remains underneath, so the hair does not get exposed."[24] Javad commented that she "designed the garment in hopes of encouraging religious Muslims who choose to wear the headscarf to get into sports," something they had been prevented from doing in Quebec and elsewhere due to *hijab* bans. She added, "The idea is to give them the power to feel confident as a woman and to go out and be active."[25]

After FIFA's announcement regarding the ResportOn *hijab*, Javad began receiving calls and orders from all over the world. IQO Design was eyeing a lucrative potential contract to supply the Iranian women's Olympic soccer team.[26] In 2008 Javad designed a head veil suitable for use in taekwondo. Although the design proved a commercial success, it paled in comparison to the profits that the ResportOn *hijab* will likely reap, as an item approved by FIFA and with multiple applications, including Formula 1 auto racing and go-carting. Canadian media reported in March 2014 that FIFA issued a final ruling to lift the ban on turbans and other religious headwear such as *hijab*. This decision extends also to male players from the Sikh community in Canada.[27]

Each year increasing numbers of Muslim women are demonstrating interest in athletics. As a result, sports *hijab* and designer lines of swimwear created especially for them are doing a booming business. Online retailers offer Islamic swimsuits with brand names such as veilkini (veil + bikini), burqini (burqa + bikini), hijood (*hijab* + hood), modestkini (modest bikini), and bodykini (body + bikini). These suits are manufactured globally—in Spain, France, China, Australia, the United States, Netherland, Canada, Singapore, the United Kingdom, Turkey, Brazil, and the United Arab Emirates. Numerous companies are reaping profits from the concept of halalness for the Muslim female athlete. To make their products even more attractive, some companies go beyond marketing modesty and offer UV protection as well, emphasizing the suits' full-body coverage to guarantee all-day protection from the brutal sun.[28]

My book *Velvet Jihad* introduces readers to Aheda Zanetti, a Muslim entrepreneur who created a company featuring fashionable, high-priced swimwear for Muslim women. Her Islamic bathing suit designs made it possible for a number of Australian Muslim women and girls to participate in a prestigious lifeguard program. Zanetti's swimwear "includes a hood-shaped Hijab design called the Hijood (a clever name combining both hijab and *hood*) and a hybrid of the Islamic burqa and the western world's bikini called a Burkini."[29]

Heather Marie Akou's study on the burqini stresses the importance of this innovative garment for Muslim women:

> The burqini . . . [was] originally created for Muslim lifeguards in Australia in 2006 by Lebanese-born fashion designer, Aheda Zanetti. Widely copied by other designers around the world, the burqini has been simultaneously embraced and reviled. Although generally accepted in Australia and by mainstream Muslims, reactions in Europe (in the era of the so-called 'burqa ban') have been much more hostile— a departure from standard swimming attire that calls to mind difficult questions concerning immigration, gender, and the limits of political correctness. As a design solution for women who want to swim while staying covered—a style of dress that disappeared from Western fashion in the mid-1900s—the burqini represents a new and fascinating case study in the aesthetics and global politics of Islamic dress.[30]

As Akou notes, response to the burqini has been hostile in parts of Western Europe. In 2009, for example, the London *Telegraph* reported that a Muslim woman was banned from entering a Parisian public swimming pool: "Pool staff said her three-piece Islamic swimsuit she bought in Dubai—consisting of a headscarf, tunic and trousers—was against pool regulations and unhygienic."[31]

Interestingly, two months after this incident, local councils in England decided to offer restricted swimming sessions for Muslims. The *Telegraph* of London reported on the regulations:

> Under the rules, swimmers—including non-Muslims—are barred from entering the pool in normal swimming attire. Instead they are told that

they must comply with the "modest" code of dress required by Islamic custom, with women covered from the neck to the ankles and men, who swim separately, covered from the navel to the knees.[32]

In a study regarding the burqini, Susie Khamis looked at the prevalence of burqini-clad Muslim women versus the "beach babe" on Australian beaches:

Burqini and its significance in relation to two dominant stereotypes in recent Australian history: the "beach babe," typically blonde, blue-eyed and bikinied; and a view of conservative Muslim culture that had taken shape in mainstream Australian media: as restrictive, regressive and misogynist. By appropriating the traditional bikini design for a contemporary Muslim clientele, the Burqini[TM] is both a confronting cultural statement and a bold example of 21st-century world fashion.[33]

Not one to miss out on profits, China has also flooded Muslim nations with ostensibly Islamic bathing suits. As might be expected, these bathing suits are generally more affordable and have saturated the swimwear market. This has definitely been the case in Egypt since the summer of 2010—despite clerics protesting that the suits violate teachings of Islam.[34] The more intensely these bathing suits, which quickly emerged in bright hues, are marketed with the imprint of Islam, the stronger their sales. In Egypt as in a multitude of other Muslim environments, the commodification of Islam is in full swing.

Intimate Wear and the Islamic Attitude

Like other women everywhere, Muslim women also often purchase intimate wear from specialty shops without embarrassment or discomfort. Historically, lingerie has been considered utilitarian, although its role has changed considerably in contemporary times. Thanks to the Internet and television, many Muslim women who earn their own money feel increasingly free to buy whatever they want, and lingerie is among those items that promise pleasure.

According to the various hadiths of the prophet Mohammad, a man and his wife have no restrictions between them in the privacy of their bedroom. Thus, a married Muslim woman may purchase erotic inti-mate wear to please herself and her husband and do so without guilt or shame. A common misconception is that a devout and veiled Muslim woman would never think about sexy lingerie or provocative styles of intimate wear. Nassib Ghossoub, owner of the Lebanese brand Vaness, said in a Just Style article, "In Arab countries there are no sex shops, so lingerie shops double as this to sell such items." When asked who buys such lingerie, Ghossoub replied, "The mohajiba (the veiled, conserva-tively dressed women) and soon-to-be brides, since wives—according to the Koran—must dance for their husbands."[35] The truth of the mat-ter is that veiled women have much the same desires relating to sexu-ality as the unveiled woman. The most obvious difference is that the veiled woman only wears such clothing in front of her husband—the only *mahram* or halal man to her and therefore the only one allowed to view her in such garments.

Contrary to Islamic stereotyping, lingerie sales are brisk in the Mid-dle East, and women in Muslim-majority countries enjoy buying sexy lingerie as much as women in the West do. This is reflected in an article by consultants offering marketing advice to Canadian companies. The consultants note, "In terms of intimate apparel and cosmetics, Muslim tastes are the same as the majority of Canadian women."[36]

The reader will note that what makes lingerie halal is not the product itself, that is, not the type of materials used, method of manufacturing, certification by an imam, and so forth. Rather, it is simply a question of how the lingerie is marketed. In the Persian Gulf and other predomi-nantly Islamic regions, open display of lingerie, particularly in upscale urban boutiques, is simply not allowed. However, in the deep recesses of bazaars and *souqs*, open-air markets, one can almost always find lin-gerie heaped in piles for passersby to examine.

Recognizing the future market for intimate wear in the Persian Gulf region, Brazilian company Scalina has invested heavily in the Arab mar-ket, manufacturing lingerie, pantyhose, and shapewear from thigh slimmers to camisoles under flagship brands TriFil and Scala. Scalina products are sold in Lebanon, Kuwait, the Emirates, Syria, Qatar, and Jordan but never openly displayed in public. The success of this com-pany indicates a healthy consumer appetite for such products. The ex-port manager of Scalina reports, "The Arabs like Brazilian lingerie a lot. The colours with greatest demand are the basic ones, like black, white and chocolate. Among all products, lingerie is what Scalina sells the most in the Middle East."[37] Brazilian-style lingerie items, particularly G-strings, enjoy marked popularity in the Middle East, with Lebanon accounting for the greatest number of Scalina sales.

Nayomi, the leading Middle Eastern retailer of brand-name lingerie and nightwear, has built fifty-eight stores in the Gulf region. Eleven of these stores are located in the UAE. The marketing pitch is that "the designs, the fabrics, and the styles take the best concepts from the international market, and give them a distinct Arabian flavour."[38] In 2011 the CEO of Frederick's of Hollywood, Linda LoRe, announced plans to disseminate products throughout the Middle East based on a "multi-year licensing arrangement with Abu-Dhabi-based Emirates Associated Business Group."[39] LoRe discussed the company's decision to expand into the Middle East:

> Womenetics: Your company recently announced that it is expanding into the Middle East. Given that much of the Middle East is very conservative when it comes to women's dress, how and why are you expanding there?
> LoRe: Frederick's of Hollywood is known as a fun, sexy brand around the world. Women everywhere aspire to be a part of the Hollywood lifestyle. That is what we are bringing to the Middle East, and that is what they are asking for.[40]

Frederick's of Hollywood's decision to tap into Muslim-dominated markets suggests careful research indicating a demand for sexy products and the promise of potentially lucrative profits. Abeleaziz Aouragh, entrepreneur of an online sex shop described earlier, said in a 2010 CNN story, "Knowing that in Mecca you can buy lingerie and buy certain sexual health products is enough. You can't get more halal than that."[41] Aouragh has big plans to offer lingerie on his website.

Lingerie displayed by vendors in their shop windows throughout the Middle East is not a new custom. In many Middle Eastern countries people are accustomed to seeing displays of bras and panties of lower quality in bazaars. Higher-quality, more expensive intimate wear items are sold in exclusive shops and beautifully displayed in the windows of small boutiques. The haram or halal aspects of such items have never been an issue until recently when certain government authorities began to object to or forbid open displays of women's garments. Predictably, the Islamic Republic of Iran took the lead in railing against such practices. In 2009 news reports followed the growing controversy regarding window displays, as does a *Guardian* article:

[Iranian] Police warned retailers . . . against displaying female mannequins wearing underwear or exposing body curves as part of a government campaign against western influence. In a statement carried by the state-owned IRNA news agency, the authorities also said that men should not sell women's underwear, and that displaying neckties and bow ties, which are considered un-Islamic, in shop windows was also prohibited. Officials have issued similar warnings in the past, but have stepped up their enforcement of strict religious dress codes since Mahmoud Ahmadinejad came to power in 2005.[42]

After wielding power for thirty years, the Iranian government unexpectedly turned on salesmen selling women's lingerie. This pronouncement may represent one more layer of paranoia regarding fancy boutiques located in upscale urban shopping districts, Iran's closest model of the forbidden Western lifestyle. Cheaper undies still may be viewed publicly hanging in traditional bazaars in less ritzy areas. No doubt the bazaar merchants, who have always sold such goods in simple displays often jumbled in boxes without regard to size or order, will continue to do so without disturbance.

After Iran's condemnation of intimate apparel in window displays, the Gaza Strip soon followed suit. Only by banning shop window displays of women's undergarments could Palestinians regain their moral compass. A news story in the *Jerusalem Post* calls attention to this justification for the decree:

The Hamas Islamic movement that controls the Gaza Strip has banned shops from displaying women's underwear in their windows, saying it offends public morality.

The prohibition is intended to "restore public morals in Palestinian society." . . . "The police will also launch investigations into the conduct of the store owners to avoid any suspicious behavior with female customers." . . . The ban is the latest measure regulating female modesty according to traditional Muslim custom enacted by Hamas . . . since it seized control of Gaza.[43]

Hamas authorities also mandated removal of scantily dressed mannequins from window displays and issued a warning against "keeping shop doors open when women are inside . . . [and] displaying bras, underwear or nightdresses, even inside the shop."[44] One wonders how women can select merchandise without seeing it first, unless Hamas intended for shopkeepers to spend their days continually opening and closing drawers in order to let the customers choose. While officials in Iran and the Gaza Strip worry about salesmen on the premises of lingerie and other women's intimate wear shops, Saudi Arabia has dealt with the same issue in a strategically different way. The Saudi edict ensures that only women may staff lingerie shops.

News from the Middle East of religious authorities clamoring about window displays or claiming that female mannequins are indecently exposed is not unusual. In February 2008, some UAE newspapers issued a statement to all clothing shops on behalf of authorities of Sharjah, the UAE's third-largest city: "The mannequins should be headless and the clothing in the window should respect the rules of decency, according to the religious principles."[45] In 2003 a fatwa related to this very issue had already been proclaimed by the Islamic Affairs Department but not implemented. Finally, religious authorities took firm action against the indecent display of mannequins, as cited in *Free Republic*: "We reinforced the ban because it was a religious issue that raised many complaints from residents, who were against shops displaying men and women's undergarments on realistic mannequins."[46]

Store window mannequins are subject to disapproval even in secular Turkey. A visit to Istanbul's Congress Center by Turkish Prime Minister Recep Tayyip Erdoğan on December 7, 2012, caused prompt removal of mannequins displaying works of certain fashion designers. The president of the Turkey Exporters Union, Mehmet Büyükekşi, deemed the "naked mannequins displaying leather belts at the Turkey Innovation Week too suggestive, so ordered officials to replace them with mannequins of ambiguous sex."[47]

Associating scantily dressed mannequins with moral concerns is not limited to the Middle East but also pervades other societies. India, a Hindu-majority nation, has experienced its own share of anger and concern toward mannequins, particularly in relation to recent sexual assaults and rape cases. The city of Mumbai set out to ban mannequins dressed in lingerie or other scanty clothes from window displays, claiming that they polluted men's minds and provoked them to attack women, while the displays also degraded women. Those in favor of removing mannequins contend that such displays do not fit the Indian traditional lifestyle. Mumbai and Delhi are known for their high number of rape cases.[48] Sadly, the mannequins are blamed for instigating rape behavior, allowing the real causes and responsibilities for such crimes to go unaddressed.

Halal Accessories

The halal-minded consumer is careful to avoid buying, wearing, or carrying any non-halal accessory items. Accessories are defined here as gloves, earrings, handbags, belts, purses, scarves, or any articles that add completeness, convenience, or attractiveness to one's basic outfit and are not gender-exclusive.[49]

Halal accessories occupy a special place in today's market. Some companies depend heavily on the availability of leather materials used in their manufacture. "Islamic" leather slippers, or *khuffs*, are worn as house shoes and sold online by various suppliers. Although this item is deemed halal, no evidence is offered regarding halal certification. According to several hadiths, this thin leather footwear dates back to the era of the Prophet Mohammad in the seventh century CE. The *khuff*, also known as *khuffain*, *kuffain*, *kuff*, and *quff*, figures prominently in the following two hadiths:

Sayyidina Mughirah bin Shu'bah said:
Dihyah Kalbi sent to Rasulullah Sayyidina Rasulullah [Prophet Mohammad] sallallahu alaihe wasallam as a gift two khuffs. . . . [He] did not inquire if the skin was from slaughtered animals or not.[50]

Buraydah (radiallahu anhu.) said:
Najaashi sent two simple black coloured [*khuffs*] as a gift to Sayyidina Rasulullah sallallahu alaihe wasallam. He wore these and made mash [a blessing] over [them] after performing wudu [ablution].[51]

In the first hadith, one notes that the Prophet "did not inquire if the skin was from slaughtered animals or not." This could indicate that it was of little importance whether the leather originated from an animal slaughtered according to the Muslim way, *zabiha*. Had it been of great significance, surely the hadith would have said so. This leads one to ask why there is so much fuss about halal leather if this hadith is accepted as authentic. If the Prophet remained silent on the slaughter issue, why give it so much attention?

In a study about commodifying Islam, Anne Meneley relays a story about her purchase of "Islamic socks"—which, as it turns out, were entirely different from *khuffs*.

These "socks," manufactured in China, a socialist state hardly known for tolerance of religious sensibilities, turned out to be black knee-high pantyhose. Islamic socks have become a part of the "intensification of veiling" in cities such as Zabid [Yemen] where Islamists are redefining public spheres for both men and women.[52]

Certainly modern textile machinery used in the production of such hosiery did not exist during the Prophet Mohammad's life. Therefore, what possible criteria could transform an ordinary pair of knee-length black stockings into "Islamic" hosiery? Perhaps it is the image of a woman in *niqab* on the package. Could that image alone qualify the product as Islamically acceptable? China, the manufacturer of such Islamic stockings, has a long record of discrimination against its Muslim population, the Uighur groups. Nevertheless, many Islamic commodities are made in China, even prayer rugs. For Muslims to be truly halal-minded, they would do well to ignore the cheaper price tags of Chinese goods and pay more attention to the political and social policies of countries where the goods originate.

Socks and shoes go together, and in Indonesia one finds a significant manufacturing sector of halal footwear certified by Indonesian authorities. This means that, as part of the certification process, authorities have ascertained that appropriate leather has been used that was harvested from a halal animal slaughtered according to *zabiha*. However, it is not unusual for Indonesian authorities to make arrests based on leather shoes having been falsely labeled. The *Jakarta Globe* reported on such an incident:

Jakarta Police arrested the head of a shoe company accused of marketing shoes as halal that contained leather made from pig's skin, police said. . . .

A man identified by police as "S. W." was arrested and charged with violating Indonesia's consumer protection law. "S. W." is the director of the Kickers shoe company. . . . [A] customer reported the company to police after noticing that two pairs of Kickers brand shoes listed "pigskin lining" on their tags. Both shoes carried a halal sticker when they were sold at the Sogo department store in Plaza Senayan, South Jakarta, police said.[53]

In Malaysia, the Domestic Trade, Cooperatives, and Consumerism Ministry is attempting to make it compulsory for merchants to disclose the halal status of leather goods, Halal Focus reports:

[S]ecretary-general Datuk Saripuddin Kasim said "this was to enable them to display separately leather items such as bags, shoes and clothing that are made from non-halal material. At the moment there are no laws that enable the ministry to enforce this. We only advise the traders to do so."[54]

Some Islamists consider women's high-heel shoes to be haram because the sound of the clicking heels draws sexual attention to the wearer. Their justification for objecting to high heels is based on a verse in the Qur'an, Surat An-Nūr (The Light), 24:31. The next-to-last line of the verse may be open to multiple interpretations:

And let them [women] not stamp their feet to make known what they conceal of their adornment. And turn to Allah in repentance, all of you, O believers that you might succeed.[55]

Whether high or low heel, what is often considered haram in terms of footwear material is the use of pigskin. This specific issue, however, is not mentioned in the Qur'an; therefore, as usual, various interpretations are offered by religious authorities without any consensus or agreement. Some argue that using pigskin in accessories is acceptable because no mention of it is found in the Qur'an, and obviously one does not eat leather. Other individuals consider items made from pig suede, such as shoes or purses, to be haram because they touch the wearer's skin. And so the controversy continues.

Brand names in sports shoes are also subject to the halal/haram debate. Online Muslim discussion groups disagree about the acceptability of Nike brand footwear. This thread appears in Islam Question and Answer:

Question:
The sign of NIKE (tick) or a word NIKE printed on T-Shits [sic] & Caps. Should muslims avoid purchasing & wearing the types of Stuffs. As if listen from many people that "It is Shirk" & it means I obey any other GOD (than Allah) (Nauzubillah) Please provide me brief answer & the history of Nike (if it is Truth).

Answer: Praise be to Allaah.

This well-known registered trademark, Nike, which may be the most well known of sporting brands in the world, bears the name of the Greek goddess of victory. The founders of this company who chose this name were Philip Knight and Bill Bowerman. They chose this name as a symbol of good luck and hope of victory for sportsmen who wore this brand and propagate the symbol of this god.

Nike was the god of victory among the ancient Greeks, who was usually presented in the form of a winged maiden, carrying a crown in one hand and a palm branch in the other. . . . Thus it is clear that it is not permissible for the Muslim to wear this symbol or to imitate those who wear it. The Muslim believes in the Oneness of Allaah (Tawheed) and believes that victory, help and strength come from Him alone. Wearing this symbol is contrary to his belief and faith. If he has no option but to buy the products of this company, then at least he should erase their symbol and name so that it is not on his chest, foot or neck. Thus his religious commitment will be safe as will his belief ('aqeedah).[56]

Few would argue that this type of phobia and extremism throws an absurd flag on the field regarding haram/halal issues around footwear.

Also of interest in the realm of accessories are amulets and charms embodying good luck, promising fertility, and protecting the wearer from the evil eye. A Qur'anic verse from chapter 113, *al Falaq* (The Dawn), is frequently included in amulets to deter evil eye. Protection is sought from *"The mischief of the envious one, As he practices envy."*[57] In certain Muslim cultures, parents will place amulets on young children to keep them safe from *jinns*, or evil spirits. Amulets may include *khamsa* depicting the open right hand of Fatima. Others might bear inscriptions of the name of God or holy people or images of sacred sites such as Kaaba in Mecca or the Dome of the Rock in Jerusalem. These symbolic icons differ widely since many are culturally dependent, reflecting local cultures rather than universally held Islamic beliefs. As I have noted elsewhere, "The gradual transmission of cultural taboos and folk beliefs from one generation to the next is a natural process in any given society. Therefore, it is not surprising to find traces of pre-Islamic customs and beliefs" in every Islamic community.[58]

In gold and silver bazaars in many Middle Eastern regions one finds extensive selections of jewelry with Islamic subjects using elegant calligraphic styles in Arabic, Persian, and Urdu. Women commonly favor this type of jewelry, while pious men are forbidden from adorning their bodies with jewelry, particularly gold. A 2004 article in *Saudi World Aramco* explains:

> To satisfy a woman's desire for jewelry that [will] embody her wealth, proclaim her identity, keep her safe from the evil eye and make her feel beautiful, silversmiths [create] a wealth of forms with designs that often [echo] ancient motifs from pre-Islamic cultures. They [add] pearls, turquoise, amber, lapis lazuli, coral, carnelian and other stones or beads as both decoration and amulet.[59]

Most merchants who manufacture and sell these commodities practice Islam themselves; therefore, they are aware that customers who feel vulnerable or who are suffering should be seeking refuge in God (Allah) only rather than in superstitious jewelry or amulets. Because Islam absolutely forbids black magic, sorcery, and witchcraft, the acts of selling and/or wearing this type of jewelry is religiously taboo. Some ulama warn against wearing any adornments with the name of Allah, his Prophets, or any other holy person. Nevertheless, merchants cater to the desires of many Muslims to seek constant reminders that God is with them at all times or to those who want to make a public show of their religiosity. In short, jewelers care little about haram or halal. Their bottom line is profit, and the ulama can take their pronouncements elsewhere.

Saudi Arabia's gold jewelry stores are chock full of pendants into which may be inserted Qur'anic verses. The pendants is then worn on a chain around the neck at all times, protecting the wearer with the words of God. Again, contradiction and confusion arise. Pendants and amulets—even those inscribed with Qur'anic verses—are considered haram by Islamic authorities. They claim that only Allah can truly protect the wearer. To trust in an amulet for safety and good luck implies distrust of Allah.

It is ironic that in the Kingdom of Saudi Arabia, with its staunch restrictions and regulations, that production and use of such items is not forbidden. Should one ask why? Perhaps the answer lies in profits resulting from marketing such commodities not only to Saudi citizens but also to visiting guest workers. In the Saudi kingdom gold jewelry is preferred over silver for those who can afford it, especially as an investment and for its resale value. Furthermore, the kingdom enjoys substantial revenues from millions of hajj pilgrims who make their way to

Mecca each year. These pilgrims often purchase gold items while visiting Mecca as Islamic commodities serving either as long-term investments or for spiritual protection.

Charms or amulets may be carried in purses. Hence, primarily due to entrepreneurial savoir-faire, one now finds advertisements for burqa bags appropriate to the task. Checking the Internet, one finds burqa bags marketed as charitable endeavors to help oppressed Muslim women like those living in Afghanistan under Taliban rule. Charity USA markets the burqa bag but is apparently not a registered charity; rather, "it is a for-profit organisation, owned by a company called Homeline Publications, which gives 'a percentage' of its profits to charity."[60] The site for this product describes how the bags are manufactured from recycled burqas.

> Stand strong with women in Afghanistan as they take back their freedom by transforming the once government-imposed burkha into stylish new accessories with heart. It's not religiously offensive to cut up a burkha, and the women doing so consider it a fun and harmless way to tell the world that they now wear a burkha by choice, rather than being governed to do so.[61]

The notion that Afghan women spend their afternoons tearing up burqas for fun and as symbols of their autonomy seems nothing less than absurd. One must admit, however, that the sales pitch is creative, evoking consumer sympathy and attention.

Another supposedly Islamic bag based on the burqa is a purse designed by Zardozi. Based in Kabul, Zardozi is a coalition of Afghan partners and suppliers crossing between Afghanistan and Pakistan. The website suggests that the company's primary objective is to find markets for the quality products of skilled Afghan craftsmen and women. The handbag is made from "an indigenous material in Afghanistan and Pakistan. It's an attempt of re-purposing the *burqa* material from a vector of anonymity to orginality! [*sic*]."[62] Zardozi's website purposefully obfuscates the phrase "indigenous material." The bag itself is 100 percent nylon. Is 100 percent nylon indigenous to Afghanistan? Again, this product is supposedly crafted from burqas belonging to Afghan women. How cleverly one makes money by twisting the purpose of the burqa and by introducing words such as "freedom" and "repurpose" into an advertising pitch!

Online retailer Zazzle, based in California,[63] and others entice consumers by offering products that exploit both halal and anti-halal themes. Created by KMILineWear for Zazzle is a cotton T-shirt that reads, "Only Eat And Drink Halal." According to the advertising copy, the consumer can "tell everyone without saying that you only eat and drink halal."[64]

Another clothing product created for Zazzle, this one by BeZizzled, is a No-Halal T-shirt, apparently for those individuals opposed to halal practices. In fact, Zazzle boasts two websites, one with a UK address on which all prices are listed in British pounds. For an average of 2.85 pounds, one can purchase the No Halal Antiqued Image Pin. Circular in shape, this pin is inscribed with "NO HALAL" in black on a white background, outlined in red with a line crossing the pin, and the Arabic script for "No Halal" at the bottom. The same inscription, "NO HALAL," also appears on other circular or square pendants for 21.95 pounds. White canvas shopping bags described as "No Halal—Crisp Image Canvas Bags" are listed at 20.95 pounds.

Not to be outdone in the pro-halal market, Redbubble, an Australian company, offers "Halal Kitty T-Shirts & Hoodies" with this pitch: "Even under her burqa, Hello Kitty's Muslim cousin Halal Kitty is easily recognized as a member of the Kitty family."[65] Another Redbubble offering is a T-shirt dyed with the familiar red and yellow colors of the fast-food chain McDonald's. The symbolic Golden Arches have been converted to the Arabic lettering for "halal," under which is "I'm lovin' it."[66] Designed by Nuh Sarche for Redbubble.com, this T-shirt doubles as an ad promoting halal foods that are occasionally available at McDonald's restaurants.

The religious commodification of objects—that is, imbuing mundane objects with religious purpose or significance—is not new. What is new are the surprisingly out-of-the-box methods entrepreneurs and companies are using to convince devout Muslims to part with their money. As we have seen, online retailers like Zazzle have, somewhat unbelievably, decided to sell to consumers on both sides of the halal issue and in doing so are quite cleverly covering their bases.

In Islamist regions dominated by conservative patriarchal authorities, young Muslim women face particular difficulties vis à vis participating in sports. Even when governments are challenged by their citizens to relax rules prohibiting athleticism in girls, the ayatollahs, ulama, muftis, sheikhs, mullahs, and *mulanas* stay firm in their conservative opinions.

The cumbersome and often uncomfortable sportswear that young Muslim women must wear represents yet another hurdle to their successful athletic achievement. Caught between the close scrutiny of religious authorities and the regulatory requirements of international organizations such as Olympic committees, the Muslim female athlete continues to face significant challenges simply in terms of her sports uniform.

Taking note of this conundrum, sportswear designers and their marketing teams have jumped on the bandwagon to accommodate the female Muslim athlete's needs. Busily creating halal sportswear that satisfies the Islamic requirement of uber modesty, guarantees safety, and meets the official standards set forth by international sporting committees, these designers are now realizing big profits.

Despite the numerous obstacles she faces, some would say that the female Muslim athlete is steadfastly making progress. Her *hijab* has gained halal status to be used at the highest level of athletics. New opportunities in the world of sports and in Middle Eastern nations specifically are opening as a result. Olympic successes are beginning to break down barriers and demolish stereotypical presumptions about Muslim women athletes. As new design concepts emerge in halal sportswear to increase comfort and performance for these determined young women, product sales will continue booming.

The sale of halal lingerie and intimate wear will follow suit, enjoying healthy profits in the Middle East and in other predominantly Muslim regions—even though displays of intimate wear in shop windows, boutiques, and public bazaars will be deemed haram by fundamentalist movements, reflecting once again a patriarchal obsession with sexuality and women's bodies. Lifelike mannequins, too, under siege by Islamist governments, will be acceptable only when they are headless, breastless, and devoid of any threatening female features. As recently as July 2014, the Sunni extremist group ISIS ordered the faces of all female—and male—mannequins in parts of Syria and Iraq to be covered.

Fashion accessories, including handbags and shoes, are entering the halal/haram discussion as well. Afghan burqas, transformed and reframed into products sold by charitable, philanthropic, technically nonprofit online enterprises, are enjoying remarkable success, with burqa bags now available on eBay. The devout Muslim may even buy footwear inscribed with "Allah" or "soldiers of Allah."

Unfortunately, one still cannot be absolutely sure if purchasing such commodities—whether a canvas shopping bag stamped with the halal logo or a colorful burqini—will guarantee the consumer a closer relationship to Allah. What seems certain is that the world of "Islamic" sportswear, lingerie, and fashion accessories has been effectively commandeered by capitalistic enterprise.

Conclusion

The race is on to develop and market religiously themed commodities. From small-scale entrepreneurs to giant multinational corporations, all are targeting specific segments of the population in order to maximize profits. Now that Internet access is all but universal, online consumers can and do place an astounding array of religiously oriented items in their virtual shopping carts. Pradip Thomas has noted, "Hindu nationalist organizations, Islamic radicals and Christian fundamentalists rank among the most creative, effective users of network technologies—telecommunications, computing, mobile telephony and the internet."[1] Some would suggest that the commodification of Islam has, in particular, been propelled by information and media technologies. Certainly, the Internet provides efficient portals for marketing, and as the halal phenomenon gains momentum, it continues to alter and be altered by expanding global markets.

In short, an unmistakable trend seems to be emerging in all religious arenas, including Islam—that is, the transformation of religious symbols into commodities and the proliferation of strategies that ensure the profitable marketing and sale of these commodities.[2] Brand Islam began as a few enterprises marketing halal food and has exploded into a massive web of Islamic services including halal banking, finance, and insurance, halal hospitals and hospice care, halal dating, halal hotels and tourism, and more. In other words, Brand Islam has morphed into an explosion of products and services, some useful and some superfluous, created by Muslim manufacturers and government-sponsored initiatives as well as by entrepreneurs solely interested in profit, not the Prophet's teachings. From halal comic books to Qur'anic psychotherapy, the commodification of Islam has become a force with which to be reckoned and one that is bursting with potential.

The Halal Race Is On

As I have demonstrated throughout this book, the concept of halal transcends ingredients found in food and drink such as alcohol and pork. Rather, halal deals with principles and processes including the packaging, handling, and storing of foods as well as moral precepts regulated by Sharia. As recently as 2012, analyses of packaging in Germany, Britain, and France revealed, a *Food Production Daily* article reports, "porcine contamination for halal foods as a result of animal fat-based lubricants used in production of some paper-based materials leaching into products."[3] Contamination had occurred in the paper packing machinery, leaking stearates, or lubricants, into the food.[4]

At present, most halal markets in the West still lack a comprehensive regulatory mechanism to guarantee safe, quality-controlled food. In the United States, the Food and Drug Administration has yet to institute halal regulations. Even if food establishments in the West boast halal certification and are operated by Muslims, naive consumers may be eating contaminated, non-halal ingredients. Halal criteria imply purity, integrity, transparency, and wholesomeness of food and drink. All of these must be present to secure the consumer's trust. This is particularly crucial, authors of a *Meat Science* article contend, "for halal brands from non-Muslim countries. Muslim consumers are willing to pay more for foods certified halal, as much as 13 percent on average; thus, significant profits may be realized in areas with large Muslim populations."[5] However, Muslim consumers will inevitably ask under what authority a product is deemed halal. Shelina Janmohamed writes, "Consumers want . . . quality, care and clarity."[6]

Responding to the demand in Belgium, Brussels Enterprises Commerce and Industry (BECI), essentially the Brussels chamber of commerce, began offering halal labels for industrial products in 2011. It was strongly criticized for doing so.[7] Many Belgians claimed this signaled yet another step in the Islamization of their nation. Islam in Europe reports that Olivier Willocx, BECI managing director, countered with a statement that the halal certificate

is meant for non-meat products for export, and not for the local market. [BECI] wanted to ensure transparency in this field . . . and now charge[s] every company that wants a halal certification for its product 1500 euro. A European certificate is recognized everywhere in the Muslim world. The charge is used to pay for the imam who comes especially from Algeria (a country which recognizes the link between church and State), and inspects the production site for three days before deciding whether to issue the certificate. BECI now gets an application for their new label every day, and they hope to get to 500 certificates a year.[8]

Directly linked to Islamic identity, halal choices are especially important to Muslims born and raised in the West. In recent decades, Muslim populations in EU nations have grown by 140 percent, primarily due to mass immigrations from Africa and Asia.[9] Among these Muslim consumers, there is a growing preference for products brandishing a halal logo. Their consumer choices are affecting markets West and East, according to the Halal Development Council (HDC) of Pakistan, an NGO dedicated to the development of halal economy. Halal Pakistan reports that "more than 80 percent of the world halal trade is done by non-Muslim countries . . . [that] by utilizing the Halal Brand to their economic benefit, have become the biggest exporters of Halal products in today's world."[10] Competition is fierce among certifying agencies in light of the growing global Muslim population and its economic power.

The halal concept has culminated in the creation of brands and in some cases, forms of co-branding, which suggests unbridled potential for both Muslims and non-Muslims.[11] A consultant's blog post in 2012 asserts,

> The race is on to establish powerful international "halal brands." The stakes are high: by some estimates, the global market for halal products is worth $500bn a year. But it's a market strewn with confusion, as separate Muslim countries try to establish recognised standards and producers from outside the Muslim world also hurry to enter the market.[12]

Muslims have traditionally been underserved in Western environments. However, this is all changing as halal items become increasingly available in restaurants including multinational chains such as Pizza Hut and McDonald's. As previously mentioned, Nestlé, Colgate Palmolive, Carrefour, Unilever, and many other corporations are investing impressive resources to capture their fair share of the Islamic market.

Also new to global markets is halal tourism, a thriving sector of the halal industry. This genre of tourism caters to the special needs of Muslim travelers, whether they are traveling for leisure or for medical and other purposes, mostly in non-Muslim-majority nations. Examples from

Belgium and Italy highlight efforts to develop this lucrative industry. In 2010, according to the website Islam in Europe, hotels in Brussels began offering halal rooms for Muslim guests, that is, hotel accommodations with "[no] porn channels, no pork, but with a Koran and a prayer rug, and a pointer towards Mecca."[13] The Brussels-based EuroHalal Market website now directs travelers to numerous halal-friendly hotels where they can easily book reservations online. Muslim travelers to Europe, especially from the Arabian Peninsula, are often well heeled and accompanied by multiple family members. These individuals are accustomed to excellent service and the best-quality conveniences. BECI's initial plan was to halal-certify hotel rooms on several floors in select Brussels hotels. However, BECI consultant Bruno Bernard says, "we don't rule out to later have a type of 'omni-halal' label for whole hotels, which have separate pools, among other things."[14]

In Italy's popular resort town of Riccione on the Adriatic coast, "the city council prepared to authorize requests to set up partitions on parts of the shoreline to satisfy requests from the town's growing numbers of Arab and Muslim tourists."[15] Local hotel and resorts owners apparently realized that their Muslim guests, now numbering in the thousands, are primarily wealthy travelers seeking beach destinations for their entire families. Preferring to stay in upscale hotels, these Muslims require private beaches for female family members who want to comfortably swim or enjoy a relaxing stroll without being heavily covered. A number of Riccione hotel and resort owners are eager to cater to this preference. Attilio Cenni, owner of the Grand Hotel des Bains, planned a TV advertising campaign in Saudi Arabia and the United Arab Emirates to attract more tourists from that part of the world.[16]

A Final Word on Fatwas

The world of e-commerce provides far-reaching forums and opportunities for countless individuals—those busily issuing fatwas, others providing consumer testimonials, and of course, merchants eagerly selling their wares. Online fatwas, even when not issued by credible religious authorities, still hold considerable sway over pious Muslims who may dismiss the source while fearing the message, especially when the message is vitriolic and delivered with the persuasive power of media technology. Fatwas may offer reassurance to a consumer concerned whether a new product or service is religiously acceptable. It is not only the halal status of commodities but also the haram aspect that is of real concern. Some would argue that the majority of Muslim laypersons obtain information regarding controversial fatwa rulings from questionable sources, as noted by Hashim and Mizerski in their study of Malaysian consumers:

> Muslim consumers tend to acquire information on more controversial fatwa rulings through less formal sources, compared to less controversial fatwa rulings. Several clusters of Muslim consumers were found to have their sources of fatwa associated with the product category, gender of respondent, and religious orientation.[17]

While these findings are limited to Malaysian Muslims, I have noted this same tendency among Muslim consumers in other nations far beyond that country's borders. In short, one should not underestimate the power of fatwas in today's marketplace and especially around halal/haram issues. The effects of an accusatory fatwa could have ruinous effects on sales. Consider what happened when a Danish cartoonist depicted the Prophet Mohammad in a satirical light in 2006. Fatwas were issued and Danish goods were boycotted, resulting in a devastating loss of revenues for some Danish products and even the removal of Danish merchandise from store shelves. One can imagine the impact of such a boycott with nearly two billion Muslim consumers globally.

The Politicization of Halal: Identity or Absurdity?

In some instances, the halal theme is being used as a political tool to protest and boycott Western products and policies. Competitive products are being developed such as Mecca Cola and the *hijabi* doll. Some of these products are direct results of anti-Western sentiment propelled by fatwas meant to preserve Islamic identity and values. Indeed, new Islamic markets are vibrant in nations with anti-Islamic histories.

In France, home to Europe's largest Muslim population and Europe's largest supplier of halal meat, the halal issue has been repeatedly politicized, resulting in inflammatory national rhetoric and xenophobic, anti-immigrant policies. During the 2012 presidential campaign, Prime Minister Francois Fillon created a furor in Jewish and Muslim communities when he urged French Muslims and Jews to consider scrapping their "outdated" slaughter rules. An exasperated Grand Rabbi of

France, Gilles Bernheim, responded in Agence France-Presse, "France's problems are so major, as we are in a period of crisis, so how can the issue of kosher meat and halal meat be a major problem for France?"[18] The *Guardian* reported much stronger views being expressed by Muslims: "Members of the booming educated and entrepreneurial Muslim middle class say they are tired of being cast as scapegoats in Sarkozy's wooing of the extreme right and have accused him of dangerous and divisive election tactics."[19] Muslim citizens accused French politicians of exploiting minorities to attract far-right voters and to avoid facing the nation's economic problems. The website *On Islam* cited a similar view: "We're just an excuse for them not to talk about the financial crisis."[20]

Even though Western businesses and political systems enjoy lucrative halal profits, they are quick to join in accusing Muslim groups of ulterior motives and hidden agendas. Claiming that halal products and services are merely fronts to support subversive, terrorist activities,[21] Western reactionaries point to the halal issue as an Islamist tactic that allows Muslim citizens to resist integrating into and embracing Western values.[22]

Regardless of how much negativity the word "halal" carries in certain parts of the world, marketers know that the concept of halal is here to stay and that at the end of the day, what matters most are sales and profit. Not addressed in this book yet worthy of brief mention are satirical reactions to the burgeoning halal culture and Islamic industries. On the Internet one finds comments and satirical images mocking halal principles on consumption of pork or alcohol.

An anonymous Iranian blogger obviously familiar with the politics, culture, and sensitivity of the Islamic Republic of Iran to anything relating to sex wrote a post titled "Iran Introduces Islamic Porn to Confront Cultural Invasion," apparently intended as a faux response to the invasion of Western pornography. The writer says the Islamic variety comes with halal guidelines to "fulfill the needs of our youth and to promote Islamic values."[23] The post continues,

> You see in Western porn what dirty practices man and woman engage in prior to intercourse. Firstly, in Islamic porn we won't see these disgusting acts, such as woman performing oral sex on men or vice versa. Secondly, group sex is forbidden in Islam and there will never be more than one man and one woman present at a scene. But I must add that there will always be a clergy present so he can wed the acting couple, filming crew and himself.[24]

A happy pink "halal" pig. The "Halal Certified" pig image appears on an anti-Islam blog in a 2013 post about pig DNA reportedly found in halal beef sausages. Image from Bare Naked Islam, http://www.barenakedislam.com/.

Budwizir. The pseudo-Arabic letters read, "Budwizir the caliph of beers. Just like the prophet used to drink! The only halal beer." Small print at the bottom adds, "Available where ever the Quaran is sold." Image from Axes and Alleys, http://www.axesandalleys.com.

Halal condom satire. Image from Think Atheist, http://www.thinkatheist.com/.

The blogger continues addressing pornography, contrasting Western and Islamic film porn actors:

[I]n Western porn, actors are performers [who] are fully naked. But in Islamic porn, in all scenes, men will have a tank top on and women will wear headscarves. This is a sensitive point that shows a porn actress, while performing her role, can still keep her Islamic hijab and that there's no incompatibility between acting in Islamic porn and observing Islamic hijab.[25]

Another satirical backlash is the so-called halal condom. The condom package shows a burqa-clad female whose body is exposed from the waist down with half her face and the rest of her upper body covered. The image, in fact, belongs to a series of paintings called "Islamic Women as Pinups Girls."[26] The condom packet reads: "There is no God but Allah and Mohammad is his Messenger . . . Zamzam DIPPED FOR EXTRA BLESSINGS . . . SHARIA APPROVED . . . Each Lubricated condom is Blessed with Sacred Verses and Masnoon prayers to keep the Satan away during Intercourse."[27] Also visible is the halal logo in English and Arabic alongside the product name "HUREX® . . . CERTIFIED HALAL GREEN CONDOMS . . . 12 REGULAR CONDOMS . . . TESTED BY A TEAM OF FUQHAA."[28]

Other absurdities abound in the Islamic marketplace, such as pork products manufactured in Asian nations with labels that read "50% halal." Obviously, an item is either 100 percent halal or not. What can be said of merchants who sell their cans of pork and beans as certified halal? On the opposite extreme are businesses that go far beyond what is required by Sharia to curry favor with their Muslim customers. The Crystal Crown Hotel in Malaysia includes elevators designated to lift halal goods only.[29] The Islamic Consumer Association of Malaysia (PPIM) offered an explanation in *Free Malaysia Today*: "The hotel definitely will do everything they can to prevent losing their halal certification as it would mean a huge loss of business for them."[30]

The Muslim *umma* seems especially interested in services and products that are advertised using Islamic cultural expressions and artifacts. Marketers attract consumers by using key principles of Islamic rituals or by promising religious favor that resonates with a devout Muslim's psyche, and in general, they synchronize their products with Islam by using a variety of advertising techniques. Some supposedly Islamic products marketed with the above criteria defy belief, such as the Auto Wudu Washer (for *wudu* or *wudhu*, ablution). This is an automatic pre-prayer personal washing system invented in Malaysia.

Not to be outdone by Malaysia, the government of Iran sponsored a project at the University of Mashad in the Mechanical Engineering Department. The result was an "Islamically approved" mechanism referred to as the Auto Mortician Operation. These robotic mechanisms, which hold potential to make huge export profits for the Shi'a-based government, contain spray jets to perform religious ablution, a process required to wash the bodies of the deceased that is customarily carried out by family members or hired professional morticians. Only one mortician is required to supervise this equipment and to facilitate a mass ritual cleansing. Before the mortician can flip the switch, an official cleric shows up to recite requisite prayers for the dead. The Auto Mortician Operation reduces human handling of the dead and, according to government officials, results in a more hygienic process. Also, a further advantage should be noted: water conservation.

At a time when many Muslim citizens, including those in Iran and other Middle Eastern nations, are struggling to free themselves from

Ear & Facial washer   Foot & Ankle washer

Auto Wudu Washer. A Sciences Club blog post describes the washer as "the world's first and only automatic pre-prayer personal washing system introduced to enable an individual to perform the Wudu ablution efficaciously in conformance to Qur'anic teachings." Malaysian manufacturer AACE Technologies makes the wall-mounted model for mosques, airports, and other public spaces and a stand-alone model for more private use. Images and quote from Sciences Club, http://www.sciencesclub.com/.

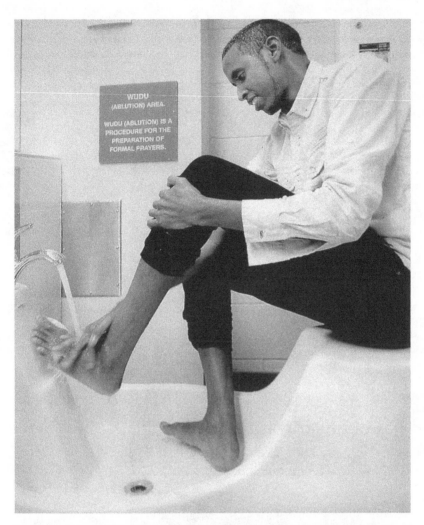

Special-needs washer. The Sciences Club blog post explains, "If a prayer room design or wudu khana needs to accommodate elderly or disabled family members, the WuduMate-R wudu sink may be the answer. The WuduMate-R is easily used by those in wheelchairs or with limited mobility." Image and quote from Sciences Club, http://www.sciencesclub.com/.

conservative fundamentalism and the patriarchal stranglehold of mullahs, muftis, ayatollahs, and *mulanas*, one might ask whether the trend toward Islamic commodification is helpful. Will it serve to minimize suffering, diminish discrimination particularly against women, or further basic human rights?

Auto-mortician equipment. Made in Iran and tested in several cities, the automated system is replacing undertakers. It was developed at the University of Mashhad with a grant from the Iranian government. Images and details from Farda News, http://www.fardanews.com/.

Racks of prepared bodies ready for burial.

The auto-mortician conveyor belt. A Qur'anic verse about the dead body is inscribed at the top.

Document permitting use of the auto-mortician. Signed by a religious authority, the handwritten inscription begins, "In the name of God"; stipulates that the process be supervised by a Muslim mortician who declares his religious intention before switching on the machinery; and ends, "May you always be successful."

General view of
the automated
mortician space
and equipment.

Future Trends

On a final note, I am convinced that Islamic commodification is here
to stay and will continue exerting a profound impact on global markets. Ultimately perhaps only two categories of goods and services will
be available—halal and haram. One can only imagine what the future
holds. Certainly, many more innovative products and processes and, inevitably, new fatwas can be expected. The Muslim-majority countries
that have not recognized the need to participate in halal economics will
likely do so.

Sharia-driven governments like those in Pakistan and Iran have
viewed halal certification as unnecessary based on the assumption
that everything in the homeland is already halal. As a result, neither
of these nations developed halal-based economies, and accordingly,
they have missed out on the trillion-dollar global halal market. As recently as 2014, however, the Iranian government made ample progress
to join the global halal certification market trend. Major Iranian industrial food products have gained the halal food standard label. This
new enterprise for the Iranian government is expected to help the Iranian economy. According to Secretary General of Halal World Institute
Abdol-Hossein Fakhri, "more than 1,000 famous Iranian industrial
food products are fully observing the requirements for obtaining the
Halal Food Standard label."[31] The Iranian halal food capacity is estimated around $30 billion with a potential to increase to $100 billion.[32]

In the future, in order to jump on the halal bandwagon, Pakistan
and other countries will need to assemble coalitions of scholars, tech-

nocrats, jurists, diplomats, and entrepreneurs to create NGOs focusing on successful promotion and exportation of their homegrown halal-certified products and services.

In the West, ironically, the more vitriolic and anti-halal the public discourse, the more attention the general public pays to all things halal. The halal cosmetic industry is building a lucrative market in the United States emphasizing natural, botanical ingredients and the absence of animal products. As the Muslim diaspora in the West continues to mushroom, halal menus and offerings will likely become prominent fixtures in mainstream society. In trendy urban restaurants, chefs will be carefully trained in and knowledgeable about creating and maintaining the purity of halal food and food preparation.

Another sign pointing to future trends is the halal food festival. In 2013 Chicago held such a festival that was attended by five thousand people, and in Newark, California, approximately ten thousand people showed up for the same type of gathering. These food festivals draw participants referred to as halal foodies, or "haloodies."[33] Indeed, it may be these individuals, Muslim and non-Muslim, who ultimately exert more influence in terms of the successful acculturation of immigrant populations than policy makers or politicians can. Who can argue the fact that food is a common denominator? All people, despite backgrounds and ethnicities, share a common love for food. Cultural events such as the 2014 Halal Food Festival in East London, which attracted twenty thousand people, will continue to increase in popularity. Many individuals drawn to these festivals are searching for clean, organic, wholesome foods and are interested in educating themselves about the farm-to-table process.

Future studies addressing the relation between Islamic piety and markets should focus on but not be limited to such topics as the growing halal demands of Muslim diaspora populations, a global standardization of halal certification, the psychological effects of increasingly manipulative Internet marketing strategies targeting Muslim consumers, and the emergence of new pharmaceuticals, nutraceuticals,[34] and biotechnological products considered halal, including "green" food packaging. Moreover, the type of technological procedures and mechanisms used in testing halal products to detect fraudulent, adulterated ingredients will continue to be improved, resulting in the establishment of new and more reliable standards.

From the very air we breathe to the bottled water we drink, no doubt the halal industry will transmute even the most mundane products into

Islamic commodities and, in doing so, continue transforming piety into profit. Some Muslims will adamantly follow and support this trend, eagerly anticipating the next halal commodity. Most, however, will continue to exercise common sense and discriminate wisely when making consumer decisions. I have written this book to inform and to question. No one can know the long-term effects of rigorously marketing Islamic-centered commodities. Perhaps the proliferation of all things Islamic will help unite and strengthen the *umma*, the Muslim community, globally. Few are willing to predict if this phenomenon will drive an even deeper wedge between East and West.

Beginning as a humble religious requirement, halal has grown into a remarkably successful and sophisticated global phenomenon. Numerous halal commodities may or may not be authentically Islamic, as I have emphasized. The reader will do well to consider that this has become a profit-based concept, one that exploits the emergence of a new Islamic economic paradigm. It is also important to keep in mind that any service or product created under Brand Islam has not necessarily been developed to honor religious practice or observance. The commodification of Islam has metamorphosed into a topic worthy of future research, study, and analysis in numerous multidisciplinary academic and non-academic fields.

Notes

Introduction

1. The term "Brand Islam" was coined by Jonathan Wilson, a senior lecturer in advertising and marketing communications at the University of Greenwich in England; Jonathan Wilson, "Brand Islam Is Fast Becoming the New Black in Marketing Terms," *Media and Tech Network* (blog), *The Guardian*, February 18, 2014, http://www.theguardian.com/media-network/media-network-blog/2014/feb/18/islamic-economy-marketing-branding.

2. "Interland," a term developed by John Grant, author of *Made With: Brands, Creatives, and Entrepreneurs from the Emerging Global Interland* (London: LID, 2013), is defined as the region between North Africa and the Middle East through Indonesia populated by Muslims, predominantly young people experiencing big economic and social changes. The new type of brand is replacing the Western established brands. The Islamic interland products are innovative and culturally appropriate to Muslims in, for example, Turkey, Iran, Lebanon, Tunisia, Qatar, Iraq, Jordan, Egypt, Dubai, Malaysia, and Indonesia.

3. Smeeta Mishra and Faegheh Shirazi, "Hybrid Identities: American Muslim Women Speak," *Gender, Place, and Culture* 17, no. 2 (April 2010): 194.

4. Jonathan Laurence, "In the Year 2030: Will Europe Become the 'Colony of Islam' That Some Predict? A Hard Look at the Future," *Boston College Magazine*, Summer 2010, http://bcm.bc.edu/issues/summer_2010/features/in-the-year-2030.html#. The article in *Il Foglio*, "In the Casbah of Rotterdam," by Giulio Meotti, published on May 14, 2009, is translated in its entirety in Sandro Magister, "Eurabia Has a Capital: Rotterdam," *Chiesa*, May 19, 2009, http://chiesa.espresso.repubblica.it/articolo/1338480?eng=y.

5. In Magister, "Eurabia Has a Capital: Rotterdam."

6. Ibid.

7. *Dhimmi* was the name applied by Arab Muslim conquerors to indigenous non-Muslim populations who surrendered by treaty (*dhimma*) to Muslim domination.

8. Bat Ye'or is a pseudonym of Gisèle Littman, née Orebi, an Egyptian-born

British writer, political commentator, and conspiracy theorist who writes about the history of Middle Eastern Christian and Jewish *dhimmis* living under Islamic governments; "Bat Yeʿor: Anti-Muslim Loon with a Crazy Conspiracy Theory Named 'Eurabia,'" Loon Watch, September 10, 2009, http://www.loonwatch.com/tag /xenophobe/.

9. Walid Saleh is affiliated with University of Toronto's Department for the Study of Religion and Department of Near and Middle Eastern Civilizations. This quotation is excerpted from the academic discussion blog Sociology of Islam and Muslim Societies, Portland State University, http://www.pdx.edu /sociologyofislam/.

10. Vali Nasr, *Forces of Fortune. The Rise of the New Muslim Middle Class and What It Will Mean for Our World* (New York: Simon and Schuster, 2009).

11. Gautam Sen, "Neo-Imperialism, the West, and Islam," *Economic and Political Weekly*, October 27, 2001, p. 4058.

12. R. Alkayyali and N. Prime, "Religion, Acculturation, and the Choice of Food Retail Outlets by Algerian Origin Muslim Women in France: Developing Research Propositions," paper presented at the European International Business Association (EIBA) 35th Annual Conference, Porto, Portugal, December 10–12, 2010.

13. Marian Salzman, "Marketing to Muslims," *Ad Week*, April 30, 2007, http://www.adweek.com/news/advertising-branding/marketing-muslims-94650. Also see Charles A. Rarick et al., "Marketing to Muslims: The Growing Importance of Halal Products," *Journal of the International Academy for Case Studies* 18, no. 1 (January 2012): 81–86.

14. Salzman, "Marketing to Muslims."

15. Fatema Mohsina, Foyez Ahmed Bhuiyan, and Mostaq Ahmad Bhuiyan, "*Shariʿa* Compliance in Building Identified Islamic Brands," special issue, "Islamic Management and Business," *European Journal of Business and Management* 5, no. 11 (2013).

16. Quoted in Nazia Hussain, "Expert Opinions on Marketing to Muslims," *Marketing Week*, June 24, 2010, http://www.marketingweek.co.uk/expert -opinions-on-marketing-to-muslims/3014949. Hussain is director of cultural strategy at Ogilvy and Mather Global.

17. "Marketing to Muslims," Associated Press, published in *Jerusalem Post*, December 28, 2010, http://www.jpost.com/Features/In-Thespotlight/Marketing-to -Muslims.

18. Raja Abdulrahim, "Marketing to Muslims Poses a Challenge for Retailers," *Los Angeles Times*, January 25, 2012, http://articles.latimes.com/keyword/ marketing.

19. Alicia Izharuddin, "Malaysia's Commodified Islam," *Malaysian Insider*, November 9, 2012, http://www.themalaysianinsider.com/sideviews/article/malaysias -commodified-islam-alicia-izharuddin.

20. Greg Fealy, "Consuming Islam: Commodified Religion in Contemporary Indonesia," in *Expressing Islam: Religious Life and Politics in Indonesia*, ed. Greg Fealy and Sally White (Singapore: Institute of Southeast Asian Studies, 2008), 17.

21. *Halal Journal*, http://www.halaljournal.com/.

22. "Neoliberalism" is defined as "a modern politico-economic theory favouring free trade, privatization, minimal government intervention in business, reduced

public expenditure on social services, etc."; Collins English Dictionary, Complete and Unabridged (HarperCollins, 2003).

23. Daromir Rudnyckyj, "Spiritual Economies: Islam and Neoliberalism in Contemporary Indonesia," *Cultural Anthropology* 24, no. 1 (February 2009): 104.

24. Daniel E. Montanno and Danuta Kasprzyk, "Theory of Reasoned Action, Theory of Planned Behavior, and the Integrated Behavioral Model," in *Health Behavior and Health Education. Theory, Research, and Practice,* ed. Karen Glanz, Barbara K. Rimer, and K. Wiswanath (San Francisco: John Wiley and Sons, 2008), 67–92.

25. Muhammad Saed Abdul-Rahman, *Islam: Questions and Answers, Divine Unity (Tawheed),* vol. 7 of Islamic Book Series (London: MSA, 2003), 8.

26. Syed Shah Alam and Nazura Mohamed Sayuti, "Applying the Theory of Planned Behavior (TPB) in Halal Food Purchasing," *International Journal of Commerce and Management* 21, no. 1 (2011): 8–20; Arshia Mukhtar and Muhammad Mohsin Butt, "Intention to Choose Halal Products: The Role of Religiosity," *Journal of Islamic Marketing* 3, no. 2 (2012): 108–120; Karijan Bonne, Iris Vermeir, and Wim Verbeke, "Impact of Religion on Halal Food Consumption Decision Making in Belgium," *Journal of International Food and Agribusiness Marketing* 21, no. 1, (2008): 5–26.

27. See Jasmin Sydee and Sharon Beder, "Ecofeminism and Globalisation: A Critical Appraisal," *Democracy and Nature: The International Journal of Inclusive Democracy* 7, no. 2 (July 2001), http://www.democracynature.org/vol7/beder_sydee_globalisation.htm. Sydee and Beder explain that material ecofeminists "identify globalisation as an outgrowth of patriarchal capitalism, insisting on the primacy of gender as the determinant of social organisation and arguing that it is the dichotomy between production and reproduction that essentially defines capitalism."

28. Morris Kalliny and Angela Hausman, "The Impact of Cultural and Religious Values on Consumer's Adoption of Innovation," *Academy of Marketing Studies Journal* 11, no. 1 (January 2007): 125.

29. *The Religious Products Market in the U.S.: Books, Music, Video and Accessories* (Packaged Facts, April 1, 2006), at Market Research, http://www.marketresearch.com/Packaged-Facts-v768/Religious-Products-Books-Music-Video-1176021/. A description at the website says the report, "a new study by Packaged Facts, explains why religion has become such a major sell and profiles companies that are profiting—Zondervan, Thomas Nelson, Tyndale House, Time Warner, and many others. It presents religious publishing market metrics in numerous tables and charts, analyzes factors in future growth, details marketing and product trends, discusses the retail situation, and thoroughly dissects consumer dynamics as related to the religious publishing and products markets, including books, music, video, software, jewelry and other gifts and accessories."

30. Nazlida Muhamad Hashim and Dick Mizerski, "The Constructs Mediating Religions' Influence on Buyers and Consumers," *Journal of Islamic Marketing* 1, no. 2 (2010): 124–135.

31. Djamchid Assadi, "Do Religions Influence Customer Behavior? Confronting Religious Rules and Marketing Concepts," *Cahiers du CEREN,* no. 5 (2003): 2–13.

32. Oriah Akir and Nor Othman, "Consumers' Shopping Behaviour Pattern on Selected Consumer Goods: Empirical Evidence on Malaysian Consumers," *Journal of Business and Policy Research* 5, no. 1 (July 2010): 123–157.

33. "Halal Honeymoon," Serendipity Tailormade, http://www.serendipity.travel/honeymoon.

34. "Halal Business: Consuming Passions," *The Economist*, May 25, 2013, http://www.economist.com/news/international/21578380-muslim-consumers-are-looking-beyond-traditional-religious-stipulations-meat-and.

35. John W. Miller, "Boosting Tourism with a Halal Label," *Real Time Brussels* (blog), *Wall Street Journal*, August 3, 2010, http://blogs.wsj.com/brussels/2010/08/03/trying-to-boost-tourism-with-halal-label/; see also Aalia Mahdi, "Five of the Best Emerging Halal Travel Destinations on the Globe," *Serendipity Tailormade* (blog), January 17, 2012, http://www.serendipity.travel/blog/2012/01/five-of-the-best-emerging-halal-travel-destinations-in-the-world/.

36. A. A. Tajzadeh-Namin, "Islam and Tourism: A Review on Iran and Malaysia," *International Research Journal of Applied and Basic Sciences* 3 (2012): 2809–2814.

37. Benjamin Jones, "Western Hoteliers Cater to Muslim Travelers," *Hotel News Now*, January 15, 2013, http://www.hotelnewsnow.com/Article/9703/western-hoteliers-cater-to-Muslim-travelers.

38. P. Kotler and D. Gertner, "Country as Brand, Product, and Beyond: A Place Marketing and Brand Management Perspective," *Journal of Brand Management* 9, nos. 4/5:249–261.

39. Ahmad Puad Mat Som and Mohammad Bader Badarneh, "Tourist Satisfaction and Repeat Visitation: Toward a New Comprehensive Model," *International Journal of Human and Social Sciences* 6, no. 1 (2011): 38–45.

40. "Halal Tourism Conference: Attracting the Market and Meeting the Need," Halal Tourism Conference 2014, http://www.htc2014.com/.

41. Mohamed M. Battour, Moustafa M. Battor, and Mohd Nazari Ismail, "The Mediating Role of Tourist Satisfaction: A Study of Muslim Tourists in Malaysia," *Journal of Travel and Tourism Marketing* 29, no. 3 (2012): 279–297.

42. "Moscow Woos Muslim Tourists with Halal Hotel," *Malay Mail*, October 20, 2014, http://www.themalaymailonline.com/travel/article/moscow-woos-muslim-tourists-with-halal-hotel.

43. Shelina Janmohamed, "Marketing in the Muslim World: Understanding the Hajj," *Spark Sheet*, November 7, 2011, http://sparksheet.com/branding-islam-sponsoring-the-hajj/. Shelina Janmohamed is a senior strategist at Ogilvy Noor, the world's first specialist consultancy for building brands with Muslim consumers. Ogilvy Noor is part of Ogilvy and Mather.

44. Charles Rarick et al., "Is It Kosher? No, It's Halal: A New Frontier in Niche Marketing." *Proceedings of the International Academy for Case Studies* 18, no. 1 (2011): 53.

45. Nestlé's range of halal products was posted on the company website along with the claim that it is the widest selection on the global market; "Nestlé Market That Produces Largest Range of Halal Products Celebrates 100 Years," Nestle, May 11, 2012, http://www.nestle.com/media/newsandfeatures/nestle-malaysia-halal.

46. Hossein Godazgar, "Islam in the Globalised World: Consumerism and Environmental Ethics in Iran," in *Religion, Consumerism, and Sustainability: Paradise Lost?*, ed. Lyn Thomas (Basington, England: Palgrave Macmillan, 2011), 117.

47. Mohammad Saeed, Zafar U. Ahmed, and Syeda-Masppda Mukhtar, "International Marketing Ethics from an Islamic Perspective: A Value Maximization Approach," *Journal of Business Ethics* 32, no. 2 (July 2001): 127.

48. Qur'an chapter 35, Sura al-Fatir or al-Mala'ikah (The Originator or The Angels), verse 28; Imam Salehudin, "Halal Literacy and Intention of Muslim Consumers to Switch from Products without Halal Label: A Measurement and Validation Study in Indonesia," Department of Management, Faculty of Economics, University of Indonesia, Social Science Research Network, June 13, 2010, http://ssrn.com/abstract=2004762.

49. An IFANCA announcement was posted on its website: "Halal/Haram Alert. Unilever uses unauthorized IFANCA Halal Logo on KNORR Products. Please be advised that Knorr Chicken Noodle Soup Mix products, (UPC CODE: 0 68400 80438 3), a product of UNILEVER CANADA, is not halal-certified by the Islamic Food and Nutrition Council of America (IFANCA). The use of IFANCA's registered halal trademark logo is an unauthorized use. For further information, please call or email us"; INFANCA, http://www.ifanca.org.

50. Salehudin, "Halal Literacy and Intention."

51. John Ireland and Soha Abdollah Rajabzadeh, "UAE Consumer Concerns about *Halal* Products," *Journal of Islamic Marketing* 2, no. 3 (2011): 274–283.

52. Ibid., 274.

53. Ahmed Ameur, "The Lifestyle Halal in European Marketing," Academic Research Centre of Canada, *Review of Economics and Finance* (2011): 83–90.

54. Sharmina Mawani and Anjoon Mukadam, "Living in a Material World: Religious Commodification and Resistance," in *Religion, Consumerism, and Sustainability: Paradise Lost?*, ed. Lyn Thomas (Basington, England: Palgrave Macmillan, 2011), 58.

55. Ibid., 56.

56. Pam Nilan, "The Reflexive Youth Culture of Devout Muslim Youth in Indonesia," in *Global Youth? Hybrid Identities, Plural Worlds*, ed. Pam Nilan and Carles Fiexa (New York: Routledge, 2006), 190.

57. Özlem Sandikci, "Researching Islamic Marketing: Past and Future Perspectives," *Journal of Islamic Marketing* 2, no. 3 (2011): 246–258.

58. Izharuddin, "Malaysia's Commodified Islam."

Chapter 1

1. Robin Richardson, "Islamophobia or Anti-Muslim Racism—or What? Concepts and Terms Revisited," lecture, University of Birmingham, England, December 9, 2009.

2. Scott Poynting and Victoria Mason, "The Resistible Rise of Islamophobia: Anti-Muslim Racism in the UK and Australia before 11 September 2001," *Journal of Sociology* 43, no. 1 (2007): 63, http://jos.sagepub.com/cgi/content/abstract/43/1/61.

3. Joel Beinin, "The New American McCarthyism: Policing Thought about the Middle East," Stanford University, http://www.stanford.edu/~beinin/New _McCarthyism.html.

4. Darrell Ezell, *Beyond Cairo: US Engagement with the Muslim World*, Series in Global Public Diplomacy (New York: Palgrave Macmillan, 2012), 48.

5. Raphael Liogier, "Islam: A Scapegoat for Europe's Decadence," *Harvard International Review*, January 6, 2011.

6. Rick Hampson, "For Families of Muslim 9/11 Victims, a New Pain," *USA Today*, September 3, 2010, updated September 9, 2010, http://www.usatoday.com /news/nation/2010-09-03-1Amuslims911_CV_N.htm.

7. Ibid.

8. Laura J. Nelson, "Federal Judge Sides with Tennessee Mosque in Time for Ramadan," *Los Angeles Times*, July 18, 2012, http://articles.latimes.com/2012 /jul/18/nation/la-na-nn-tennessee-mosque-ramadan-20120718.

9. In Reshma Kirpalani, "'Ground Zero Mosque' Clears Legal Hurdle to Build," ABC News, July 13, 2011, http://abcnews.go.com/US/ground-mosque -wins-legal-battle-build/story?id=14062701#.UAhgi7_iObI.

10. Sean Hannity, "'Ground Zero Mosque' Imam Sets the Record Straight on 'Hannity,'" Fox News, May 24, 2012, http://www.foxnews.com/on-air /hannity/2012/05/24/ground-zero-mosque-imam-sets-record-straight-hannity.

11. Isabel Vincent, "No Community Programs at 'Ground Zero' Mosque a Year after the Controversy," *New York Post*, December 9, 2012, http://www.nypost .com/p/news/local/manhattan/.

12. Herman Cain, interview by Chris Wallace, *Fox News Sunday*, July 17, 2011, http://www.foxnews.com/on-air/fox-news-sunday/.

13. Ibid.

14. John R. Bowen, *Blaming Islam* (Cambridge: MIT Press, 2012).

15. "Texas Man Stages Pig Races to Protest Islamic Neighbor's Plans to Build Mosque," Fox News, January 5, 2007, http://www.foxnews.com/story /0,2933,241897,00.html.

16. Cindy Horswell, "Not Ground Zero, but Katy Mosque Also Stirs Passions," *Houston Chronicle*, September 7, 2010, http://www.chron.com/life/houston -belief/article/Not-Ground-Zero-but-Katy-mosque-also-stirs-1717134.php.

17. Rick Dewsbury, "Belgian Politician Risks Muslim Backlash after Using Teenage Daughter Dressed in Burka and Bikini for Campaign against Islam," *Daily Mail*, February 3, 2012, http://www.dailymail.co.uk/news/.

18. European Monitoring Centre on Racism and Xenophobia (EUMC), "Muslims in the European Union Discrimination and Islamophobia," report, 2006, 3.

19. Ibid.

20. Ibid.

21. Poynting and Mason, "Resistible Rise of Islamophobia."

22. "Islam in Europe," Islamophobia Watch, June 5, 2008, http://www .islamophobia-watch.com/islamophobia-watch/author/martin-sullivan.

23. "Campaigns for Ban on Mosques across Europe," *The Guardian*, October 11, 2007, reposted at Islamophobia Watch, http://www.islamophobia-watch .com/islamophobia-watch/islam-is-peace-campaign-upsets-fascist.html.

24. In "Austrian State Bans Mosques," Islamophobia Watch, February 14, 2008,

http://www.islamophobia-watch.com/islamophobia-watch/2008/2/14/austrian
-state-bans-mosques.html.

25. Ibid.

26. Nick Cumming-Bruce and Steven Erlanger, "Swiss Ban Building of Minarets on Mosques," *New York Times*, November 30, 2009, http://www.nytimes
.com/2009/11/30/world/europe/30swiss.html.

27. Yori Yanover, "Swiss Politician Wants 'Kristallnacht for Mosques,'" *Jewish Press*, June 28, 2012, http://www.jewishpress.com/news/breaking-news/swiss
-politician-wants-kristallnacht-for-mosques/2012/06/28. The U.S. Holocaust Memorial Museum website posts this description:

> Kristallnacht, literally "Night of Crystal," is often referred to as the "Night of
> Broken Glass." The name refers to the wave of brutal violence against Jewish
> populations that took place November 9 and 10, 1938, throughout Germany,
> in German-annexed Austria, and in areas of the Sudetenland in Czechoslovakia
> that had recently been occupied by German troops.

U.S. Holocaust Memorial Museum, "Kristallnacht: A Nationwide Pogrom," Washington, DC, http://www.ushmm.org/wlc/en/article.php?ModuleId=10005201.

28. Nicholas Kulish, "In Germany, Xenophobia Diverted by Open Doors,"
New York Times, March 23, 2010, http://www.nytimes.com/2010/03/24/world
/europe/24germany.html. See also "Mosque Madness German Group Hopes for
EU Referendum on Minarets," *Spiegel*, December 15, 2009, http://www.spiegel
.de/international/germany/mosque-madness-german-group-hopes-for-eu-referen
dum-on-minarets-a-667158.html.

29. "Right Wing Warns against Threat of 'Islamisation'—in the Czech Republic, where Muslims Are 0.1% of the Population," *Prague Post*, July 28,
2011, reposted in Islamophobia Watch, http://www.islamophobia-watch.com
/islamophobia-watch/author/bob-pitt.

30. Gwendolyn Albert, "Regional Authority in Czech Republic Provides Financial Support to Anti-Mosque Movement," *Romano Vod'i*, July 19, 2011, http://
www.romea.cz/en/news/czech/regional-authority-in-czech-republic-financially
-supports-anti-mosque-movement.

31. "SANEP (The Centre for Analysis and Empirical Studies) is the first on-line
Internet research center for public opinion in the Czech Republic. SANEP is the
exclusive partner of the University of Economics in Prague, Faculty of International
Relations and the Governance Research Project in the context of a globalized soci-
ety and economy and it is also a member of AIMRI (The Alliance of International
Market Research Institutes)"; http://www.sanep.cz/project/.

32. "Kotka Mulls Mosque Ban," Islamophobia Watch, August 10, 2012,
http://www.islamophobia-watch.com/islamophobia-watch/2012/8/10/kotka
-mulls-mosque-ban.html.

33. "Netanyahu Backs Law to Ban Loudspeakers at Mosques across Israel," *The
Independent*, December 13, 2012, http://www.independent.co.uk/news/world
/middle-east/netanyahu-backs-law-to-ban-loudspeakers-at-mosques-across-israel
-6276173.html.

34. Ibid.

35. "Colorado State Sen. Says Banning New Mosques Is Something to Think About." Denver CBS, July 16, 2012, http://denver.cbslocal.com/2012/07/16/colorado-state-sen-says-banning-new-mosques-is-something-to-think-about; Pat Dollard, "Banning Mosques? Colo. State Senator's Remarks Have CAIR Whining and Complaining," *Pat Dollard* (blog), July 2012, http://patdollard.com/2012/07/banning-mosques-colo-state-senators-remarks-have-terrorist-ties-cair-whining-complaining (site discontinued).

36. Henry Samuel, "Praying in Paris Streets Outlawed," *The Telegraph*, September 15, 2011, http://www.telegraph.co.uk/news/worldnews/europe/france/8766169/Praying-in-Paris-streets-outlawed.html.

37. "Marine Le Pen: Muslims in France 'Like Nazi Occupation,'" *The Telegraph*, December 12, 2010, http://www.telegraph.co.uk/news/worldnews/europe/france/8197895/Marine-Le-Pen-Muslims-in-France-like-Nazi-occupation.html.

38. Guy Hedgecoe, "Local Mosque Row a Spanish Problem," *Irish Times*, July 10, 2012, http://www.irishtimes.com/newspaper/world/2012/0710/1224319719491.html.

39. Ibid.

40. Ibid.

41. Marisa Caroço Amaro, "Reflections about the European Debate on Integration Policies: The Case of the Swiss Ban on Minarets," *Revista Migrações* (Lisbon, ACIDI), no. 8 (April 2011): 149. http://www.oi.acidi.gov.pt/docs/Revista_8/Migracoes_8web147a150.pdf.

42. Ibid.

43. Bernard Lewis, "Islam and the West: A Conversation with Bernard Lewis," Pew Forum on Religion and Public Life, April 27, 2006, Washington, DC, http://www.catholiceducation.org/en/culture/catholic-contributions/islam-and-the-west-a-conversation-with-bernard-lewis.html. Bernard Lewis is a British American historian, scholar in Oriental studies, and political commentator. He is the Cleveland E. Dodge Professor Emeritus of Near Eastern Studies at Princeton University. Lewis specializes in the history of Islam and the interaction between Islam and the West.

44. Ibid.

45. Tawfik Hamid, "How Western Tolerance Breeds Intolerance in the Muslim World," *Free Thought Nation*, September 27, 2011, http://freethoughtnation.com/contributing-writers/72-tawfik-hamid/598-how-western-tolerance-breeds-intolerance-in-the-muslim-world.html. Hamid is a Muslim and self-proclaimed ex-radical who educates people about the doctrines of Islamic fundamentalism as he experienced them from the inside; he advocates reform based on modern interpretations of Islamic texts. He has written numerous articles, and many of his lectures may be viewed on YouTube; see his website, http://www.tawfikhamid.com.

46. Tawfik Hamid, "Western Tolerance Breeds Muslim Intolerance," *Newsmax*, September 20, 2011, http://www.newsmax.com/TawfikHamid/Western-Tolerance-Muslim-Intolerance/2011/09/20/id/411707.

47. Lewis, "Islam and the West."

48. Richard W. Bulliet, *The Case for Islamo-Christian Civilization* (Columbia University Press, 2004).

49. In Ezell, *Beyond Cairo*, 52.

50. Lewis, "Islam and the West."

51. Paul Belien, "Don't Burn Muhammad," *Brussels Journal*, February 16, 2006, http://www.brusselsjournal.com/node/823.

52. "The Muhammad Cartoon Controversy," NPR, March 1, 2006, http://www.npr.org/templates/rss/podlayer.php?id=5196793.

53. Ibid.

54. Ibid.

55. Sina Lucia Kottman, "Mocking and Miming the Moor: Staging of the 'Self' and 'Other' on Spain's Borders with Morocco," *Journal of Mediterranean Studies* 20, no. 1 (2011): 107–136, http://www.academia.edu/903191/Mocking_and_Miming_the_Moor_Staging_of_the_Self_and_Other_on_Spains_Borders_with_Morocco.

56. Belien, "Don't Burn Muhammad."

57. Lewis, "Islam and the West."

58. Flore Murard-Yovanovitch. "Institutional Racism and Ethnic Profiling in Italy," *Reset DOC*, April 24, 2011, http://www.resetdoc.org/story/00000022114.

59. "Controversial Italian Politician Rallies Opposition to Mosque Construction," *Catholic World News*, September 14, 2007, http://www.catholicculture.org/news/features/index.cfm?recnum=53532#sthash.BoG6dydf.dpuf.

60. Ibid.

61. Ibid.

62. Karen Wren, "Cultural Racism: Something Rotten in the State of Denmark?" *Social and Cultural Geography* 2, no. 2 (2001): 141–162.

63. Muhammad Wajid Akhtar, "5 Examples of Supreme Muslim Tolerance," *Muslim Matters*, September 20, 2012, http://muslimmatters.org/author/muhammad-wajid-akhter.

Chapter 2

1. Johan Fischer, "Feeding Secularism: Consuming Halal among the Malays in London," *Diaspora: A Journal of Transnational Studies* 14, no. 2/3 (2005): 275–297, http://muse.jhu.edu/journals/dsp/summary/v014/14.2.fischer.html.

2. Abuʿabd Allah Muhammad ibn Ismaʿil, known as Imam Bukhari, was born in Bukhara on July 21, 810. His collection on *ahadith* of the Prophet Muhammed is recognized by a majority of Sunni and even to a great extent the Shia population. Sahih al-Bukahri (the correct or authentic collection of sayings of the Prophet Mohammad) is well accepted in the academic world. Al-Bukhari's collection is quoted here and easily available online.

3. Sahih International.

4. Ibid.

5. For verses in the Qur'an that describe what is halal (lawful) and haram (unlawful), see ParsQuran, http://www.parsquran.com/eng/subject/halal.htm.

6. Quran.com, http://quran.com/35/12-21.

7. Mian N. Riaz and Muhammad M. Chaudry, *Halal Food Production* (New York: CRC Press, 2004).

8. Ibid, 6.

9. Ibid.

10. Ibid., especially chapter 6, "Halal Production Requirements for Meat and Poultry," 57–78.

11. Ibid., 58.

12. Ibid., 57.

13. Scott Casey, "Halal: A Growing Market With A Caveat: Halal Is a Market Full of Eastern Promise, but It's Also a Market Full of Potential Pitfalls," *Poultry World*, June 1, 2010, http://business.highbeam.com/435132/article -1G1-230778606/halal-growing-market-caveat-halal-market-full-eastern.

14. Abul Taher, "Chicken McHalal: McDonald's Denied Using Halal Meat," *Daily Mail*, October 9, 2010, http://www.dailymail.co.uk/news/article-1319218 /Chicken-McHalal-An-MoS-investigation-reveals-halal-meat-IS-used-McDonalds -popular-meals.html.

15. Houchang Chahabi, "How Caviar Turned Out to Be Halal," *Journal of Food and Culture* 7, no. 2 (2007): 17.

16. In Qasim Muhammed, "America's Costly Halal Food," *Halal Journal*, March 29, 2009, http://www.halaljournal.com/article/3426/america-costly-halal -food.

17. Mian N. Riaz, "Fundamentals of Halal Foods and Certification," *Prepared Foods* 179, no. 1 (January 2010): 71, http://www.preparedfoods.com/articles /article-fundamentals-of-halal-foods-and-certification-january-2010.

18. Darhim Hashim, "Redefining Regulatory Procedures in the Halal Industry," paper presented at the 6th World Halal Forum, Kuala Lumpur, April 4, 2011, organized by Islamic Chamber of Commerce and Industry, proceedings, International Halal Integrity Alliance (2011), http://worldhalalforum.org/WHF 2011speakerpresentation/Session%203-RedefiningRegulatoryProceduresinthe HalalIndustrybyDarhim%20Hashim.pdf.

19. International Halal Integrity Alliance Business Consultant, Kuala Lumpur, http://www.facebook.com/IHIAlliance/info.

20. In 2009 approximately 203 million Indonesians identified as Muslim, more than 88 percent of the total population.

21. "MUI to Set Single National Halal Standard," *Jakarta Post*, July 1, 2011, http://www.thejakartapost.com/news/2011/01/07/mui-set-single-national-halal -standard.html.

22. Ibid.

23. Noor Tengku and Abdullah Shamsiah Tengku, "HDC to Issue Country's Halal Certificate and Logo," Halal Focus, April 5, 2008, http://halalfocus .net/2008/04/04/hdc-to-issue-country-s-halal-certificate-and-logo.

24. "Malaysia: Only Jakim Halal Logo Recognised from 1 Jan 2012," Halal Focus, October 2, 2011, http://halalfocus.net/malaysia-only-jakim-halal-logo -recognised-from-1-jan-2012/.

25. Ibid. I have converted Malay ringgits (MYR or RM) to US dollars to give readers a clear understanding of the specific amount of each fine.

26. "Malaysia: Jakim Does Not Commercialise Halal Certs," Halal Focus, May 4, 2012, http://halalfocus.net/malaysia-jakim-does-not-commercialise-halal -certs-jamil-khir/.

27. "Muslims in Malaysia Advised against Drinking Halal Beer," *Indian Ex-*

press, May 30, 2011, http://www.indianexpress.com/news/muslims-in-malaysia
-advised-against-drinking-halal-beer/797111.

28. "Barbican's Beer Is Halal, Says National Fatwa Council," *Malaysia Insider*,
July 26, 2011, http://www.themalaysianinsider.com/malaysia/article/barbicans
-beer-is-halal-says-national-fatwa-council.

29. Dan Harrington, "Civet Coffee the Most Expensive Coffee in the World,"
Gourmet Coffee Lovers, October 18, 2009, http://www.gourmetcoffeelovers.com
/civet-coffee-the-most-expensive-coffee-in-the-world.

30. "Coffee Luwak Is Considered One," Civet Coffee blog, March 16, 2011,
http://civetcoffeestarbucks.blogspot.com. I have searched other sources, all of
which suggest an average price of $50 per cup.

31. Bari Muchtar, "A Fatwa on Coffee?" Radio Netherlands Worldwide, July 23,
2010, http://www.rnw.nl/english/article/a-fatwa-coffee. Also see "Indonesian
Muslims Drop Fatwa against Expensive Coffee," July 20, 2010, *News*, http://www
.news.com.au/breaking-news/indonesian-muslims-drop-fatwa-against-expensive
-coffee/story-e6frfku0-1225894764601; "Fatwa Boosts Luwak Coffee Sales in Indonesia," *Jakarta Globe*, August 2, 2010, http://www.thejakartaglobe.com/home
/fatwa-boosts-luwak-coffee-sales-in-indonesia/388985.

32. "Is Kopi Luwak Coffee Halal?" Hatem al-Haj, February 28, 2012, http://
www.drhatemalhaj.com/qa/index.php/2012/02/28/is-kopi-luwak-coffee-halal.

33. Ibid.

34. Press release, IFANCA, n.d., http://www.ifanca.org/cms/wpages/detail
/4ca2ce9e-2120-4458-ae07-593c1b830f0c. For more details and information
about this organization see the YouTube video "Islamic Food and Nutrition Council of America (IFANCA)—PSA," IFANCA, posted October 20, 2010, http://
www.youtube.com/watch?v=dT53R9JaNaw.

35. "How Reliable Is IFANCA??" Eat Halal, September 17, 2009, http://www
.eathalal.ca/2009/09/how-reliable-is-ifanca.html.

36. "Mazhar Hussaini Resigns from IFANCA," Sound Vision, September 17,
2009, http://soundvision.com/Info/halalhealthy/resignation.asp.

37. Pew Forum on Religion and Public Life, "The Future of the Global Muslim
Population Projections for 2010–2030," analysis, January 27, 2011, http://www
.pewforum.org/The-Future-of-the-Global-Muslim-Population.aspx.

38. Ben Berry, "Agri-Food Trade Service Global Halal Food Market," Market
Indicator Report, April 2011, International Markets Bureau, Agriculture and Agri-
Food Canada, http://www.ats.agr.gc.ca/inter/4352-eng.htm.

39. D. Minkus-McKenna, "The Pursuit of Halal," *Progressive Grocer* 86 (2007):
17.

40. Ibid. Key halal markets include Indonesia, United Arab Emirates, Algeria,
Saudi Arabia, Iraq, Morocco, Iran, Malaysia, Egypt, Turkey, Tunisia, Kuwait, Jor-
dan, Lebanon, Yemen, Qatar, Bahrain, Syria, Oman, and Pakistan. Besides India,
China, and Russia, emerging halal markets with relatively large Muslim populations
include the Philippines (5 million), France (5 million), Germany (4 million) and the
United Kingdom (3 million).

41. Ashfak Bokhari, "Opinion: Political Bias against Halal Meat Market," Halal Focus, March 30, 2012, http://halalfocus.net/2012/03/30/opinion-political
-bias-against-halal-meat-market.

42. "Paris Halal Expo Underlines Lucrative Prospect of French Halal Market,"

Halal Media, n.d., http://halalmedia.net/paris-halal-expo-underlines-lucrative-prospect-french-halal-market.

43. Berry, "Agri-Food Trade Service."

44. Campbell Soup of Canada, "Extraordinary, Authentic Nourishment for All," http://www.campbellsoup.ca/nourishment-for-all. The company website also says, "Campbell Canada donated more than 4000 cans of Halal-certified soup to Food Banks Canada for distribution to Muslims who access local food banks across the country. The company has also made food donations to a number of mosques for Ramadan when many families go to their mosques to eat their evening meal after sundown."

45. See Riaz and Chaudry, *Halal Food Production*, 92–94.

46. Aaron Smith, "Starbucks to Phase Out Bug Extract as Food Dye," CNN Money, April 19, 2012, http://money.cnn.com/2012/04/19/news/companies/starbucks-bugs/index.htm. Starbucks food items that contained cochineal red dye were Strawberries and Crème Frappuccino, Strawberry Banana Smoothie, Raspberry Swirl Cake, Birthday Cake Pop, Mini Donut with pink icing, and Red Velvet Whoopie Pie.

47. An undated report says the FDA "required food manufacturers to disclose whether red cochineal beetles, often disguised as artificial coloring in food, are among their products' ingredients"; "Beetles as Artificial Coloring Must Be Disclosed—FDA," Halal Media, http://halalmedia.net/beetles-artificial-coloring-disclosed-fda.

48. Ibid.

49. Mike Adams, "True Fact: A Common Ingredient in Commercial Breads Is Derived from Human Hair Harvested in China," *Natural News*, June 16, 2011, http://www.naturalnews.com/032718_L-cysteine_commercial_bread.html#ixzz22ncxBslz.

50. The purified form of the resin is exuded by the female of the insect *Laccifer lacca*, found in India and the Far East. After drying into sheets, it is normally supplied as an alcohol solution, although varying chemical processes can produce different grades. Used as a glazing agent and polish, it is found in cake decorations, fruit, pills, and sweets. It may cause skin irritation; La Leve di Archimede, n.d., http://www.laleva.cc/food/enumbers/E901-970.html.

51. "Food Ingredient Numbers: (E-numbers)," World of Islam, http://special.worldofislam.info/Food/numbers.html, citing Muslim Consumer Group.

52. The Mars UK page at http://www.mars.com/uk/en/our-commitments/health-and-nutrition/product-suitability.aspx has been removed. An anti-halal group on Facebook posted Mars in 2011 on its list of halal products; https://www.facebook.com/BOYCOTT.HALAL.UK/posts/201636513254928. Halal Food Authority lists "Approved Suppliers of Food Additives, Flavourings, and Chemicals"; http://halalfoodauthority.com/.

53. Adams, "True Fact." One likely reason the rabbi issued the order is the source—a Hindu temple where statues of various gods are worshipped. The act of idol worshipping is forbidden in Judaism and Islam.

54. A cryoprotectant is a substance that is used to protect biological tissue from freezing.

55. "9 Things to Know About Surimi [Fake Crab]," *Get Fooducated* (blog),

October 22, 2011, http://blog.fooducate.com/2011/10/22/9-things-to-know -about-surimi-fake-crab.

56. N. Huda, A. Aminah, and A. S. Babji, "Halal Issues in Processing of Surimi and Surimi-Based Food Product," *Infofish* 5 (1999): 45–47; Food Science and Nutrition Department, University of Kebangsaan, Kuala Lumpur, 2009.

57. Dessy Sagita, "BPOM Discovers More Pork in 3 'Halal' Beef Jerky Brands," *Jakarta Globe*, June 2, 2009, http://jakartaglobe.beritasatu.com/archive /bpom-discovers-more-pork-in-3-halal-beef-jerky-brands/.

58. Ibid.

59. Kelli B. Grant, "8 Food Frauds on Your Shopping List," Market Watch, April 16, 2012, http://www.smartmoney.com/spend/deal-of-the-day/8-food -frauds-on-your-shopping-list-1334616484577.

60. "Whole Foods Market China Organic California Blend?" video, posted to YouTube by ABC 1 Team, August 28, 2008, http://www.youtube.com /watch?v=JQ31Ljd9T_Y; Kasey Culliney, "The GM Rice Problem: Food Fraud in China?" Food Navigator, May 7, 2012, http://www.foodnavigator-asia.com /Markets/The-GM-rice-problem-Food-fraud-from-China.

61. Liz Gooch, "Malaysia Seeks to Gain Bigger Role in Halal Food," *New York Times*, January 1, 2011, http://query.nytimes.com/gst/fullpage.html?res=9C05E6 DE1739F932A35752C0A9679D8B63&pagewanted=all.

62. Halal Monitoring Committee (HMC, UK), http://www.halalmc.net /halal_certification/costs_fees.html; the article quoted is no longer posted, and HMC has a new website, http://www.halalhmc.org/.

63. "Indonesia: MUI Criticizes NU's Plan to Draft Halal Certification," Halal Focus, February 2, 2012, http://halalfocus.net/2012/02/02/indonesia-mui -criticizes-nus-plan-to-draft-halal-certification. See also a document published by the Malaysian government to address common questions regarding halal certification, at http://www.halal.gov.my/ehalal/pdf/FAQ_english.pdf.

64. Lincoln Tan, "Halal Certification Group under Fire," *New Zealand Herald*, January 11, 2010, http://www.nzherald.co.nz/lincoln-tan/news/article.cfm?a _id=308&objectid=10619444.

65. Ibid.

66. Tim Lindsey, "Monopolising Islam: The Indonesian Ulama Council and State Regulation of the 'Islamic Economy,'" *Bulletin of Indonesian Economic Studies* 48, no. 2 (2012): 256–257.

Chapter 3

1. Abdul-Rahman, *Islam: Questions and Answers*, 8.

2. W. Schulze, H. Schultze-Petzold, A. S. Hazem, and R. Gross, "Experiments for the Objectification of Pain and Consciousness during Conventional (Captive Bolt Stunning) and Religiously Mandated ('Ritual Cutting')," translated by Sahib M. Bleher, *Deutsche Tieraerztliche Wochenschrift* (German Veterinary Weekly) 85 (1978): 62–66, posted at Mustaquim Art and Literature, http://www.mustaqim .co.uk/halalstudy.htm.

3. N. G. Neville, M. von Wenzlawowicz, R. M. Alam, H. M. Anil, T. Yesildere,

and A. Silva-Fletcher, "False Aneurysms in Carotid Arteries of Cattle and Water Buffalo during Shechita and Halal Slaughter," *Meat Science* 79, no. 2 (June 2008): 285–288.

4. Tariq Ramadan, "My Compatriots' Vote to Ban Minarets Is Fuelled by Fear," *The Guardian*, November 29, 2009, http://www.theguardian.com /commentisfree/belief/2009/nov/29/swiss-vote-ban-minarets-fear.

5. William Turvill, "Denmark Accused of Anti-Semitism as It Bans Religious Slaughter of Animals for Kosher and Halal Meat," *Daily Mail*, February 18, 2014, http://www.dailymail.co.uk/news/article-2562350/Denmark-accused-anti -Semitism-bans-religious-slaughter-animals-kosher-halal-meat.html.

6. "Protesters Demand Poland Keeps Kosher and Halal Slaughter Ban," Radio Poland, January 31, 2013, http://www.thenews.pl/1/12/Artykul/125879 ,Protesters-demandWh-Poland-keeps-kosher-and-halal-slaughter-ban.

7. "International Halal Integrity Alliance on Animal Welfare in Religious Slaughter," *Halal Focus*, June 7, 2011, http://halalfocus.net/2011/.

8. Bruno Waterfield, "Dutch Parliament Votes to Ban Ritual Slaughter of Animals," *The Telegraph*, June 28, 2011, http://www.telegraph.co.uk/news/religion /8603969/Dutch-parliament-votes-to-ban-ritual-slaughter-of-animals.html.

9. Pablo Lerner and Alfredo Mordechai Rabello, "The Prohibition of Ritual Slaughtering (Kosher Shechita and Halal) and Freedom of Religion of Minorities," *Journal of Law and Religion* 22, no. 1 (2006–2007), posted at Instituto Italiano di Bioetica, http://www.istitutobioetica.org/Bioetica%20sociale/multiculturalismo /Lerner%20Rabello%20Macellazione.htm.

10. Adam Withnall, "Denmark Bans Kosher and Halal Slaughter as Minister Says 'Animal Rights Come before Religion,'" *The Independent*, July 27, 2015, http://www.independent.co.uk/news/world/europe/.

11. Tetty Havinga, "Regulating Halal and Kosher Foods: Different Arrangements between State, Industry and Religious Actors," *Erasmus Law Review* 3, no. 4 (2010).

12. Waterfield, "Dutch Parliament Votes."

13. European Convention for the Protection of Animals for Slaughter, *Official Journal of the European Union* L 137 (June 2, 1988): 27–38.

14. "Germany Faces Hurdles to Halal Slaughter," Public Radio International, April 17, 2012, http://www.pri.org/stories/politics-society/religion/despite-court -ruling-islamic-butcher-in-germany-faces-hurdles-to-halal-slaughter-9483.html.

15. Ibid.

16. "Popular French Fast Food Chain Causes Controversy by Introducing Halal-Only Food," *Daily Mail*, September, 2, 2010, http://www.dailymail.co.uk /news/article-1308366/Popular-French-fast-food-chain-Quick-causes-controversy -introducing-halal-food.html.

17. Angela Doland, "French Debate: First It Was Burqas, Now Burgers," *Bloomberg Business*, September 1, 2010.

18. Ibid.

19. In "Minister under Fire for 'Halal' Comment on Immigrant Vote," France 24, March 3, 2012, http://www.france24.com/en/20120303-minister-controversy -halal-comment-immigrant-voting-gueant-france-local-elections-sarkozy-ump.

20. Edward Cody, "In France, Halal Meat Drama Enters Election Cam-

paign," *Washington Post*, March 6, 2012, https://www.washingtonpost.com/world /europe/.

21. "New EU Labels for Halal and Kosher Foods Spark Anger," *The National*, http://www.thenational.ae/news/world/europe/new-eu-labels-for-halal-and -kosher-foods-spark-anger#ixzz2RXDRTbJB.

22. "On the European Kangaroo Trail," Kangaroo Protection Coalition, http://www.kangaroo-protection-coalition.com/kangaroos-in-europe.html (page discontinued); A Well Fed World, Feeding Families, Saving Animals, http://awfw .org/.

23. Pieer Haski, "This Halal Meat Upset Leaves Nicolas Sarkozy in a Bad Way," *The Guardian*, March 8, 2012, http://www.guardian.co.uk/commentisfree/2012 /mar/08/halal-meat-nicolas-sarkozy-marine-le-pen.

24. Article 9 of the European Convention on Human Rights provides a right to freedom of thought, conscience, and religion. This includes the freedom to change a religion or belief and to manifest a religion or belief in worship, teaching, practice, and observance, subject to certain restrictions that are "in accordance with law" and "necessary in a democratic society"; Jim Murdoch, "Protecting the Right to Freedom of Thought, Conscience, and Religion under the European Convention on Human Rights," Council of Europe Human Rights Handbooks (Strasbourg: Council of Europe, 2012), http://www.coe.int/t/dgi/hr-natimplement/Source /documentation/hb09_rightfreedom_en.pdf.

25. Eman El-Shenawi, "British Muslims Defend Halal Slaughter after Calls for Ban," *Al Arabiya*, May 6, 2012, http://english.alarabiya.net/articles /2012/05/06/212477.html.

26. Ibid.

27. Harrow is a borough, or neighborhood, in northwest London, England.

28. "UK: Parents Outraged over Halal-Only Food Being Forced on Their Children in Schools Fight Back," *Bare Naked Islam* (blog), August 16, 2010, http:// barenakedislam.com/2010/08/16/uk-parents-outraged-over-halal-only-food-bein.

29. "Pork DNA in Halal Sausages at Westminster Primary School," BBC News, March 14, 2013, http://www.bbc.co.uk/news/uk-england-london-21791513.

30. Lucy Crossley, "Halal Pies and Pasties Given to Muslim Prisoners Found to Contain PORK in Latest Meat Contamination Scandal," *Daily Mail*, February 2, 2013, http://www.dailymail.co.uk/news/.

31. The comment posted by Michael Smith is no longer available at 4BC 1116 News Talk, http://www.4bc.com.au/.

32. Paul Farhi, "A Canadian Line of Campbell's Soups Has Activists Stewing over Islamic Connection," *Washington Post*, October 17, 2010, http://www .washingtonpost.com/wp-dyn/content/article/2010/10/17/AR2010101702840 .html.

33. "Hate Map," n.d., Southern Poverty Law Center, http://www.splcenter.org /get-informed/hate-map#s=NY.

34. Pamela Geller, "Happy Halal Thanksgiving," *American Thinker*, November 21, 2011, http://www.americanthinker.com/articles/2011/11/happy_halal _thanksgiving.html.

35. "Pamela Geller," Southern Poverty Law Center, n.d., http://www.splcenter .org/get-informed/intelligence-files/profiles/pamela-geller#.UXqy4b88x8p.

36. Joe Kaufman, "Can Buying Food Contribute to Terrorism?" *Frontpage Mag*, March 2013, frontpagemag.com.

37. Eric Carpenter, "Meat Not up to Islamic Law, Market Pays $527,000," *Orange County Register*, November 21, 2011, http://www.ocregister.com/articles/market-328147-anaheim-meat.html. See also Ayub Khan, "TMO Story About Fake Halal Causes $500,000 Fine against Fraudster," *Muslim Observer*, November 23, 2011, http://muslimmedianetwork.com/mmn/?p=9426.

38. "When Is Halal Meat Not Halal Meat?" BBC News, May 20, 2009, http://news.bbc.co.uk/2/hi/uk_news/magazine/8059218.stm; Charles Rarick et al., "Is it Kosher? No, It's Halal: A New Frontier in Niche Marketing," *Proceedings of the International Academy for Case Studies* 18, no. 1 (2011): 51–56.

39. David Sapsted, "Halal Dispute over Kentucky Fried Chicken," *The National*, March 15, 2010, http://www.thenational.ae/news/world/europe/halal-dispute-over-kentucky-fried-chicken.

40. Ibid.

41. Ibid.

42. "KFC Scraps Controversial Halal Only Menu after Mass Brit Boycott," *DNA India*, June 26, 2010, http://www.dnaindia.com/lifestyle/1401572/report-kfc-scraps-controversial-halal-only-menu-after-mass-brit-boycott.

43. "Fake Halal Imports Anger China's Muslims," Halal Focus, January 21, 2013, in Muslim Village, http://muslimvillage.com/2013/01/21/34421/fake-halal-imports-anger-chinas-muslims. The Han Chinese are a majority ethnic group native to East Asia. Uyghurs are a Turkic ethnic minority group living in Eastern and Central Asia.

44. "Traders Warned against Fake Halal Products," *Fiji Live*, 2011, http://fijilive.com/news/2011/.

45. Sibusiso Nkomo, "MJC Denies 'Ducking and Diving,'" *IoL News*, January 19, 2012, http://www.iol.co.za/news/south-africa/western-cape/.

46. Hazel Corall, "White Collar Crime, Consumers, and Victimization," *Crime, Law and Social Change* 51, no. 1 (2009): 142.

47. On the subject of "laundered meat" see, for example, Richard Tyler, "Britain: Thousands of Tons of Condemned 'Meat Laundered' for Human Consumption," World Socialist Web Site, May 5, 2001, http://www.wsws.org/articles/2001/may2001/meat-m05.shtml.

48. John Pointing and Yunes Teinaz, "Halal Meat and Food Crime in UK," paper presented for the International Halal Food Seminar, Islamic University College of Malaysia, September 2004.

49. Ibid.

50. "Horsemeat Scandal: Dutch Uncover Large-Scale Meat Fraud," BBC News, April 10, 2013, http://www.bbc.co.uk/news/world-europe-22098763.

51. In Anne Sewell, "Pork Found in Halal Food in Norway and UK," *Digital Journal*, March 15, 2013, http://digitaljournal.com/article/345771#ixzz2RY3XT8A2.

52. Johan Fischer, "Religion, Science, and Markets: Modern Halal Production, Trade, and Consumption," *EMBO Reports* 9, no. 9 (September 2008): 829.

53. Ibid.

54. Ibid.

55. Shelina Janmohamed, "Opinion: The Politics of Halal," *Halal Focus*, March 29, 2013, http://halalfocus.net/opinion-the-politics-of-halal.

56. Wim Verbeke et al., "Credence Quality Coordination and Consumers' Willingness-to-Pay for Certified Halal Labelled Meat," *Meat Science* 95, no. 4 (December 2013): 790–797, at BioMedSearch.com, http://www.biomedsearch.com/nih/.

57. Ibid.

58. Mohd Nasir et al., "An RFID-Based Validation System for Halal Food," *International Arab Journal of Information Technology* 8, no. 2 (2011): 204–211, http://www.iajit.org/PDF/vol.8,no.2/13-1394.pdf.

59. Azah Anir Norman et al., "Consumer Acceptance of RFID-Enabled Services in Validating Halal Status," Communications and Information Technology, ISCIT 9th International Symposium, Incheon, South Korea, September 28–30, 2009, 911–914.

60. Ibid., 913.

61. Ibid.

62. Ibid.

63. "Tanka Precious Metals to Supply Pork Detection Kits," Pig Site News Desk, April 6, 2010, http://www.thepigsite.com/swinenews/23515/tanaka-precious-metals-to-supply-pork-detection-kits/.

64. Abdul Rohman and Yaakob B. Che Man, "Analysis of Pig Derivatives for Halal Authentication Studies," *Food Reviews International* 28, no. 1 (2012): 97–112; Yuny Erwanto et al., "Identification of Pork Contamination in Meatballs of Indonesia Local Market Using Polymerase Chain Reaction-Restriction Fragment Length Polymorphism (PCR-RFLP) Analysis," *Asian-Australas Journal of Animal Sciences* 27, no. 10 (October 2014): 1487–1492; Ellen Podivinsky and John Mackay, "High Resolution Melting Analysis as a Novel DNA Assay for Meat Speciation," Queenstown Molecular Biology Meeting, Queenstown, New Zealand, August 29–31, 2011; S. N. Depamede, "Development of a Rapid Immunodiagnostic Test for Pork Components in Raw Beef and Chicken Meats: a Preliminary Study," *Media Peternakan*, August 2011, 83–87; Yasemin Demirhan, Pelin Ulca, and Hamide Z. Senyuva, "Detection of Porcine DNA in Gelatine and Gelatine-Containing Processed Food Products—Halal/Kosher Authentication," *Meat Science* 90 (2012): 686–689; Chandrika Murugaiah, Zainon Mohd Noor, Maimunah Mastakim, Lesley Maurice Bilung, Jinap Selamat, and Son Radu, "Meat Species Identification and Halal Authentication Analysis Using Mitochondrial DNA," *Meat Science* 83 (2009): 57–61; Nurrulhidayah A. Fadzlillah, Yaakob B. Che Man, Mohammad Aizat Jamaludin, and Suhaimi A. Rahman, "The Contribution of Science and Technology in Determining the Permissibility (Halalness) of Food Products," *Revelation and Science* 2, no. 1 (2012): 1–9; M. Nurjuliana, Y. B. Che Man, D. Mat Hashim, and A. K. S. Mohamed, "Rapid Identification of Pork for Halal Authentication Using the Electronic Nose and Gas Chromatography Mass Spectrometer with Headspace Analyzer," *Meat Science* 88 (2011): 638–644; Yongsheng Yang and Wenxing Bao, "The Design and Implementation of Halal Beef Wholly Quality Traceability System," *IFIP Advances in Information and Communication Technology* 346 (2011): 464–472.

65. Karijn Bonne and Wim Verbeke, "Religious Values Informing Halal Meat Production and the Control and Delivery of Halal Credence Quality," *Agriculture and Human Values* 25 (2008): 35.

66. Khadijah Nakyinsige, Yaakob Bin Che Man, and Awis Qurni Sazili, "Halal Authenticity Issues In Meat and Meat Products," *Meat Science* 91 (2012): 207–214.

67. Temple Grandin and Joe M. Regenstein, "Religious Slaughter And Animal Welfare: A Discussion For Meat Scientists," *Meat Focus International* (March 1994): 123.

Chapter 4

1. Mecca to Medina game, created 2005 by Baba Ali of Sherman Oaks, CA; Board Game Geek, https://boardgamegeek.com/boardgame/17564/mecca -medina.

2. Sawab Quest, online Islamic quiz game; 2 Muslims, http://www.2muslims .com/directory/Detailed/226618.shtml.

3. Kalliny and Hausman, "Impact of Cultural and Religious Values," 132.

4. Faegheh Shirazi, "Islam and Barbie: The Commodification of Hijabi Dolls," *Islamic Perspective*, no. 3 (2010): 10–23, http://iranianstudies.org/wp-content /uploads/2010/04/Islamic-perspective-Journal-number-3-2010.pdf.

5. Valerie Sperling, "Women's Organizations: Institutionalized Interest Groups or Vulnerable Dissidents?," in *Russian Civil Society: A Critical Assessment*, ed. Alfred B. Evans, Laura A. Henry, and Lisa McIntosh Sundstrom (New York: M. E. Sharpe, 2006), 166.

6. Sarah El-Deeb, "Saudis Bust Barbie's 'Dangers,'" CBS News, September 10, 2003, http://www.cbsnews.com/stories/2003/09/10/world/main572564.shtml.

7. Ibid.

8. "Jewish Barbie" is a reference to Ruth Marianna Handler (1916–2002), an American businesswoman born to Jewish-Polish immigrants Jacob and Ida Moskowicz and president of the toy manufacturer Mattel Inc. She is remembered primarily for her role in marketing the Barbie doll; "Ruth Handler," Wikipedia, http:// en.wikipedia.org/wiki/Ruth_Handler.

9. Gregory Starrett, "The Political Economy of Religious Commodities in Cairo," *American Anthropologist* 97, no. 10 (March 1995): 53.

10. Pradip Thomas, "Selling God/Saving Souls." *Global Media and Communication* 5, no. 1 (2009): 57–76.

11. Doris Y. Wilkinson, "The Doll Exhibit: A Psycho-Cultural Analysis of Black Female Role Stereotypes," *Journal of Popular Culture* 21, no. 2 (1987): 19.

12. The social and cultural significance of dolls was shown when a Public Action Coalition on Toys in 1975 decided to "protest toys considered to be dangerous, violent, sexist or racist. . . . The year before, in Cuba, the ministry proclaimed that dolls made in that country would be designed in the image of Cuban people. In the past, girls played most often with Aryan-image dolls made from European modes. New ones will have Cuban-type faces and clothing"; "New Image Planned for Cuban Dolls," *Minneapolis Star*, July 2, 1974, quoted in Wilkinson, "Doll Exhibit," 26–27.

13. Laura Smith-Spark, "Instead of Spiderman or Bratz Dolls, Children in the US Could Soon Be Clutching a Talking Jesus Toy, a Bearded Moses or A Muscle-Bound Figure of Goliath," BBC News, July 30, 2007, http://news.bbc.co.uk/2/hi /americas/6916287.stm.

14. Ibid.

15. Shreya Shoundial, "Meet Salma, the 'Muslim' Barbie Doll," *IBN Live*, October 10, 2007, http://ibnlive.in.com/news/meet-salma-the-muslim-barbie-doll /50287-3-1.html.

16. The Qur'an 8:83 says Islam is the religion of Allah: "Do they seek for other than the Religion of Allah?—while all creatures in the heavens and on earth have, willing or unwilling, bowed to His Will (Accepted Islam), and to Him shall they all be brought back."

17. Christina Caron, "Barbie 'Obsession': Collectors Reflect on Hobby as Pregnant Midge Doll Is Reported Stolen," ABC News, June 24, 2011, http:// abcnews.go.com/US/barbie-obsession-collectors-reflect-hobby-pregnant-midge -doll/story?id=13912462. In 2002 Midge was introduced as a pregnant doll and instantly became controversial. She was removed from store shelves. Many parents complained that the doll, packaged alone without family members, sent the wrong message. Pregnant Midge, as a part of the Barbie collection, has a compartment inside her belly with an upside-down baby that can be removed. For more information on this doll see also Mike Smith, "Eight Controversial Toys," *Unplugged* (blog), *Yahoo! Games*, February 15, 2012, http://games.yahoo.com/blogs /unplugged/eight-controversial-toys-232432086.html.

18. "Bosnian Dolls," *Doll World: The Magazine for Doll Lovers*, posted in "Doll Ambassadors," *Sarajevska Tribina*, n.d., http://sarajevskatribina.info/ba/bosnian -dolls/. The *Tribina* says the Bosnian Dolls were one of its most successful projects; they were produced by the women's association DRINA from Gorazde.

19. Amy Silverstein, "The Simpsons Toys Banned in Iran," *Global Post*, February 6, 2012, http://www.globalpost.com/dispatches/globalpost-blogs/weird -wide-web/the-simpsons-toys-banned-iran.

20. "Iran Bans Simpsons Dolls, Fearing Infiltration of Western Culture," Associated Press, published in *Haaretz*, February 6, 2012, http://www.haaretz .com/news/middle-east/iran-bans-simpsons-dolls-fearing-infiltration-of-western -culture-1.411339.

21. "Elif' the Doll Registered At Turkish Patent Office," *Hurriyet Daily News*, November 21, 2010, http://www.hurriyetdailynews.com/.

22. "Barbie Is Out, Elif Is In—In Turkey," Middle East Media Research Institute (*MEMRI* blog, article archived), http://www.thememriblog.org/turkey/.

23. "Elif Bebek, Turkey's Doll," *Skylife*, November 2009, http://www .turkishairlines.com/zh-cn/skylife/2009/november/cityscope/elif-bebek-turkeys -doll.aspx.

24. I am thankful to Dr. Jeannette Okur for translating the text from Turkish to English; Dr. Okur is on the faculty of the Department of Middle Eastern Languages and Culture, University of Texas at Austin.

25. Anne Menely, "Fashions and Fundamentalism in Fin de Siècle Yemen: Chador Barbie and Islamic Socks," *Cultural Anthropology* 22, no. 2 (May 2007): 214–243.

26. "Prayers and Playthings. Making Money from Believers," *The Economist*, July 14, 2012, http://www.economist.com/node/21558563.

27. "Hearts for Hearts Girls," Playmates Toys, http://www.playmatestoys .com/brands/hearts-for-hearts-girls; World Vision, http://www.worldvision.org/.

28. Joel Best, "Too Much Fun: Toys as Social Problems and the Interpretation of Culture," *Symbolic Interaction* 21, no. 2 (1998): 197–212. Best cites the studies of Donald Ball (1967), Norman Denzin (1977), and Gary Alan Fine (1987).

29. Best, "Too Much Fun," 198.

30. Roscoe B. Starek, "The ABCs at the FTC: Marketing and Advertising to Children," speech, July 25, 1997, Federal Trade Commission, https://www.ftc .gov/public-statements/1997/07/abcs-ftc-marketing-and-advertising-children.

31. Anup Shah, "Children as Consumers," *Global Issues*, November 21, 2010, http://www.globalissues.org/article/237/children-as-consumers. On the Swedish ban see "Sweden Pushes Its Ban on Children's Ads," *Wall Street Journal*, May 29, 2001, reposted at Common Dreams, http://www.commondreams.org /headlines01/0529-05.htm.

32. "Television Advertising Leads to Unhealthy Habits in Children, Says APA Task Force," American Psychological Association, February 23, 2014, http://www .apa.org/news/press/releases/2004/02/children-ads.aspx.

33. Richard Robbins, *Global Problem and the Culture of Capitalism* (Boston: Allyn and Bacon, 2005), 24.

34. Kim Campbell and Kent Davis-Packard, "How Ads Get Kids To Say, I Want It!" *Christian Science Monitor*, September 18, 2000, http://www.csmonitor .com/2000/0918/p1s1.html.

35. James U. McNeal, "From Savers to Spenders: How Children Became a Consumer Market," Center for Media Literacy, n.d., http://www.medialit.org /reading-room/savers-spenders-how-children-became-consumer-market.

36. Sandra L. Calvert, "Children as Consumers: Advertising and Marketing," *Future Child* 18, no. 1 (Spring 2008): 207, http://www.futureofchildren.org.

37. Campbell and Davis-Packard, "How Ads Get Kids to Say, I Want It!"

38. Muslim Kids TV: Videos and Crafts for Muslim Children, http:// muslimkidstv.com.

39. Ibid.

40. Ibid.

41. "Prayers and Playthings: Making Money from Believers," *The Economist*, July 14, 2012, http://www.economist.com/node/21558563.

42. "Little Big Kids (Muslim Toy Company)," *Muslim Heroes*, March 24, 2011, http://muslimheroes.org/2011/03/24/162-little-big-kids-muslim-toy-company.

43. Elizabeth S. Moore, "It's Child's Play: Advergaming and the Online Marketing of Food to Children," Kaiser Family Foundation, July 2006, http:// kaiserfamilyfoundation.files.wordpress.com/2013/01/7536.pdf.

44. Ibid.

45. Michael McGinnis, Jennifer Appleton Gootman, and Vivica I. Kraak, eds., "Food and Beverage Marketing to Children and Youth," in *Food Marketing to Children and Youth: Threat or Opportunity?*, Committee on Food Marketing and the Diets of Children and Youth, Institute of Medicine of the National Academies (Washington, DC: National Academies Press, 2006), 210.

46. Calvert, "Children as Consumers," 207.

47. Pamela Geller, "A Muslim Barbie Is a Breastless Barbie!" April 21, 2004, http://pamelageller.com/2009/04/a-muslim-barbie-is-a-breastless-barbie.html.

48. M. Smith, "Eight Controversial Toys."

49. Brian Reynolds, "Children's Toys Contain Hidden Muslim Religious Agenda to Brainwash America's Youth Islam Is the Light!" comment, *Voices*, Yahoo, http://voices.yahoo.com/childrens-toys-contain-hidden-muslim-religious-agenda-2603859.html?cat=9 (page discontinued).

50. "Hidden Message Of Islam In Children's Toys!" video, News 10, posted to YouTube September 16, 2010, by Society Secrets, http://www.youtube.com/watch?v=GZLXffdEBgA. A comment on this page reads, "Start checking any and ALL of your children's toys! Keep them for the pending law suits, which are being filed as class action."

51. "Mystery of Muslim Children's Toys Disappearing Solved!" http://www.malagent.com/archives/2214 (site unavailable).

52. "UAE Wants to Control Toys that Mock Islam," *Iran Aware*, June 19, 2012, http://iranaware.com/2012/06/19/uae-wants-to-control-toys-that-mock-islam.

53. H. Scott English, "Saudis Demand McDonald's Be Punished For Happy Meal Toy That Insults Muhammed," *Inquisitr*, May 28, 2012, http://www.inquisitr.com/244094/saudis-demand-mcdonalds-be-punished-for-happy-meal-toy-that-insults-muhammed.

54. Ibid.

55. "Teddy Bear Update—Thousands Call for Death of Teacher," BBC, posted at *Elder of Ziyon* (blog), November 30, 2007, http://elderofziyon.blogspot.com/2007/11/teddy-bear-update-thousands-call-for.html.

56. Nazlida Muhamad Hashim and Dick Mizerski, "Exploring Muslim Consumers' Information Sources For Fatwa Rulings on Products and Behaviors," *Journal of Islamic Marketing* 1, no. 1 (2010): 37–50.

57. Sheikh Muhammad Abdul Majed Zakir is a senior *qari* (Qur'an reciter) from Riyadh. He is of Pakistani descent, but he migrated to Jeddah and then to Medina, Saudi Arabia.

58. *Adam's World* is a unique Islamic video series with the aim of introducing children to Islamic morals, values, and culture in a manner that is both entertaining and educational; the project is supported by Sound Vision, http://www.soundvision.com/info/adam/.

59. "Naming Toys with Muslim Names," Islamic Research Foundation International, n.d., http://www.irfi.org/articles2/articles_3701_3750/naming%20toys%20with%20muslim%20nameshtml.htm.

60. Ibid.

61. Bikya Masr, "Lebanese Sheikh Calls for Toy to Be Banned, Says It Insults Prophet's Wife," *Masress*, June 23, 2012, http://www.masress.com/en/bikyamasr/70562.

62. Pamela Nilan, "Muslim Media and Youth in Globalizing Southeast Asia," in *Media Consumption and Everyday Life in Asia*, ed. Youna Kim (New York: Routledge, 2008), 48.

63. Nilan, "Reflexive Youth Culture," 91.

Chapter 5

1. "Saudi Arabia and UAE Top World List in Consumption of Cosmetics," *Al Arabiya*, November 7, 2012, http://english.alarabiya.net/articles/2012/07/11/225712.html.
2. Vidya Rao, "Halal Beauty Products Appeal Goes beyond the Muslim Market," *Today Show*, MSNBC, posted in *Muslim Village*, August 19, 2010, http://muslimvillage.com/2010/08/19/5478/halal-beauty-products-appeal-goes-beyond-the-muslim-market.
3. Venessa Gera, "Breathable Nail Polish a Surprise Hit with Muslims," *Yahoo News*, February 27, 2013, http://news.yahoo.com/breathable-nail-polish-surprise-hit-muslims-080455659.html.
4. Puziah Hashim, "Alternative Ingredients for Halal Cosmetic and Personal Care Products," *Proceedings*, 3rd International Symposium on IMT-GT, Halal Science and Management, Universiti Putra, Malaysia, December 21–22, 2009, 135.
5. Michelle Yeomans, "Halal Cosmetics Proves to Be a Market Trend in the US," *Cosmetics Design*, February 16, 2012, http://www.cosmeticsdesign.com/Market-Trends/Halal-cosmetics-proves-to-be-a-market-trend-in-the-US.
6. Colette Bouchez, "Natural Cosmetics: Are They Healthier for Your Skin?" WebMD, http://www.webmd.com/beauty/makeup/natural-cosmetics-are-they-healthier-for-your-skin.
7. Ibid.
8. Chandra Tiwary, "Premature Sexual Development in Children Following the Use of Estrogen-or Placenta-Containing Hair Products," *Clinical Pediatrics* 37. no. 12 (1998): 733–739.
9. Essential Serum, Skinmedica, http://www.skinmedica.com/skin-care-products/rejuvenation/tns-essential-serum.
10. "Anti-Aging Property of Human Sperm," Plasmetic, June 1, 2009, http://www.plasmetic.com/skin/antiaging/anti-aging-property-of-human-sperm.html.
11. Zoe Ruderman, "WTF?! Beauty Treatment: Spermine Facials," *Cosmopolitan*, September 14, 2009, http://www.cosmopolitan.com/hairstyles-beauty/beauty-blog/spermine-facials.
12. Daniel Slack, "Another Good Reason to Keep Men Around: Everyday Commercial Uses Of Semen," *Newsvine*, April 29, 2009, http://daniel-slack.newsvine.com/news/.
13. "Bull Semen: The Latest Hair Miracle," Naturally Curly, June 22, 2009, http://www.naturallycurly.com.
14. Prasun Bandyopadhyay, Vaclav Janout, Lan-hui Zhang, and Steven L. Regen, "Ion Conductors Derived from Cholic Acid and Spermine: Importance of Facial Hydrophilicity on Na^+ Transport and Membrane Selectivity." *Journal of American Chemical Society* 123, no. 31 (2001): 7691–7696.
15. "Plazan: The Company World Leader in Placenta Cosmeceutical Skin Care," Plazan Cosmetics, February 2005, http://www.plazancosmetics.com/plazan-skin-care-about.html.
16. Ibid.
17. "Rejuvenation Tour to Japan," Dr. Makise Supplement Clinic, http://www.drmakise.com/en/travel.

18. Ibid.

19. Valerie Richardson, "Aborted Fetus Cells Used in Beauty Creams," *Washington Times*, November 3, 2009, http://www.washingtontimes.com/news/2009/nov/3/aborted-fetus-cells-used-in-anti-aging-products/?page=all.

20. "Cosmetics Firm Using Remains Of Executed Chinese," *World Tribune*, March 23, 2006, http://www.worldtribune.com/worldtribune/06/front2453818.0847222223.html.

21. Ibid.

22. Ian Cobain and Adam Luck, "The Beauty Products from the Skin of Executed Chinese Prisoners," *The Guardian*, September 13, 2005, http://www.guardian.co.uk/science/2005/sep/13/medicineandhealth.china.

23. In Rao, "Halal Beauty Products Appeal."

24. Ibid.

25. Katie Nichol, "Opportunity Knocks for Natural and Organic Halal Cosmetics," *Cosmetics Design*, November 8, 2012, http://www.cosmeticsdesign.com/Market-Trends/Opportunity-knocks-for-natural-and-organic-halal-cosmetics.

26. Ibid. The potential for halal was discussed at the Asian Pacific Sustainable Cosmetics Summit in Hong Kong on November 12–13, 2012. The Sustainable Cosmetics Summit is a series of international summits that focus on leading issues the beauty industry faces concerning sustainability and natural, organic, fair trade, and ecological products. The aim of the summits is to encourage sustainability in the beauty industry by bringing together key stakeholders and debating these major issues in a high-level forum; http://www.sustainablecosmeticssummit.com.

27. Feliciano Blanco-Davila, "Beauty and the Body: The Origins of Cosmetics," *Plastic and Reconstructive Surgery* 105, no. 3, (March 2000): 1196–1204.

28. "Skin Rejuvenating Collagen Boosting Drink. We Investigate the Latest Beauty Craze to Hit the Headlines," *Laser Skin Solutions* (blog), February 7, 2013, http://www.laserskinsolutions.co.uk/blog/2013/02/07/.

29. Ibid.

30. UTHM Institutional Repository, Universiti Tun Hussein Onn Malaysia, http://eprints.uthm.edu.my/5797/.

31. Salafism is a movement among Sunni Muslims named by its proponents in reference to the *salef* (predecessors or ancestors), the earliest Muslims considered to be examples of Islamic practice; "Salafi Movement," note 1, Wikipedia, http://en.wikipedia.org/wiki/Salafi_movement-cite_note-1.

32. Eva F. Nisa, "The Internet Subculture of Indonesian Face-Veiled Women," *International Journal of Cultural Studies* (February 8, 2013): 9.

33. Ibid.

34. Katie Nichol, "First International Conference on Halal Cosmetics and Toiletries," *Cosmetics Design*, March 10, 2010, http://www.cosmeticsdesign-europe.com/Market-Trends/First-international-conference-on-Halal-cosmetics-and-toiletries.

35. Ibid.

36. Nichol, "Opportunity Knocks."

37. Norzaidi Mohd Daud et al., "Identifying the Determinant Attributes of Halal Cosmetics Product That Influence Its Positioning Strategy in Malaysian Market," *Journal of Applied Sciences Research* 8, no. 1 (2012): 302.

38. "Tom's of Maine Products Earn Halal Certification," Tom's of Maine,

July 26, 2006, http://www.tomsofmaine.com/press/releases/detail/toms-of-maine
-products-earn-halal-certification.

39. "Colgate Toothpaste FAQS," Colgate, http://www.colgate.com.sg/app
/Colgate/SG/OC/Products/Toothpastes/ColgateHalal/FAQPage.cvsp.

40. "Cosmetics (Women Care Products) Market for Halal Cosmetics in India,"
Halal India, http://www.halalinindia.com/cosmetics.php.

41. In Shilpa Phadnis, "Indian Brands Get 'Halal' Stamp, Set to Woo Muslims
in Global Markets," *Times of India*, May 21, 2012, http://timesofindia.indiatimes
.com/business/india-business/.

42. Ibid.

43. Unilever is an Anglo-Dutch multinational consumer goods company. Its
products include foods, beverages, cleaning agents, and personal care products. It
is the world's third-largest consumer goods company measured by 2011 revenues
(after Procter & Gamble and Nestlé) and the world's largest maker of ice cream;
Unilever, https://www.unilever.com/about/. Sunsilk is sold under a variety of different names in markets around the world including Elidor, Seda, and Sedal. The
brand is strongest in Asia, Latin America, and the Middle East and is the number one hair care brand in Pakistan, India, Brazil, Argentina, Bolivia, Bangladesh,
Sri Lanka, Indonesia, and Thailand; "Sunsilk," Wikipedia, http://en.wikipedia.org
/wiki/Sunsilk.

44. Translation by Tanweer Aslam and Fawzia Afzal Khan. Text is taken from
an image posted at *Jawa Report*, http://mypetjawa.mu.nu/.

45. Noor al-Qasimi, "Shampoo: Editing, Advertising, and Codes of Modesty
on Saudi Arabian Television," *Camera Obscura* 26, no. 2 (2011): 91–92.

46. Hamid Naficy, "Veiled Visions/Powerful Presences: Women in Postrevolutionary Iranian Cinema," in *In the Eye of the Storm: Women in Post-Revolutionary
Iran*, ed. Mahnez Afkhami and Erika Friedl (London: I. B. Tauris, 1994), 131–150.

47. "Brunei: Thumbs Up for Halal Cosmetics," Halal Focus, http://halalfocus
.net/brunei-thumbs-up-for-halal-cosmetics.

48. E. Huff, "Toxic Burden: Women Put 515 Chemicals on Their Faces Every
Day," *Natural News*, December 29, 2009, http://www.naturalnews.com/027822
_cosmetics_chemicals.html.

49. Ibid. The Environmental Working Group (EWG) is an American environmental organization that specializes in research and advocacy in the areas of toxic
chemicals, agricultural subsidies, public lands, and corporate accountability. EWG
is a nonprofit organization, 501(c)(3), whose mission, according to the website, is
"to use the power of public information to protect public health and the environment." Founded in 1993 by Ken Cook and Richard Wiles, EWG is headquartered
in Washington, DC. A sister organization, the EWG Action Fund, is the lobby-
ing arm, 501(c)(4), of the organization and was founded in 2002. Annually the
EWG publishes its "Dirty Dozen" list of foods with the highest pesticide residue.
The EWG recommends that consumers look for organically produced varieties of
these products. The EWG also publishes the "Clean 15" list of foods with the least
pesticide residue; Environmental Working Group, http://www.ewg.org/foodnews
/summary.php.

50. N. Lekouch et al., "Lead and Traditional Moroccan Pharmacoepia," *Science
of the Total Environment* (December 2001): 39–43.

51. Ibid.

52. A. D. Hardy et al., *Journal of Ethnopharmacology* 60, no. 3 (1998): 223.

53. A. D. Hardy, H. H. Sutherland, and R. Vaishnav, "A Study of the Composition of Some Eye Cosmetics (Kohls) Used in the United Arab Emirates," *Journal of Ethnopharmacology* 80 (2002): 145. See also Karim N. Jallad and Hartmut G. Hedderich, "Characterization of a Hazardous Eyeliner (Kohl) by Confocal Raman Microscopy," *Journal of Hazardous Materials* B124 (2005): 236–240; I. C. Nnorom, J. C. Igwe, and C. G. Oji-Nnorom, "Trace Metal Contents of Facial (Make-Up) Cosmetics Commonly Used in Nigeria," *African Journal of Biotechnology* 4, no. 10 (October 2005): 1133–1138; A. Selwa, F. al-Hazzaa, and Peter M. Krahn, "Kohl: A Hazardous Eyeliner," *International Ophthalmology* 19, no. 2. (1995): 83–88.

54. C. Parry and J. Eaton, "Kohl: A Lead-Hazardous Eye Makeup from the Third World to the First World," *Environmental Health Perspectives* 94 (August 1991): 121–123.

55. Jamiatul Ulama of KwaZulu, Natal, South Africa, http://jamiat.org.za/blog/permissibility-of-permanent-makeup.

56. Guy Montague-Jones, "Consumer Lobby Group Slams Cosmetics Safety in US," *Cosmetics Design*, October 1, 2007, http://www.cosmeticsdesign.com/Market-Trends/Consumer-lobby-group-slams-cosmetics-safety-in-US.

57. Ibid.

58. Simon Pitman, "Industry Hits Back at EWG Product Safety Review," *Cosmetics Design*, October 26, 2005, http://www.cosmeticsdesign.com/Market-Trends/Industry-hits-back-at-EWG-product-safety-review.

59. Simon Pitman, "Study Points to Cancer-Risk from Petroleum-Based Cosmetics," *Cosmetics Design*, February 12, 2007, http://www.cosmeticsdesign.com/Formulation-Science/Study-points-to-cancer-risk-from-petroleum-based-cosmetics.

60. Simon Pitman, "California Cosmetics Bill Becomes Law," *Cosmetics Design*, October 12, 2005, http://www.cosmeticsdesign.com/Market-Trends/California-cosmetics-Bill-becomes-law.

61. "Governor Signs Safe Cosmetics Bill," Campaign for Safe Cosmetics, http://safecosmetics.org/.

62. "Toxic Chemicals in Cosmetics, Shampoos, Targeted by Congress," Campaign for Safe Cosmetics, http://safecosmetics.org/.

63. The Campaign for Safe Cosmetics website describes how rules and regulations are changing regarding the cosmetic industry; http://safecosmetics.org/.

64. A Cosmetics Industry Review panel of experts meets quarterly in Washington, DC; these meetings are open to the public and all attendees are encouraged to participate. The CIR is a panel established and funded by the Personal Care Products Council (PCPC, sometimes referred to by its old acronym, CTFA). On its website, PCPC states that "the Cosmetic Ingredient Review thoroughly reviews and assesses the safety of ingredients used in cosmetics in an open, unbiased, and expert manner, and publishes the results in the open, peer-reviewed scientific literature." The CIR was established in 1976 "with support of the US Food and Drug Administration and the Consumer Federation of America. Although funded by CTFA, CIR and the review process are independent from CTFA and the cosmetic industry"; CIR, http://www.cir-safety.org/about. Also see "Cos-

metic Ingredient Review," Source Watch, http://www.sourcewatch.org/index.php
?title=Cosmetic_Ingredient_Review.

65. Ingredients, Cosmetics Info, http://www.cosmeticsinfo.org/.

66. In "Something's Fishy about This Lipstick," SciTech, *IoL*, February 14, 2002, http://www.iol.co.za/scitech/technology/something-s-fishy-about-this-lipstick-1.81796#.VjgpDSvQMtc.

67. Abdul Rohman and Yaakob B. Che Man, "Analysis of Cod Liver Oil Adulteration Using Fourier Transform Infrared (FTIR) Spectroscopy," *Journal of the American Oil Chemists' Society* 86, no. 12 (2009): 1149.

68. Ibid., 1150.

69. Abdul Rohman and Yaakob B. Che Man, "Analysis of Lard in Cream Cosmetics Formulations Using FT-IR Spectroscopy and Chemometrics," *Middle-East Journal of Scientific Research* 7, no. 5 (2011): 726–732.

70. Ibid., 731.

71. Katie Bird, "Cosmetics Companies Could Benefit from Targeting Muslim Market," *Cosmetics Design*, March 6, 2008, http://www.cosmeticsdesign.com/Business-Financial/Cosmetics-companies-could-benefit-from-targeting-Muslim-market.

72. Yeomans, "Halal Cosmetics."

73. Bird, "Cosmetics Companies Could Benefit."

74. M. E. S. Mirghani et al., "Special Oils for Halal Cosmetics," Proceedings, 3rd International Symposium on IMT-GT, Halal Science and Management, Halal Products Research Institute, Universiti Putra, Malaysia, December 21–22, 2009.

75. Ibid., 141.

76. In Jessica Hume, "Marriage Advice by the Book," *The National*, July 11, 2009, http://www.thenational.ae/news/uae-news/marriage-advice-by-the-book.

77. In Meher Ahmad, "Muslim Women Like Having Sex, and Halal Lube Is a Thing that Exists," *Jezebel*, May 15, 2013, http://jezebel.com/muslim-women-like-having-sex-and-halal-lube-is-a-thing-505979520.

78. Michael Blass, "Halal Sex Website—No Contradiction," Radio Netherlands Worldwide, July 9, 2010, http://www.rnw.nl/africa/article/halal-sex-website-no-contradiction-0. See also "Amsterdam's Muslim Sex Shop," video, posted September 7, 2010, to YouTube, http://www.youtube.com/watch?v=X8ioahw7AfA.

79. Hanina Ajaral and Joke Mat, "Online Islamic Sex Shop Opens for Business," NRC, March 19, 2010, http://vorige.nrc.nl/international/article2507049.ece.

80. Blass, "Halal Sex Website."

81. Sex Toys Islam, http://sextoysislam.ecrater.com.

82. Paramount Supplements, http://www.paramount-supplements.com/esforwo30ta.html.

83. In Phadnis, "Indian Brands Get 'Halal' Stamp."

84. Al-Kauthar Institute is a pioneering Islamic educational provider of Islamic Studies in the English language; it operates on a not-for-profit basis in nine countries and five continents; Al-Kauthar, http://www.alkauthar.org/alkauthar-institute.

85. "Netherlands: Halal Cosmetics," Islam in Europe, January 25, 2008, http://islamineurope.blogspot.com/2008/01/netherlands-halal-cosmetics.html.

86. Ibid.

87. Ehsan Yaghmaie, "Culture of Iran: How Women Applied Makeup 3000 Years Ago," Iran Chamber Society, http://www.iranchamber.com/culture/articles /how_women_applied_makeup_3000.php.

88. Faegheh Shirazi, *The Veil Unveiled: The Hijab in Modern Culture* (Gainesville: University Press of Florida, 2003), 93.

Chapter 6

1. Kambiz Heidarzadeh Hanzaee and Shahrzad Chitsaz, "A Review of Influencing Factors and Constructs on the Iranian Women's Islamic Fashion Market," *Interdisciplinary Journal of Research in Business* 1, no. 4. (April 2011): 95.

2. Mary Ellen Roach-Higgins and Joanne B. Eicher, "Dress and Identity," *Textiles Research Journal* 10, no. 4 (Summer 1992): 1.

3. G. P. Stone, "Appearance and the Self," in *Human Behavior and the Social Process: An Interactionist Approach,* ed. A. M. Rose (New York: Houghton Mifflin, 1962), 86–116; Erving Goffman, *Behavior in Public Places: Notes on the Social Organization of Gatherings* (New York: Free Press of Glencoe, 1963); S. Stryker, *Symbolic Interactionism: A Social Structural Version* (Menlo Park, CA: Benjamin Cummings, 1980).

4. Cyber group promoting chastity and the veil, Hijab Poster, http://hijab -poster.ir.

5. Erving Goffman, "Attitudes and Rationalizations Regarding Body Exposure," in *Dress and Identity,* ed. Mary Ellen Roach-Higgins, Joanne B. Eicher, and Kim K. P. Johnson (New York: Fairchild, 1995), 261.

6. Dorothea E. Schuiz, "Competing Sartorial Assertions of Femininity and Muslim Identity in Mali," *Fashion Theory* 11, no. 2/3 (2007): 253–280.

7. See Faegheh Shirazi, "The Islamic Veil in Civil Societies," in *Governance in the Middle East and North Africa: A Handbook,* ed. Abbas Kadhim (London: Routledge, 2012): 155–172; Faegheh Shirazi and Smeeta Mishra, "Young Muslim Women on the Face Veil (Niqab): A Tool of Resistance in Europe but Rejected in the United States," *International Journal of Cultural Studies* 13, no. 1 (2010): 43–62; Mishra and Shirazi, "Hybrid Identities"; Lila Abu-Lughod, "Do Muslim Women Really Need Saving? Anthropological Reflections on Cultural Relativism and Its Others," *American Anthropologist* 104, no. 3 (September 2002): 783–790; Jens Kreinath, "(Un)veiled: Muslim Women Talk about Hijab by Ines Hofmann Kanna," *American Anthropologist* 112112, no. 4 (December 2010): 654–655; Kaye Haw, "From Hijab To Jilbab and the 'Myth' of British Identity: Being Muslim in Contemporary Britain a Half-Generation On," *Race Ethnicity and Education* 12. no. 3 (2009): 363–378; Emma Tarlo, "Hijab in London: Metamorphosis, Resonance and Effects," *Journal of Material Culture* 12, no. 2 (2007): 131–156; Yildiz Atasoy, "Governing Women's Morality: A Study of Islamic Veiling in Canada," *European Journal of Cultural Studies* 9, no. 2 (May 2006): 203–221; Nilüfer Göle, "The Voluntary Adoption of Islamic Stigma Symbols," *Social Research: An International Quarterly* 70, no. 3 (Fall 2003): 809–828; Ajay Singh Chaudhary, "Simulacra of Morality: Islamic Veiling, Religious Politics and the Limits of Liberalism," *Dialectical Anthropology* 29, nos. 3–4 (2005): 349–372; Banu Gökariksel and

Anna J. Secor, "'You Can't Know How They Are Inside': The Ambivalence of Veiling and Discourses of the Other in Turkey," *Religion and Place* (2013): 95–113; Rachel Bailey Jones, "Case Study: The Veiled Women in the Visual Imagination of the West," *Postcolonial Representations of Women Explorations of Educational Purpose* 18 (2011): 135–167; Theresa R. Milallos, "Muslim Veil as Politics: Political Autonomy, Women and *Syariah* Islam in Aceh," *Contemporary Islam* 1, no. 3 (December 2007): 289–301; Géraldine Mossière, "Modesty and Style in Islamic Attire: Refashioning Muslim Garments in a Western Context," *Contemporary Islam* 6, no. 2 (July 2012): 115–134; Z. Fareen Parvez, "Debating the Burqa in France: the Antipolitics of Islamic Revival," *Qualitative Sociology* 34, no. 2 (June 2011): 287–312; Fadwa El Guindi, "Veiling Resistance," *Fashion Theory: The Journal of Dress, Body, and Culture* 3, no. 1 (1999): 51–80; Banu Gökariksel and Anna J. Secor, "Islamic-ness in the Life of a Commodity: Veiling-Fashion in Turkey," *Transactions of the Institute of British Geographers* 35. no. 3 (2010): 313–333.

8. Shirazi, *Veil Unveiled*, 180.

9. Norah Vincent, "Veiled Intentions," *Salon*, February 1, 2002, http://www.salon.com/2002/02/01/burqa.

10. Caroline Osella and Filippo Osella, "Muslim Style in South India," *Fashion Theory* 11, no. 2/3 (2007): 2.

11. Annelies Moors, "'Discover the Beauty of Modesty' Islamic Fashion Online," in *Modest Fashion: Styling Bodies, Mediating Faith*, ed. Reina Lewis (London: I. B. Tauris, 2013), 19.

12. Pierre Tristam, "Does the Quran Require Women to Wear the Veil?" About News, http://middleeast.about.com/od/religionsectarianism/f/me080209.htm.

13. Qur'an Surat An-Nūr or al-Noor (The Light) 24:60; http://quran.com/24/60.

14. Quoted in Shirazi and Mishra, "Hybrid Identities," 43.

15. Ibid., 44.

16. Mohammad Alyousei, "'Burkas for Babies': Saudi Cleric's New Fatwa Causes Controversy," *Al Arabiya*, February 3, 2013, http://english.alarabiya.net/articles/2013/02/03/264031.html.

17. Ibid.

18. "Fatwa against Designer Burqas," *Haindava Keralam*, December 19, 2012, http://www.haindavakeralam.com/HKPage.aspx?PageID=16698.

19. "Deoband Fatwa against Modelling by Muslim Women," *Z News*, April 6, 2010, http://zeenews.india.com/news/nation/deoband-fatwa-against-modelling-by-muslim-women_616908.html.

20. Jonathan Turley, "Fatwa Issued against Women Running Beauty Salons," *Jonathan Turley* (blog), April 9, 2010, http://jonathanturley.org/2012/04/09/fatwa-issued-against-women-running-beauty-salons.

21. "Islamic Fashion Shows Displaying Hijab," *Islamic Fatwas* (blog), http://islamicfatwas.blogspot.com/2008/03/islamic-fashion-shows-displaying-hijab.html.

22. "Fashion Parades, the Ulama, and the Madrasah," *The Majlis* 16, no. 3 (2005), posted at Sunni Forum, http://www.sunniforum.com/forum/showthread.php?5069-Fashion-Parades-the-Ulama-and-the-Madrasah.

23. Ibid.

24. Ibid.

25. Ibid.

26. Gemma Champ, "World's First Muslim Model Agency Opens in New York," *The National*, February 14, 2012, http://www.thenational.ae/lifestyle /fashion/worlds-first-muslim-model-agency-opens-in-new-york.

27. "The Future of the Global Muslim Population: Projections for 2010–2030," Pew Research Center, January 27, 2011, http://www.pewforum.org/future -of-the-global-muslim-population-russia.aspx.

28. "International Festival 'Islamic Style,'" Halal Expo, http://www.halalexpo .org/doc/program/style.

29. "Islamic Fashion Comes to Moscow," *Muslim.ru*, http://www.muslim.ru /en/articles/138/4200.

30. Champ, "World's First Muslim Model Agency."

31. "Muslim Modeling Agency, Mixing Modeling and Modesty," *Female Daily* (blog), February 23, 2012, http://www.fashionesedaily.com/blog/2012/02/23 /muslim-modeling-agency-mixing-modeling-modesty.

32. In Monica Sarkar, "H&M's Latest Look: Hijab-Wearing Muslim Model Stirs Debate," CNN, October 4, 2015, http://www.cnn.com/2015/09/29/europe /hm-hijab-model/.

33. In Leanne Bayley, "Trending: Maria Hidrissi, H&M's First Muslim Model," *Glamour*, September 28, 2015, http://www.glamourmagazine.co.uk /news/fashion/2015/09/maria-hidrissi-hm-new-muslim-model.

34. Afia R. Fitriati, "HijUp.com Announces Modelling Contest," *Aquila Style*, December 5, 2012, http://www.aquila-style.com/fashionbeauty/hijup-com -modelling-contest. Tumblr has photos at "Hijab Model," https://www.tumblr .com/tagged/hijab-model/.

35. "My Jakarta: Dendy Oktariady, Modeling Agency Head," *Jakarta Globe*, n.d., http://www.thejakartaglobe.com/archive/my-jakarta-dendy-oktariady -modeling-agency-head.

36. "Muslim Fashions Light Up Jakarta Fashion Week," *Legally Couture* (blog), November 14, 2012, http://cempakaulika.blogspot.com/2012/11/muslim -fashions-light-up-jakarta.html.

37. "Government and Private Sector Collaborate to Promote Indonesian Fashion Industry," *Kemendag*, May 20, 2013, http://www.kemendag.go.id/files/pdf /2013/05/20/pemerintah-dan-swasta-berkolaborasi-dorong-industri-fesyen -indonesia-en0-1369031792.pdf.

38. "Indonesia Strives to Become World's Muslim Apparel Centre," *Fiber 2 Fashion*, June 27, 2013, http://www.fibre2fashion.com/news/garment-apparel -news/indonesia/newsdetails.aspx?news_id=147865.

39. "Iran Organizing Islamic Women's Fashion Festival," *Tehran Times*, http:// tehrantimes.com/arts-and-culture/95557-iran-organizing-islamic-womens-fashion -festival (page unavailable).

40. For some of the studies on this topic see A. Jafari, "Two Tales of a City: An Exploratory Study of Cultural Consumption among Iranian Youth," *Iranian Studies* 40, no. 3 (2007): 367–383; Sanam Zahir, *The Music of the Children of Revolution: The State of Music and Emergence of the Underground Music in the Islamic Republic of Iran with an Analysis of Its Lyrical Content* (Saarbrücken, Germany: Lembert Academic, 2008); Laudan Nooshin, "Underground: Rock Music and Youth Discourses in Iran," *Iranian Studies* 38, no. 3 (2005): 463–494; Sholeh

Johnston, "Persian Rap: The Voice of Modern Iran's Youth," *Journal of Persianate Studies* 1, no. 1 (2008): 102–119; Massimo Leone, "My Schoolmate: Protest Music in Present-Day Iran," *Critical Discourse Studies* 9, no. 4 (2012): 347–362.

41. Borzou Daragahi, "Catwalk Skirts the Mullahs," *Los Angeles Times*, May 11, 2007, http://articles.latimes.com/print/2007/may/11/world/fg-fashion11.

42. Rohin Guha, "Keen for Green: Iran's Underground Fashion Week," *Black-Book*, September 23, 2009, http://www.bbook.com/fashion/keen-for-green-irans-underground-fashion-week/.

43. "Iranian Fashion Thrives Underground," *Newsweek*, September 17, 2009, http://www.newsweek.com/iranian-fashion-thrives-underground-79513.

44. Frances Harrison, "Crackdown in Iran over Dress Codes," BBC News, April 27, 2007, http://news.bbc.co.uk/2/hi/middle_east/6596933.stm.

45. Thomas Erdbrink, "Ahmadinejad and Clerics Fight over Scarves," *Washington Post*, July 22, 2011, https://www.washingtonpost.com/world/middle-east/.

46. "Muslim Fashions Light Up Jakarta Fashion Week."

47. Banu Gökariksel and Anna J. Secor, "New Transnational Geographies of Islamism, Capitalism, and Subjectivity: The Veiling-Fashion Industry in Turkey," *Royal Geographical Society* 41, no. 1 (2009): 6.

48. Angel Rabasat and F. Stephen Larrabee, "The Rise of Political Islam in Turkey," National Defense Research Institute, published by RAND Corporation, 2008, p. iii.

49. Alexandra Hudson, "'Allah's Tailors' Gaining Profile in Turkey," Reuters, posted in *Veiling Fashion*, November 13, 2010, http://veilingfashion.unc.edu/news-allahs-tailors.php.

50. Özlem Sandikci and Güliz Ger, "Constructing and Representing the Islamic Consumer in Turkey," *Fashion Theory* 11, no. 2/3 (2007): 205.

51. "A Marriage of Modesty and Style," BBC News, June 5, 2008, http://news.bbc.co.uk/2/hi/uk_news/england/leicestershire/7427576.stm.

52. In Sebastian Smith, "Islam and Sensuality: Muslim Fashion Designer Covers Up," *Islam.ru*, September 5, 2012, http://islam.ru/en/content/story/islam-and-sensuality-muslim-fashion-designer-covers.

53. In Margot Adler, "Designer Brings Muslim Fashion to the Runway," NPR, November 3, 2011, http://www.npr.org/2011/11/03/141545276/designer-brings-muslim-fashion-to-the-runway.

54. Jorge Rivas, "Young Muslim Designer Puts Her Fashions on New York Runways," *Colorlines*, November 4, 2011, http://colorlines.com/archives/2011/11/muslim_designer_puts_her_fashions_on_the_runway.html.

55. Women *abaya* designers and their fashion houses include Bahraini fashion designer Kubra al-Qaseer, Saudi fashion designer Hania al-Braikan, and Emirati fashion designer Zaina al-Marzouqi.

56. "Hijab on the Runway," Pinterest, https://www.pinterest.com/ahfif/hijab-on-the-runway/.

57. Sisters Couture ad, cited in Urban Muslim Woman, http://www.urbanmuslimwoman.co.uk/old-site/Fashion_Show.html.

58. Ibid. Oudh, or oud, comes from the wood of the tropical agar (aquilaria) tree, believed to have originated in the Assam region of India and to have spread throughout Southeast Asia. When the wood of this tree gets infected with a cer-

tain mold variety (*Phialophora parasitica*), it reacts by producing a precious, dark, and fragrant resin, which is the perfume ingredient oud, also called agarwood. Oud (in Arabian *oudh*) is highly valued by perfumers for its sweet, woody, aromatic, and complex scent. Due to its rarity, high demand, and the difficulty of harvesting it, oud oil is perhaps the most expensive oil in the world. Its value is estimated as 1.5 times the value of gold, and it is sometimes referred to as "liquid gold"; Catherine Helbig, "What Is Oud (Oudh)?" About Style, http://beauty.about.com/od /fragrancl/a/What-is-Oud.htm.

59. "Islamic Fashions Rock the Catwalk?!" *Lombok Island* (blog), December 2008, http://lombok-island.blogspot.com/2008/12/islamic-fashions-rock -catwalk.html.

60. Balqees Fashion Design, http://www.balqees.ae/about-balqees-fashion -design.html.

61. Annelies Moors and Emma Tarlo, "Muslim Fashion," *Fashion Theory: The Journal of Dress, Body, and Culture* 11, no. 2/3 (2007): 133.

Chapter 7

1. Ergun Yurdadon, "History of Sport in Islamic-Period Turkey," *Sports Journal* 6, no. 4 (Fall 2003).

2. Andrew Pillow, "Muslim Women Participation in 2012 London Olympics Is the Start, Not the Goal," *Bleacher Report*, July 27, 2012, http://bleacherreport .com/articles/1275194-muslim-women-participation-in-2012-london-olympics-is -the-start-not-the-goal.

3. Manal Hamzeh and Kimberly L. Oliver, "'Because I Am Muslim, I Cannot Wear a Swimsuit': Muslim Girls Negotiate Participation Opportunities," *Research Quarterly for Exercise and Sport* 83, no. 2 (2012): 337.

4. Ibid.

5. Hadi Yahmid, "Mixed Swimming Worries Swiss Muslims," Swimwear for Muslim Women, January 14, 2009, http://swimwearformuslimwomen.wordpress .com/2009/01/14/mixed-swimming-worries-swiss-muslims/#more-25.

6. Sarah J. Murray, "Unveiling Myths: Muslim Women and Sport," Women's Sports Foundation, 2003, http://www.womenssportsfoundation.org/cgibin/iowa /issues/part/article.html?record=863. Murray spent ten years as the web producer for the Women's Sports Foundation in the United States. Her editorial leadership and marketing strategies helped the organization secure the top Google search results spot for "women's sports"; Women Win, http://womenwin.org/about/team /staff/sarah-murray.

7. "Beijing Volleyball: Algeria's women breaking new ground in China," *The Telegraph*, July 31, 2008, http://www.telegraph.co.uk/sport/olympics/2479735 /Beijing-Volleyball-Algerias-women-breaking-new-ground-in-China.html.

8. Jamiat Ulema-I-Hind (Organization of Indian Scholars) is one of the leading Islamic organizations in India.

9. Bhaumik Subir, "Protection for Indian Tennis Star," BBC News, September 17, 2005, http://news.bbc.co.uk/2/hi/south_asia/4256052.

10. Shirazi, *Velvet Jihad*, 139–140.

11. Joanna Paraszczuk, "Saudi and Iranian Women Fight for Right to Compete," *Jerusalem Post*, August 3, 2012, http://www.jpost.com/Middle-East/Saudi -and-Iranian-women-fight-for-right-to-compete.

12. Ibid.

13. Ibid.

14. Faezeh Hashemi-Rafsanjani is an Iranian journalist, women's rights activist, former member of the Iranian Parliament, and daughter of former Iranian president Akbar Hashemi Rafsanjani. Between 1996 and 2000, she was a parliamentary representative from Tehran and founded the women's newspaper *Zan*. Hashemi-Rafsanjani favors women's rights and has been a staunch advocate of relaxing Iran's strict dress code. She has traveled widely in Europe, Africa, and India to promote dialogue and is interested in ties with all regions. She has written positively about the effective movements of Nelson Mandela, Martin Luther King, and Gandhi; "Faezeh Hashemi," Wikipedia, http://en.wikipedia.org/wiki/Faezeh_Hashemi.

15. "Faezeh Hashemi," Answers.com, http://www.answers.com/topic/faezeh -hashemi.

16. In Ghada Talhami, *Historical Dictionary of Women in the Middle East and North Africa* (Plymouth, England: Scarecrow, 2013), 160.

17. James Dorsey, "Middle East Soccer Associations Campaign for Women's Right to Play," *Huffington Post*, January 22, 2013, http://www.huffingtonpost .com/james-dorsey/middle-east-soccer-women_b_2471577.html.

18. Geoff Harkness and Samira Islam, "Muslim Female Athletes and the Hijab," *Contexts* 10, no. 4 (October 2011): 64–65.

19. Ibid.

20. "Moroccan Female Soccer Players Fight Uphill Battle for Resources," WBEZ91.5, May 14, 2010, http://www.wbez.org/episode-segments/moroccan -female-soccer-players-fight-uphill-battle-resource.

21. Nicole Matuska, "The Development of Women's Football in Morocco," *Viewpoints* special edition, *Sports and the Middle East*, May 2010, pp. 37–39. Middle East Institute, Washington, DC, posted at https://www.mcgill.ca/sociology /files/sociology/2010_—_sports_and_the_middle_east.pdf.

22. "UN Special Adviser on Sport Supports Initiative to Allow Safe Headscarf in Football," United Nations, www.un.org/wcm/content/site/sport/home /template/news_item.jsp?cid=32703 29.

23. Capsters, https://www.capsters.com/philosophy.jsp.

24. "FIFA's Hijab Ban Reversal Good News for Local Designer," CTV News Montreal, July 5, 2012, http://montreal.ctvnews.ca/.

25. Ibid.

26. "Sports Hijab Lets Islamic Women Throw Some Punches," *Arab Times*, http://www.arabtimesonline.com/news.

27. Benjamin Shingler, "FIFA Panel Officially Allows Turbans, Hijabs In Soccer after Quebec Controversy," Canadian Press, posted at CTV News Montreal, March 1, 2014, http://montreal.ctvnews.ca/fifa-panel-officially-allows-turbans -hijabs-in-soccer-after-quebec-controversy-1.1709704.

28. "Health Concern about Swim Wear," Swimwear for Muslim Women, http://swimwearformuslimwomen.wordpress.com/2007/02/01/health-concern -about-swim-wear/#more.

29. Shirazi, *Velvet Jihad*, 148.

30. Heather Marie Akou, "A Brief History of the Burqini," *Dress* 39, no. 1 (May 2013): 25.

31. Henry Samuel, "French Ban Muslim Woman from Pool for Wearing 'Burkini' Swimsuit," *The Telegraph*, August 12, 2009, http://www.telegraph.co.uk /news/worldnews/europe/france/6017524/French-ban-Muslim-woman-from -pool-for-wearing-burkini-swimsuit.html.

32. Patrick Sawer, "Swimmers Are Told to Wear Burkinis," *The Telegraph*, August 15, 2009, http://www.telegraph.co.uk/news/politics/6034706/Swimmers -are-told-to-wear-burkinis.html.

33. Susie Khamis, "Braving the Burqini: Re-Branding the Australian Beach," *Cultural Geographies* 13, no. 3 (2010): 379.

34. Antar al-Sayed, "Islamic Bathing Suits Make Huge Sales in Egypt," *Al Arabiya*, July 15, 2010, http://www.alarabiya.net/articles/2010/07/15/113943.html.

35. "Middle East Lingerie Bucks Islamic Stereotype," *Just Style*, August 22, 2006, http://www.just-style.com/article.aspx?id=94591&d=1. I am not aware of any such claim in the Koran.

36. "When Consumption Embraces the Faith," Markethnik, October 31, 2011, http://markethnik.com/?p=484&lang=en.

37. "Carlyle Group Buys Scalina," *PEU Report* (blog), August 29, 2010, http:// peureport.blogspot.com/2010/08/carlyle-group-buys-scalina.html.

38. "Nayomi Has Opened at Wafi Mall," AME Info, http://www.ameinfo .com/.

39. Jan Jaben-Eilon, "Luxe Lingerie Goes Global," Womanetics, https://www .womenetics.com/Global-Initiatives/luxe-lingerie-goes-global.

40. Ibid.

41. In Atika Shubert, "Website Sells Shariah-Approved Sex Aids to Muslims," CNN, September 7, 2010, http://www.cnn.com/2010/WORLD/europe/09/07 /muslim.sexual.health/index.html.

42. "Shops in Iran Told Not to Display Female Underwear," Associated Press, published in *The Guardian*, September 23, 2009, http://www.guardian.co.uk /world/2009/sep/23/iran-police-government-female-underwear; "Iran Warns Men Not to Sell Women's Undies," CBS News, September 23, 2009, http://www .cbsnews.com/2100-202_162-5331471.html.

43. "Hamas Bans Women's Underwear from Shop Windows. Prohibition Aims to 'Restore Palestinian Morals,'" *Jerusalem Post*, July 29, 2010, http://www .jpost.com/Middle-East/Hamas-bans-womens-underwear-from-shop-windows. Also see "Gaza: Hamas Demands Gaza Shops Stop Displaying Female Lingerie," *Little Green Footballs*, August 19, 2010, http://littlegreenfootballs.com/page /222551_Gaza-_Hamas_demands_Gaza_shop.

44. "Hamas Bans Women's Underwear."

45. Ken McCracken, "The UAE Orders Mass Beheadings—of Store Mannequins That Are Just Oh So Sexy," *Say Anything Blog*, February 23, 2008, http://sayanythingblog.com/entry/the_uae_orders_mass_beheadings_of_store _mannequins_that_are_just_oh_so_sexy.

46. Mariam M. al-Serkal, "Sharjah Shops Told to 'Behead' Mannequins," *Free Republic*, February 20, 2008, http://www.freerepublic.com/focus/f-news /1973596/posts.

47. "Risque Mannequins Removed for Visit of Turkish PM," *Hurriyet Daily*

News, December 9, 2012, http://www.hurriyetdailynews.com/risque-mannequins
-removed-for-visit-of-turkish-pm.aspx?pageID=238&nid=36441.

48. Dean Nelson, "Mumbai, Home of India's Increasingly Raunchy Bollywood
Film Industry, Is to Ban Mannequins Modeling Lingerie from Its Shop Windows
to Stop the City's Men Having 'Impure Thoughts,'" *The Telegraph*, May 28, 2013,
http://www.telegraph.co.uk/news/worldnews/asia/india/.

49. "Accessory," Dictionary.com, http://dictionary.reference.com/browse
/accessory. According to the *Dictionary of Costume*, "accessory" is "a term which
covers all items that complete a costume and, if not carefully chosen, such hat,
shoes, gloves, handbag or whatever, can mar a costume"; R. Turner Wilcox, *Dictionary of Costume* (New York: Charles Scribner's Sons, 1969), 2.

50. Book 9, Hadith 70; Sunnah, http://sunnah.com/shamail/10. In another
narration it is stated that with the khuffs a *jubbah* (a long coat) was also sent.

51. Ibid., Book 9, Hadith 69.

52. Menely, "Fashions and Fundamentalism," 215, 217.

53. "Shoe Company Head Arrested over Fake Halal Certification Allegations,"
Jakarta Globe, December 20, 2012, http://www.thejakartaglobe.com/archive
/shoe-company-head-arrested-over-fake-halal-certification-allegations/.

54. "Malaysia: Traders to Be Required to Disclose Halal Status of Leather
Products!" *Halal Focus*, February 6, 2012, http://halalfocus.net/malaysia-traders
-to-be-required-to-disclose-halal-status-of-leather-products.

55. Qur'an, Surat An-Nūr (The Light), 24:31; http://quran.com/24/31.

56. Fatwa No. 114631, Islam Question and Answer, http://islamqa.info/en/
ref/114631.

57. Ibid.

58. Shirazi, *Velvet Jihad*, 56.

59. Anne Mullin Burnham, "Silver Speaks," *Saudi Aramco World* 55, no. 6
(November/December 2004): 8–16, http://www.saudiaramcoworld.com/issue
/200406/silver.speaks.htm.

60. "Get Your Blissful Burqa Bag Here," Dinah Lord, October 14, 2009,
http://dinahlord.typepad.com/dinah_lord/2009/10/get-your-blissful-burka-bag
-here.html#sthash.nJQFdxBP.dpuf.

61. Ibid.

62. "Blue Burqa—Fancy Evening Hand Bag by Zardozi," Gundara, http://
gundara.com/SHOP/small-bags/blue-burqa-fancy-evening-hand-bag-zardozi.

63. Zazzle, http://www.zazzle.com/. The Wikipedia entry says, "Zazzle is an
online retailer that allows users to upload images and create their own merchandise
(clothing, posters, etc.), or buy merchandise created by other users, as well as use
images from participating companies."

64. KMILineWear, Facebook, https://www.facebook.com/KMILineWear.

65. Redbubble, http://www.redbubble.com/.

66. Ibid.

Conclusion

1. Thomas, "Selling God/Saving Souls," 58.

2. See Greg Fealy's discussion in "Consuming Islam."

3. Rory Harrington, "Packaging Highlighted as Increasing Source of Halal Food Contamination," *Food Production Daily*, July 6, 2012, http://www.food productiondaily.com/Safety-Regulation/Packaging-highlighted-as-increasing -source-of-Halal-food-contamination.

4. Stearate is the saturated fatty acid. It is a waxy solid, and its chemical formula is $CH_3(CH_2)_{16}CO_2H$. Much of it is extracted from animal fats, particularly from pig; "Stearic Acid," Thai Polychemicals, http://thaipolychemicals.weebly.com /stearic-acid.html.

5. Wim Verbeke et al., "Credence Quality Coordination and Consumers' Willingness-to-Pay for Certified Halal Labelled Meat," *Meat Science* (April 2013): 790–797, at BioMedSearch, http://www.biomedsearch.com/nih/.

6. Shelina Janmohamed, "Guest Post: Building Halal Brands," *Beyond Brics* (blog), *Financial Times*, February 10, 2012, http://blogs.ft.com/beyond -brics/2012/02/10/guest-post-building-halal-brands/#axzz2RhNuEgJc.

7. "Brussels: Halal Hotel Rooms," *Islam in Europe* (blog), August 31, 2010, http://islamineurope.blogspot.com/2010/08/brussels-halal-hotel-rooms.html.

8. Ibid.

9. Rarick et al., "Marketing to Muslims."

10. "Halal Development Council, an NGO Dedicated to the Development of Halal Economy," Halal Pakistan, n.d., http://www.halalpakistan.com/html /halal_market.htm.

11. Jonathan A. J. Wilson and Jonathan Liu, "Shaping the Halal into a Brand?" *Journal of Islamic Marketing* 1, no. 2 (2010): 107.

12. Janmohamed, "Guest Post: Building Halal Brands."

13. "Brussels: Halal Hotel Rooms."

14. Ibid.

15. Ariel David, "Italy Opens Beach For Muslim Women," *Sydney Morning Herald*, August 11, 2006, http://www.smh.com.au/news/italy/italy-opens-beach -for-muslim-women/2006/08/11/1154803064177.html.

16. Ibid.

17. Hashim and Mizerski, "Exploring Muslim Consumers' Information Sources."

18. "French Jews, Muslims Unite in Anger over Halal Meat Row," Agence France-Presse, published in *France 24*, March 5, 2012, http://www.france24.com /en/20120305-fillon-france-kashrut-kosher-halal-jews-muslims-election.

19. Kim Willsher, "France's Muslims Hit Back At Nicolas Sarkozy's Policy on Halal Meat," *The Guardian*, March 10, 2012, http://www.theguardian.com /world/2012/mar/10/nicolas-sarkozy-halal-meat-france-election.

20. "Halal Market Defies France Politics," *On Islam*, April 4, 2012, http:// www.onislam.net/english/news/europe/456493-thriving-french-halal-market -defies-politics.html (site discontinued).

21. Dale Hurd, "Muslim Halal Food Sales Supporting Terrorism?" CBN News, January 9, 2011, http://www.cbn.com/cbnnews/world/2011/january/muslim -halal-food-sales-supporting-terrorism.

22. Soeren Kern, "France Goes Halal—The Halal Issue Is about More than Just Meat," Gatestone Institute, February 28, 2012, http://www.gatestoneinstitute .org/2886/france-halal.

23. "Iran Introduces Islamic Porn to Confront Cultural Invasion," *Poyl* (blog),

January 2010, http://poyl.blogspot.com/2010/01/in-order-to-confront-western-cultural.html.

24. Ibid.

25. Ibid.

26. "Islamic Calendar Girl Paintings," *Makan (Max) Emadi Art Blog*, June 2007, http://maxemadi.arikiart.com/2007/06/islamic-calendar-girl-paintings.htm. Makan Emadi's art packs a punch or pokes a stick at some political figure or cultural standard. His Islamic Calendar Girl series is a provocative view of the image of Islamic women and traditional Islamic dress.

27. Zamzam is the name of a well located within the Masjid al-Haram in Mecca. *Masnoon* in Arabic means "protective"; this is in reference to Qur'anic verses recited for safety and protection of the devout against unseen misfortunes and Satan.

28. *Fuqaha* refers to religious scholars.

29. Jared Pereira, "'Halal' Elevators at Four-Star Hotel," *FMT News*, January 9, 2013, http://www.freemalaysiatoday.com/category/nation/2013/01/09/halal-elevators-at-four-star-hotel.

30. Ibid.

31. "Major Iranian Food Products Receive Halal Food Standard Label," Islamic Republic News Agency, August 14, 2014, http://www3.nkhorasan.irna.ir/en/News/81271944/Economic/Major_Iranian_food_products_receive_Halal_Food_Standard_label.

32. Ibid.

33. Susie Mesure, "Move over Organic—the New Big Business in Food is Halal," *The Independent*, September 26, 2013, http://www.independent.co.uk/life-style/food-and-drink/news/.

34. Stephen DeFelice from the Foundation for Innovation in Medicine defines "nutraceuticals as "food, or parts of food, that provide medical or health benefits, including the prevention and treatment of disease"; Foundation for Innovation in Medicine, http://www.fimdefelice.org/p2410.html. Also see Baby Chauhan et al., "Current Concepts and Prospects of Herbal Nutraceutical: A Review," *Journal of Advanced Pharmaceutical Technology and Research* 4, no. 1 (2010): 4–8; and Manisha Pandey, Rohit K. Verma, and Shubhini A. Saraf, "Nutraceuticals: New Era of Medicine and Health," *Asian Journal of Pharmaceutical and Clinical Research* 3, no. 1 (January–March): 11–15.

Bibliography

Abduh, Muhamad. "Factors Influence Depositors' Withdrawal Behavior in Islamic Banks Using Theory of Reasoned Action." *World Academy of Science Engineering and Technology* 60 (2011): 2074–2079.

Abdulrahim, Raja. "Marketing to Muslims Poses a Challenge for Retailers." *Los Angeles Times*, January 25, 2012. http://articles.latimes.com/keyword/marketing.

Abdul-Rahman, Muhammad Saed. *Islam: Questions and Answers, Divine Unity (Tawheed)*. Vol. 7, Islamic book series. London: MSA, 2003.

Abul, Taher. "Chicken McHalal: McDonald's Denied Using Halal Meat." *Daily Mail*, October 9, 2010. http://www.dailymail.co.uk/news/.

Abu-Lughod, Lila. "Do Muslim Women Really Need Saving? Anthropological Reflections on Cultural Relativism and Its Others." *American Anthropologist* 104, no. 3 (September 2002): 783–790.

Abu-Nasr, Donna. "Saudi Women to Spurn Lingerie Shops over Salesmen." http://www.middle-east-online.com/english/features/?id=31228.

Adams, Mike. "True Fact: A Common Ingredient in Commercial Breads Is Derived from Human Hair Harvested in China." *Natural News*, June 16, 2011. http://www.naturalnews.com/032718_L.cysteine_commercial_bread.html #ixzz22ncxBslz.

Adler, Margot. "Designer Brings Muslim Fashion to the Runway," NPR, November 3, 2011. http://www.npr.org/2011/11/03/141545276/designer-brings -muslim-fashion-to-the-runway.

Agnaou, Fatima. *Gender, Literacy, and Empowerment in Morocco*. New York: Routledge, 2004.

Ahmad, Meher. "Muslim Women Like Having Sex, and Halal Lube Is a Thing That Exists." *Jezebel*, May 15, 2013. http://jezebel.com/muslim-women-like -having-sex-and-halal-lube-is-a-thing-505979520.

Ajaral, Hanina, and Joke Mat. "Online Islamic Sex Shop Opens for Business." NRC, March 19, 2010. http://vorige.nrc.nl/international/article2507049.ece.

Akhtar, Muhammad Wajid. "5 Examples of Supreme Muslim Tolerance." *Muslim Matters*, September 20, 2012. http://muslimmatters.org/author/muhammad -wajid-akhter.

Akir, Oriah, and Nor Othman. "Consumers' Shopping Behaviour Pattern on Selected Consumer Goods: Empirical Evidence on Malaysian Consumers." *Journal of Business and Policy Research* 5, no. 1 (July 2010): 123–157.

Akou, Heather Marie. "A Brief History of the Burqini." *Dress* 39, no. 1 (May 2013): 25–35.

Alam, Syed Shah, and Nazura Mohamed Sayuti. "Applying the Theory of Planned Behavior (TPB) in Halal Food Purchasing." *International Journal of Commerce and Management* 21, no. 1 (2011): 8–20.

Albert, Gwendolyn. "Regional Authority in Czech Republic Provides Financial Support to Anti-Mosque Movement." *Romano Vod'i*, July 19, 2011. http://www.romea.cz/en/news/czech/regional-authority-in-czech-republic -financially-supports-anti-mosque-movement.

Alkayyali, R., and N. Prime. "Religion, Acculturation and the Choice of Food Retail Outlets by Algerian Origin Muslim Women in France: Developing Research Propositions." Paper presented at the European International Business Association (EIBA) 35th Annual Conference, Porto, Portugal, December 10–12, 2010.

Altman, Jennifer S. "For Families of Muslim 9/11 Victims, a New Pain." *USA Today*, September 3, 2010. http://www.usatoday.com/news/nation/2010-09-03 -1Amuslims911_CV_N.htm.

Alyousei, Mohammad. "'Burkas for Babies': Saudi Cleric's New Fatwa Causes Controversy." *Al Arabiya News*, February 3, 2013. http://english.alarabiya.net /articles/2013/02/03/264031.html.

Amara, Mahfoud. "Veiled Women Athletes in the 2008 Beijing Olympics: Media Accounts." *International Journal of the History of Sport* 29, no. 4, March (2012): 638–651.

American Psychological Association. "Television Advertising Leads to Unhealthy Habits in Children; Says APA Task Force." Press release. February 23, 2004. http://www.apa.org/news/press/releases/2004/02/children-ads.aspx.

Ameur, Ahmed Ameur. "The Lifestyle Halal in European Marketing." *Review of Economics and Finance*, Academic Research Centre of Canada (2011): 83–90.

Assadi, Djamchid. "Do Religions Influence Customer Behavior? Confronting Religious Rules and Marketing Concepts." *Cahiers du CEREN*, no. 5 (2003): 2–13.

Atasoy, Yildiz. "Governing Women's Morality: A Study of Islamic Veiling in Canada." *European Journal of Cultural Studies* 9, no. 2 (May 2006): 203–221.

Bandyopadhyay, Prasun, Janout Vaclav, Zhang Lan-hui, and Steven L. Regen. "Ion Conductors Derived from Cholic Acid and Spermine: Importance of Facial Hydrophilicity on Na^+ Transport and Membrane Selectivity." *Journal of American Chemical Society* 123, no. 31 (2001): 7691–7696.

Battour, Mohamed M., Moustafa M. Battor, and Mohd Ismail. "The Mediating Role of Tourist Satisfaction: A Study of Muslim Tourists in Malaysia." *Journal of Travel and Tourism Marketing* 29, no. 3 (2012): 279–297.

Bayley, Leanne. "Trending: Maria Hidrissi, H&M's First Muslim Model." *Glamour*, September 28, 2015. http://www.glamourmagazine.co.uk/news/fashion /2015/09/maria-hidrissi-hm-new-muslim-model.

Beinin, Joel. "The New American McCarthyism: Policing Thought about the Middle East." Stanford University, n.d. http://www.stanford.edu/~beinin/New _McCarthyism.html.

Belien, Paul. "Don't Burn Muhammad." *Brussels Journal*, February 16, 2006. http://www.brusselsjournal.com/node/823.

Berry, Ben. "Agri-Food Trade Service Global Halal Food Market," Market Indicator Report, April 2011. International Markets Bureau, Agriculture and Agri-Food Canada. http://www.ats.agr.gc.ca/inter/4352-eng.htm.

Best, Joel. "Too Much Fun: Toys as Social Problems and the Interpretation of Culture." *Symbolic Interaction* 21, no. 2 (1998): 197–212.

Bird, Katie. "Cosmetics Companies Could Benefit from Targeting Muslim Market." *Cosmetics Design*, March 6, 2008. http://www.cosmeticsdesign.com /Business-Financial/Cosmetics-companies-could-benefit-from-targeting -Muslim-market.

Blanco-Davila, Feliciano. "Beauty and the Body: The Origins of Cosmetics." *Plastic and Reconstructive Surgery* 105, no. 3, (March 2000): 1196–1204.

Blass, Michael. "Halal Sex Website—No Contradiction." Radio Netherlands Worldwide, July 9, 2010. http://www.rnw.nl/africa/article/halal-sex-website -no-contradiction-0.

Bokhari, Ashfak. "Opinion: Political Bias against Halal Meat Market." *Halal Focus*, March 30, 2012. http://halalfocus.net/2012/03/30/opinion-political-bias -against-halal-meat-market.

Bonne, Karijn, and Wim Verbeke. "Religious Values Informing Halal Meat Production and the Control and Delivery of Halal Credence Quality." *Agriculture and Human Values* 25 (2008): 35–47.

Bonne, Karijn, Iris Vermeir, and Wim Verbeke. "Impact of Religion on Halal Food Consumption Decision Making in Belgium." *Journal of International Food and Agribusiness Marketing* 21, no. 1, (2008): 5–26.

Bouchez, Colette. "Natural Cosmetics: Are They Healthier for Your Skin?" WebMD. http://www.webmd.com/beauty/makeup/natural-cosmetics-are-they -healthier-for-your-skin.

Bowen, John R. *Blaming Islam*. Cambridge, MA: MIT Press, 2012.

Bulliet, Richard W. *The Case for Islamo-Christian Civilization*. New York: Columbia University Press, 2004.

Burnham, Anne Mullin. "Silver Speaks." *Saudi Aramco World* 55, no. 6 (November/December 2004): 8–16. http://www.saudiaramcoworld.com/issue /200406/silver.speaks.htm.

Cain, Herman. Interview by Chris Wallace. *Fox News Sunday*, July 17, 2011. http:// www.foxnews.com/on-air/fox-news-sunday/.

Calvert, Sandra L. "Children as Consumers: Advertising and Marketing." *Future Child* 18, no. 1 (Spring 2008): 205–234.

Campbell, Kim, and Kent Davis-Packard. "How Ads Get Kids to Say, I Want It!" *Christian Science Monitor*, September 18, 2000. http://www.csmonitor .com/2000/0918/p1s1.html.

Caroço Amaro, Marisa. "Reflections about the European Debate on Integration Policies: The Case of the Swiss Ban on Minarets." *Revista Migrações* (Lisbon, ACIDI), no. 8 (April 2011): 147–150. http://www.oi.acidi.gov.pt/docs /Revista_8/Migracoes_8web147a150.pdf.

Caron, Christina. "Barbie 'Obsession': Collectors Reflect on Hobby as Pregnant

Midge Doll Is Reported Stolen." ABC News, June 24, 2011. http://abcnews .go.com/US/.

Carpenter, Eric. "Meat Not up to Islamic Law, Market Pays $527,000." *Orange County Register*, November 21, 2011. http://www.ocregister.com/articles /market-328147-anaheim-meat.html.

Carrington, Daisy. "Iran Tightens Grip on Cyberspace with 'Halal Internet.'" CNN, June 3, 2013. http://www.cnn.com/2013/06/03/world/meast/iran -internet-restrictions-halal-internet.

Casey, Scott. "Halal: A Growing Market With A Caveat: Halal Is a Market Full of Eastern Promise, but It's Also a Market Full of Potential Pitfalls." *Poultry World* 164, no. 6 (June 2010): 23–35.

Chahabi, Houchang. "How Caviar Turned Out to Be Halal." *Journal of Food and Culture* 7, no. 2 (2007).

Champ, Gemma. "World's First Muslim Model Agency Opens in New York." *The National*, February 14, 2012, http://www.thenational.ae/lifestyle/fashion/.

Chaudhary, Ajay Singh. "Simulacra of Morality: Islamic Veiling, Religious Politics and the Limits of Liberalism." *Dialectical Anthropology* 29, nos. 3–4 (2005): 349–372.

Chauhan, Baby, Gopal Kumar, Nazia Kalam, and Shahid H. Ansari. "Current Concepts and Prospects of Herbal Nutraceutical: A Review." *Journal of Advanced Pharmaceutical Technology and Research* 4, no. 1 (2010): 4–8.

Cobain, Ian, and Adam Luck. "The Beauty Products from the Skin of Executed Chinese Prisoners." *The Guardian*, September 13, 2005. http://www.guardian .co.uk/science/2005/sep/13/medicineandhealth.china.

Cody, Edward. "In France, Halal Meat Drama Enters Election Campaign." *Washington Post*, March 6, 2012. https://www.washingtonpost.com/world/europe/.

Conner, Mark, and Christopher Armitage. "Extending the Theory of Planned Behavior: A Review and Avenues for Further Research." *Journal of Applied Social Psychology* 28, no. 15, (1998): 1429–1464.

Corall, Hazel. "White Collar Crime, Consumers, and Victimization." *Crime, Law, and Social Change* 51, no. 1, (2009): 127–142.

Crossley, Lucy. "Halal Pies and Pasties Given to Muslim Prisoners Found to Contain PORK in Latest Meat Contamination Scandal." *Daily Mail*, February 2, 2013. http://www.dailymail.co.uk/news/.

Culliney, Kasey. "The GM Rice Problem: Food Fraud from China?" Food Navigator, May 7, 2012. http://www.foodnavigator-asia.com/Markets/.

Cumming-Bruce, Nick, and Steven Erlanger. "Swiss Ban Building of Minarets on Mosques." *New York Times*, November 30, 2009. http://www.nytimes.com /2009/11/30/world/europe/.

Daragahi, Borzou. "Catwalk Skirts the Mullahs." *Los Angeles Times*, May 11, 2007. http://articles.latimes.com/print/2007/may/11/world/fg-fashion11.

Daud, Norzaidi Mohd, Abdul Aziz Hazni, Noor Hana Baharudin, and Siti Fazila Shamsudin. "Identifying the Determinant Attributes of Halal Cosmetics Product That Influence Its Positioning Strategy in Malaysian Market." *Journal of Applied Sciences Research* 8, no. 1 (2012).

David, Ariel. "Italy Opens Beach For Muslim Women," *Sydney Morning Herald*, August 11, 2006, http://www.smh.com.au/news/italy/.

Deasy, Kristin. "Iranian Ex-President Rafsanjani's Daughter Released from Jail." *Global Post*, March 19, 2013. http://www.globalpost.com/dispatch/news /regions/middle-east/iran/.

Demirhan, Yasemin, Ulca Pelin, and Hamide Z. Senyuva. "Detection of Porcine DNA in Gelatine and Gelatine-Containing Processed Food Products—Halal/ Kosher Authentication." *Meat Science* 90 (2012): 686–689.

Depamede, S. N. "Development of a Rapid Immunodiagnostic Test for Pork Components in Raw Beef and Chicken Meats: A Preliminary Study." *Media Peternakan* (August 2011): 83–87.

Dewsbury, Rick. "Belgian Politician Risks Muslim Backlash after Using Teenage Daughter Dressed in Burka and Bikini for Campaign against Islam." *Daily Mail*, February 3, 2012. http://www.dailymail.co.uk/news/.

Doland, Angela. "French Debate: First It Was Burqas, Now Burgers." *Bloomberg Business*, September 1, 2010.

Dorsey, James. "Middle East Soccer Associations Campaign for Women's Right to Play." *Huffington Post*, January 22, 2013. http://www.huffingtonpost.com /james-dorsey/.

El Guindi, Fadwa. "Veiling Resistance." *Fashion Theory* 3, no. 1 (1999): 51–80.

El-Deeb, Sarah. "Saudis Bust Barbie's 'Dangers.'" CBS News, September 10, 2003. http://www.cbsnews.com/stories/2003/09/10/world/.

El-Shenawi, Eman. "British Muslims Defend Halal Slaughter after Calls for Ban." *Al Arabiya*, May 6, 2012, http://english.alarabiya.net/articles/2012/05/06 /212477.html.

English, H. Scott. "Saudis Demand McDonald's Be Punished For Happy Meal Toy That Insults Muhammed." *Inquisitr*, May 28, 2012. http://www .inquisitr.com/244094/saudis-demand-mcdonalds-be-punished-for-happy -meal-toy-that-insults-muhammed.

Erdbrink, Thomas. "Ahmadinejad and Clerics Fight over Scarves." *Washington Post*, July 22, 2011. https://www.washingtonpost.com/world/middle-east/.

Erwanto, Yuny, Mohammad Zainal Abidin, Eko Yasin Prasetyo Muslim Sugiyono, and Abdul Rohman. "Identification of Pork Contamination in Meatballs of Indonesia Local Market Using Polymerase Chain Reaction-Restriction Fragment Length Polymorphism (PCR-RFLP) Analysis." *Asian-Australas Journal of Animal Sciences* 27, no. 10 (October 2014): 1487–1492.

European Monitoring Centre on Racism and Xenophobia (EUMC). "Muslims in the European Union Discrimination and Islamophobia," Report. 2006.

Ezell, Darrell. *Beyond Cairo: US Engagement with the Muslim World*. Series in Global Public Diplomacy. New York: Palgrave Macmillan, 2012.

Fadzlillah, Nurrulhidayah A., Yaakob B. Che Man, Mohammad Aizat Jamaludin, and Suhaimi A. Rahman. "The Contribution of Science and Technology in Determining the Permissibility (Halalness) of Food Products." *Revelation and Science* 2, no. 1 (2012): 1–9.

Farhi, Paul. "A Canadian Line of Campbell's Soups Has Activists Stewing over Islamic Connection." *Washington Post*, October 17, 2010. http://www.washington post.com/wp-dyn/.

Fealy, Greg. "Consuming Islam: Commodified Religion in Contemporary Indonesia." In *Expressing Islam: Religious Life and Politics in Indonesia*. Edited by Greg Fealy and Sally White. Singapore: Institute of Southeast Asian Studies, 2008.

Fischer, Johan. "Feeding Secularism: Consuming Halal among the Malays in London." *Diaspora: A Journal of Transnational Studies* 14, no. 2/3 (2005): 275–297. http://muse.jhu.edu/journals/dsp/summary/v014/14.2.fischer.html.

———. "Religion, Science, and Markets: Modern Halal Production, Trade, and Consumption." *EMBO Reports* 9, no. 9 (September 2008): 828–831.

Fitriati, Afia R. "HijUp.com Announces Modelling Contest." *Aquila Style*, December 5, 2012. http://www.aquila-style.com/fashionbeauty/hijup-com-modelling-contest.

Geller, Pamela. "Ground Zero Mosqueteer Sharif El-Gamal Bombshell: Plan to build 39-Story Tower and [Ground Zero] Mosque." *Pamela Geller* (blog), April 5, 2015. http://pamelageller.com/2015/04/.

———. "Happy Halal Thanksgiving." *American Thinker*, November 21, 2011. http://www.americanthinker.com/2011/11/happy_halal_thanksgiving.html.

———. "A Muslim Barbie Is a Breastless Barbie!" *Pamela Geller* (blog), April 21, 2004. http://pamelageller.com/2009/04/.

Gera, Venessa. "Breathable Nail Polish a Surprise Hit with Muslims." Yahoo News, February 27, 2013. http://news.yahoo.com/breathable-nail-polish-surprise-hit-muslims-080455659.html.

Godazgar, Hossein. "Islam in the Globalised World: Consumerism and Environmental Ethics in Iran." In *Religion, Consumerism, and Sustainability: Paradise Lost?* Edited by Lyn Thomas. Basington, England: Palgrave Macmillan, 2011.

Goffman, Erving. "Attitudes and Rationalizations Regarding Body Exposure." In *Dress and Identity*. Edited by Mary Ellen Roach-Higgins, Joanne B. Eicher, and Kim K. P. Johnson. New York: Fairchild, 1995.

———. *Behavior in Public Places: Notes on the Social Organization of Gatherings*. New York: Free Press of Glencoe, 1963.

Gökariksel, Banu, and Anna J. Secor. "Islamic-ness in the Life of a Commodity: Veiling-Fashion in Turkey." *Transactions of the Institute of British Geographers* 35. no. 3 (2010): 313–333.

———. "New Transnational Geographies of Islamism, Capitalism, and Subjectivity: The Veiling-Fashion Industry in Turkey." *Royal Geographical Society* (2008): 6–18.

———. "'You Can't Know How They Are Inside': The Ambivalence of Veiling and Discourses of the Other in Turkey." *Religion and Place* (2013): 95–113.

Göle, Nilüfer. "The Voluntary Adoption of Islamic Stigma Symbols." *Social Research: An International Quarterly* 70, no. 3 (Fall 2003): 809–828.

Gooch, Liz. "Malaysia Seeks to Gain Bigger Role in Halal Food." *New York Times*, January 1, 2011. http://query.nytimes.com/gst/fullpage.html?res=9C05E6DE1739F932A35752C0A9679D8B63&pagewanted=all.

Gökariksel, Banu, and Anna J. Secor. "New Transnational Geographies of Islamism, Capitalism and Subjectivity: The Veiling-Fashion Industry in Turkey." *Royal Geographical Society* 41, no. 1 (2009): 6–18.

Grandin, Temple, and Joe M. Regenstein. "Religious Slaughter And Animal Welfare: A Discussion For Meat Scientists." *Meat Focus International* (March 1994): 115–123.

Grant, John. *Made With: Brands, Creatives, and Entrepreneurs from the Emerging Global Interland*. London: LID, 2013.

Grant, Kelli B. "8 Food Frauds on Your Shopping List." *Market Watch*, April 16, 2012, http://www.smartmoney.com/spend/deal-of-the-day/8-food-frauds-on -your-shopping-list-1334616484577.

Guha, Rohin. "Keen for Green: Iran's Underground Fashion Week." *BlackBook*, September 23, 2009. http://www.bbook.com/fashion/keen-for-green-irans -underground-fashion-week/.

Halasa, Malu, and Rana Salam. *The Secret Life of Syrian Lingerie: Intimacy and Design*. San Francisco: Chronicle Books, 2008.

Hamid, Tawfik. "How Western Tolerance Breeds Intolerance in the Muslim World." *Free Thought Nation*, September 27, 2011. http://freethoughtnation.com /contributing-writers/72-tawfik-hamid/598-how-western-tolerance-breeds -intolerance-in-the-muslim-world.html.

———. "Western Tolerance Breeds Muslim Intolerance." *Newsmax*, September 20, 2011. http://www.newsmax.com/TawfikHamid/Western-Tolerance-Muslim -Intolerance/2011/09/20/id/411707.

Hampson, Rick. "For Families of Muslim 9/11 Victims, a New Pain." *USA Today*, September 3, 2010, updated September 9, 2010. http://www.usatoday.com /news/nation/2010-09-03-1Amuslims911_CV_N.htm.

Hamzeh, Manal, and Kimberly L. Oliver. "'Because I Am Muslim, I Cannot Wear a Swimsuit': Muslim Girls Negotiate Participation Opportunities." *Research Quarterly For Exercise and Sport* 83, no. 2 (2012): 330–339.

Hannity, Sean. "'Ground Zero Mosque' Imam Sets the Record Straight on 'Hannity.'" Fox News, May 24, 2012. http://www.foxnews.com/on-air /hannity/2012/05/24/.

Hardy, A. D., H. H. Sutherland, and R. Vaishnav. "A Study of the Composition of Some Eye Cosmetics (Kohls) Used in the United Arab Emirates." *Journal of Ethnopharmacology* 80 (2002): 137–145.

Hardy, A. D., R. Vaishnav, S. S. Z. al-Kharusi, H. H. Sutherland, and M. A. Worthing. "Composition of Eye Cosmetics (Kohls) Used in Oman." *Journal of Ethnopharmacology* 60, no. 3, (1998): 223–234.

Harkness, Geoff, and Samira Islam. "Muslim Female Athletes and the Hijab." *Contexts* 10, no. 4 (October 2011): 64–65.

Harrington, Dan. "Civet Coffee the Most Expensive Coffee in the World." Gourmet Coffee Lovers, October 18, 2009. http://www.gourmetcoffeelovers.com /civet-coffee-the-most-expensive-coffee-in-the-world.

Harrington, Rory. "Packaging Highlighted as Increasing Source of Halal Food Contamination." *Food Production Daily*, July 6, 2012. http://www.food productiondaily.com/Safety-Regulation/Packaging-highlighted-as-increasing -source-of-Halal-food-contamination.

Harrison, Frances. "Crackdown in Iran over Dress Codes." BBC News, April 27, 2007, http://news.bbc.co.uk/2/hi/middle_east/6596933.stm.

Hashim, Darhim. "Redefining Regulatory Procedures in the Halal Industry." Paper presented at the 6th World Halal Forum, Kuala Lumpur, April 4, 2011, organized by Islamic Chamber of Commerce and Industry. Proceedings, International Halal Integrity Alliance (2011), http://worldhalalforum.org

/WHF2011speakerpresentation/Session%203-RedefiningRegulatory ProceduresintheHalalIndustrybyDarhim%20Hashim.pdf.

Hashim, Nazlida Muhamad, and Dick Mizerski. "The Constructs Mediating Religions' Influence on Buyers and Consumers." *Journal of Islamic Marketing* 1, no. 2 (2010): 124–135.

———. "Exploring Muslim Consumers' Information Sources for Fatwa Rulings on Products and Behaviors." *Journal of Islamic Marketing* 1, no. 1 (2010): 37–50.

Hashim, Puziah. "Alternative Ingredients for Halal Cosmetic and Personal Care Products." Proceedings, 3rd International Symposium on IMT-GT. Halal Science and Management, Universiti Putra, Malaysia, December 21–22, 2009.

Haski, Pieer. "This Halal Meat Upset Leaves Nicolas Sarkozy in a Bad Way." *The Guardian*, March 8, 2012. http://www.guardian.co.uk/commentisfree/2012/mar/08/halal-meat-nicolas-sarkozy-marine-le-pen.

Havinga, Tetty. "Regulating Halal and Kosher Foods: Different Arrangements between State, Industry and Religious Actors." *Erasmus Law Review* 3, no. 4 (2010). http://papers.ssrn.com/sol3/papers.cfm?abstract_id=1815253.

Haw, Kaye. "From Hijab To Jilbab and the 'Myth' of British Identity: Being Muslim in Contemporary Britain a Half-Generation On." *Race Ethnicity and Education* 12. no. 3 (2009): 363–378.

Hedgecoe Guy. "Local Mosque Row a Spanish Problem." *Irish Times*, Tuesday, July 10, 2012. http://www.irishtimes.com/newspaper/world/2012/0710/1224319719491.html.

Heidarzadeh, Kambiz Hanzaee, and Shahrzad Chitsaz. "A Review of Influencing Factors and Constructs on the Iranian Women's Islamic Fashion Market." *Interdisciplinary Journal of Research in Business* 1, no. 4. (April 2011): 94–100.

Helbig, Catherine. "What Is Oud (Oudh)?" About Style. http://beauty.about.com/od/fragranc1/a/What-is-Oud.htm.

Heyer, Hazel. "Muslim Bikini Stirs Controversy in Europe." ETN, October 19, 2009, http://www.eturbonews.com/12321/muslim-bikini-stirs-controversy-europe.

Horswell, Cindy. "Not Ground Zero, but Katy Mosque Also Stirs Passions." *Houston Chronicle*, September 7, 2010. http://www.chron.com/life/houston-belief/article/Not-Ground-Zero-but-Katy-mosque-also-stirs-1717134.php.

Hoye, Sarah. "More than Able to Hold Her Own, Girl Gets Boot from Catholic Football League." CNN, February 14, 2013, http://www.cnn.com/2013/02/14/us/philadelphia-archdiocese-boys-only-football.

Huda, N., A. Aminah, and A. S. Babji, "Halal Issues in Processing of Surimi and Surimi-Based Food Product," *Infofish* 5 (1999): 45–47.

Hudson, Alexandra. "'Allah's Tailors' Gaining Profile in Turkey." Reuters. Posted in *Veiling Fashion*, November 13, 2010. http://veilingfashion.unc.edu/news-allahs-tailors.php.

Huff, E. "Toxic Burden: Women Put 515 Chemicals on Their Faces Every Day." *Natural News*, December 29, 2009. http://www.naturalnews.com/027822_cosmetics_chemicals.html.

Hume, Jessica. "Marriage Advice by the Book." *The National*, July 11, 2009. http://www.thenational.ae/news/uae-news/marriage-advice-by-the-book.

Hurd, Dale. "Muslim Halal Food Sales Supporting Terrorism?" CBN News, January 9, 2011. http://www.cbn.com/cbnnews/world/2011/january/muslim-halal-food-sales-supporting-terrorism.

Hussain, Nazia. "Expert Opinions on Marketing to Muslims." *Marketing Week*, June 24, 2010. http://www.marketingweek.co.uk/expert-opinions-on-market ing-to-muslims/3014949.article.

Ireland, John, and Soha Abdollah Rajabzadeh. "UAE Consumer Concerns about *Halal* Products." *Journal of Islamic Marketing* 2, no. 3 (2011): 274–283.

Izharuddin, Alicia. "Malaysia's Commodified Islam." *Malaysian Insider*, November 9, 2012, http://www.themalaysianinsider.com/sideviews/article/malaysias -commodified-islam-alicia-izharuddin.

Jaben-Eilon, Jan. "Luxe Lingerie Goes Global." Womanetics. http://www .womenetics.com/Global-Initiatives/luxe-lingerie-goes-global.

Jafari, A. "Two Tales of a City: An Exploratory Study of Cultural Consumption among Iranian Youth." *Iranian Studies* 40, no. 3 (2007): 367–383.

Jallad, Karim N., and Hartmut G. Hedderich. "Characterization of a Hazardous Eyeliner (Kohl) by Confocal Raman Microscopy." *Journal of Hazardous Materials* B124 (2005): 236–240.

Janmohamed, Shelina. "Guest Post: Building Halal Brands." *Beyond Brics* (blog), *Financial Times*, February 10, 2012. http://blogs.ft.com/beyond-brics/2012/02 /10/guest-post-building-halal-brands/#axzz2RhNuEgJc.

———. "Marketing in the Muslim World: Understanding the Hajj." *Spark Sheet*, November 7, 2011. http://sparksheet.com/branding-islam-sponsoring-the-hajj.

———. "Opinion: The Politics of Halal." *Halal Focus*, March 29, 2013. http:// halalfocus.net/opinion-the-politics-of-halal.

Johnson, Toni. "Europe: Integrating Islam." *Backgrounder*, July 25, 2011. Council on Foreign Relations. http://www.cfr.org/religion/europe-integrating-islam /p8252.

Johnston, Sholeh. "Persian Rap: The Voice of Modern Iran's Youth." *Journal of Persianate Studies* 1, no. 1 (2008): 102–119.

Jones, Benjamin. "Western Hoteliers Cater to Muslim Travelers." *Hotel News Now*, January 15, 2013. http://www.hotelnewsnow.com/Article/9703/western -hoteliers-cater-to-Muslim-travelers.

Jones, Rachel Bailey. "Case Study: The Veiled Women in the Visual Imagination of the West." *Postcolonial Representations of Women Explorations of Educational Purpose* 18 (2011): 135–167.

Kalliny, Morris, and Angela Hausman. "The Impact of Cultural and Religious Values on Consumer's Adoption of Innovation." *Academy of Marketing Studies Journal* 11, no. 1 (January 2007): 125–136.

Kaufman, Joe. "Can Buying Food Contribute to Terrorism?" *Frontpage Mag*, March 25, 2013, http://frontpagemag.com/2013/joe-kaufman/can-buying -food-contribute-to-terrorism.

Kern, Soeren. "France Goes Halal—The Halal Issue Is about More than Just Meat." Gatestone Institute, February 28, 2012. http://www.gatestoneinstitute .org/2886/france-halal.

Khamis, Susie. "Braving the Burqini: Re-Branding the Australian Beach." *Cultural Geographies* 13, no. 3 (2010): 379–390.

Khan, Ayub. "TMO Story about Fake Halal Causes $500,000 Fine against Fraudster." *Muslim Observer*, November 23, 2011, http://muslimmedianetwork.com /mmn/?p=9426.

Kirpalani, Reshma. "'Ground Zero Mosque' Clears Legal Hurdle to Build." ABC

News, July 13, 2011. http://abcnews.go.com/US/ground-mosque-wins-legal
-battle-build/story?id=14062701#.UAhgi7_iObI.

Kotler, P., and D. Gertner. "Country as Brand, Product, and Beyond: A Place Marketing and Brand Management Perspective." *Journal of Brand Management* 9,
nos. 4/5:249–261.

Kottman, Sina Lucia. "Mocking and Miming the Moor: Staging of the 'Self' and
'Other' on Spain's Borders with Morocco." *Journal of Mediterranean Studies*
20, no. 1 (2011): 107–136. http://www.academia.edu/903191/Mocking_and
_Miming_the_Moor_Staging_of_the_Self_and_Other_on_Spains_Borders
_with_Morocco.

Kreinath, Jens. "(Un)veiled: Muslim Women Talk about Hijab by Ines Hofmann
Kanna." *American Anthropologist* 112, no. 4 (December 2010): 654–655.

Kulish, Nicholas. "In Germany, Xenophobia Diverted by Open Doors." *New
York Times*, March 23, 2010. http://www.nytimes.com/2010/03/24/world
/europe/24germany.html.

Laurence, Johnathan. "In the Year 2030: Will Europe Become the 'Colony of Islam' That Some Predict? A Hard Look at the Future." *Boston College Magazine*, Summer 2010. http://bcm.bc.edu/issues/summer_2010/features/in-the
-year-2030.html#.

Lekouch, N., A. Sedki, A. Nejmeddine, and S. Gamon. "Lead and Traditional Moroccan Pharmacopoeia." *Science of the Total Environment* (December 2001):
39–43.

Leone, Massimo. "My Schoolmate: Protest Music in Present-Day Iran." *Critical
Discourse Studies* 9, no. 4 (2012): 347–362.

Lerner, Pablo, and Alfredo Mordechai Rabello. "The Prohibition of Ritual Slaughtering (Kosher Shechita and Halal) and Freedom of Religion of Minorities."
Journal of Law and Religion 22, no. 1 (2006–2007). Posted at Instituto Italiano di Bioetica, http://www.istitutobioetica.org/Bioetica%20sociale/multi
culturalismo/Lerner%20Rabello%20Macellazione.htm.

Lewis, Bernard. "Islam and the West: A Conversation with Bernard Lewis." Pew
Forum on Religion and Public Life, April 27, 2006, Washington, DC. Posted at
http://catholiceducation.org/articles/history/world/wh0117.htm.

Lindsey, Tim. "Monopolising Islam: The Indonesian Ulama Council and State
Regulation of the 'Islamic Economy.'" *Bulletin of Indonesian Economic Studies*
48, no. 2 (2012): 256–257.

Liogier, Raphael. "Islam: A Scapegoat for Europe's Decadence." *Harvard International Review*, January 6, 2011. http://hir.harvard.edu/islam-a-scapegoat-for
-europe-s-decadence/.

Magister, Sandro. "Eurabia Has a Capital: Rotterdam." *Chiesa*, May 19, 2009.
http://chiesa.espresso.repubblica.it/articolo/1338480?eng=y.

Masr, Bikya. "Lebanese Sheikh Calls for Toy to Be Banned, Says It Insults Prophet's
Wife." *Masress*, June 23, 2012. http://www.masress.com/en/bikyamasr/70562.

Mat Som, Ahmad Puad, and Mohammad Bader Badarneh. "Tourist Satisfaction
and Repeat Visitation: Toward a New Comprehensive Model." *International
Journal of Human and Social Sciences* 6, no. 1 (2011): 38–45.

Matuska, Nicole. "The Development of Women's Football in Morocco." *Viewpoints* special edition, *Sports and the Middle East*, May 2010, 37–39. Middle East

Institute, Washington, DC. Posted at https://www.mcgill.ca/sociology/files/sociology/2010_—_sports_and_the_middle_east.pdf.

Mawani, Sharmina, and Anjoon Mukadam. "Living in a Material World: Religious Commodification and Resistance." In *Religion, Consumerism, and Sustainability: Paradise Lost?*. Edited by Lyn Thomas. Basington, England: Palgrave Macmillan, 2011.

McGinley, Shane. "World's First Modeling Agency Target Gulf Talent," *Arabian News*, February 26, 2012, http://www.arabianbusiness.com/world-s-first-muslim-modeling-agency-target-gulf-talent-445661.html.

McGinnis, Michael, Jennifer Appleton Gootman, and Vivica I. Kraak, eds. "Food and Beverage Marketing to Children and Youth." In *Food Marketing to Children and Youth: Threat or Opportunity?*. Committee on Food Marketing and the Diets of Children and Youth. Institute of Medicine of the National Academies. Washington, DC: National Academies Press, 2006.

McKenna, Minkus D. "The Pursuit of Halal." *Progressive Grocer* 86 (2007): 17–27.

McNeal, James U. "From Savers to Spenders: How Children Became a Consumer Market." Center for Media Literacy, n.d. http://www.medialit.org/reading-room/savers-spenders-how-children-became-consumer-market.

Menely, Anne. "Fashions and Fundamentalism in Fin-De-Siècle Yemen: Chador Barbie and Islamic Socks." *Cultural Anthropology* 22, no. 2 (May 2007): 214–243.

Mesure, Susie. "Move Over Organic—Halal Is the Latest Food Craze." *The Independent*, September 26, 2013. http://www.independent.co.uk/life-style/food-and-drink/news/move-over-organic-the-new-big-business-in-food-is-halal-8831791.html.

Milallos, Theresa R. "Muslim Veil as Politics: Political Autonomy, Women and *Syariah* Islam in Aceh." *Contemporary Islam* 1, no. 3 (December 2007): 289–301.

Mirghani, M. E. S., I. Jaswir, H. M. Salih, Z. H. Yumi, B. Hashim, and Y. B. Che Man. "Special Oils for Halal Cosmetics." *Proceedings*, 3rd International Symposium on IMT-GT, Halal Science and Management, Halal Products Research Institute, Universiti Putra, Malaysia, December 21–22, 2009: 140–142.

Mishra, Smeeta, and Faegheh Shirazi. "Hybrid Identities: American Muslim Women Speak." *Gender, Place, and Culture: A Journal of Feminist Geography* 17, no. 2 (April 2010): 191–209.

Mohsina, Fatema, Foyez Ahmed Bhuiyan, and Mostaq Ahmad Bhuiyan. "*Shari'a* Compliance in Building Identified Islamic Brands." *Islamic Management and Business*. Special issue of *European Journal of Business and Management* 5, no. 11 (2013): 10–16.

Montague-Jones, Guy. "Consumer Lobby Group Slams Cosmetics Safety in US." *Cosmetics Design*, October 1, 2007. http://www.cosmeticsdesign.com/Market-Trends/Consumer-lobby-group-slams-cosmetics-safety-in-US.

Montanno, Daniel E., and Danuta Kasprzyk. "Theory of Reasoned Action, Theory of Planned Behavior, and the Integrated Behavioral Model." In *Health Behavior and Health Education. Theory, Research, and Practice*. Edited by Karen Glanz, Barbara K. Rimer, and K. Wiswanath, 67–92. San Francisco: John Wiley and Sons, 2008.

Moore, Elizabeth S. "It's Child's Play: Advergaming and the Online Marketing of Food to Children." Report. Kaiser Family Foundation, July 2006. http://kaiserfamilyfoundation.files.wordpress.com/2013/01/7536.pdf.

Moors, Annelies. "'Discover the Beauty of Modesty' Islamic Fashion Online." In *Modest Fashion: Styling Bodies, Mediating Faith.* Edited by Reina Lewis. London: I. B. Tauris, 2013.

Moors, Annelies, and Emma Tarlo. "Muslim Fashion," *Fashion Theory* 11, no. 2/3 (2007): 1–30.

Mossière, Géraldine. "Modesty and Style in Islamic Attire: Refashioning Muslim Garments in a Western Context." *Contemporary Islam* 6, no. 2 (July 2012): 115–134.

Muchtar, Bari. "A Fatwa on Coffee?" Radio Netherlands Worldwide, July 23, 2010. http://www.rnw.nl/english/article/a-fatwa-coffee.

Muhammed, Qasim. "America's Costly Halal Food." *Halal Journal,* March 29, 2009. http://www.halaljournal.com/article/3426/america-costly-halal-food.

Mukhtar, Arshia, and Muhammad Mohsin Butt. "Intention to Choose Halal Products: The Role of Religiosity." *Journal of Islamic Marketing* 3, no. 2 (2012): 108–120.

Murard-Yovanovitch, Flore. "Institutional Racism and Ethnic Profiling in Italy." *Reset DOC,* April 24, 2011. http://www.resetdoc.org/story/00000022114.

Murdoch, Jim. "Protecting the Right to Freedom of Thought, Conscience, and Religion under the European Convention on Human Rights." Council of Europe Human Rights Handbooks. Strasbourg: Council of Europe, 2012. http://www.coe.int/t/dgi/hr-natimplement/Source/documentation/hb09_right freedom_en.pdf.

Murray, Sarah J. "Unveiling Myths: Muslim Women and Sport." Women's Sports Foundation, 2003. http://www.womenssportsfoundation.org/cgibin/iowa/issues/part/article.html?record=863.

Murugaiah, Chandrika, Noor Zainon Mohd, Mastakim Maimunah, Lesley Maurice Bilung, Selamat Jinap, and Radu Son. "Meat Species Identification and Halal Authentication Analysis Using Mitochondrial DNA." *Meat Science* 83, (2009): 57–61.

Naficy, Hamid. "Veiled Visions/Powerful Presences: Women in Postrevolutionary Iranian Cinema." In *In the Eye of the Storm: Women in Post-Revolutionary Iran.* Edited by Mahnez Afkhami and Erika Friedl, 131–150. London: I. B. Tauris, 1994.

Nakyinsige, Khadijah, Yaakob Bin Che Man, and Awis Qurni Sazili. "Halal Authenticity Issues in Meat and Meat Products." *Meat Science* 91 (2012): 207–214.

Nasir, Mohd, Azah Norman, Shukor Fauzi, and Masilyana Azmi. "An RFID-Based Validation System for Halal Food," *International Arab Journal of Information Technology* 8, no. 2 (2011): 204–211. http://www.iajit.org/PDF/vol.8,no.2/13-1394.pdf.

Nasr, Vali. *Forces of Fortune. The Rise of the New Muslim Middle Class and What It Will Mean for Our World.* New York: Simon and Schuster, 2009.

Nelson, Dean. "Mumbai, Home of India's Increasingly Raunchy Bollywood Film Industry, Is to Ban Mannequins Modeling Lingerie from Its Shop Windows to Stop the City's Men Having 'Impure Thoughts.'" *The Telegraph,* May 28, 2013. http://www.telegraph.co.uk/news/worldnews/asia/india/10084272/

Mumbai-bans-lingerie-clad-mannequins-to-save-men-from-impure-thoughts
.html.

Nelson, Laura J. "Federal Judge Sides with Tennessee Mosque in Time for Ramadan." *Los Angeles Times*, July 18, 2012. http://articles.latimes.com/2012/jul/18/nation/la-na-nn-tennessee-mosque-ramadan-20120718.

Neville, N. G., M. von Wenzlawowicz, R. M. Alam, H. M. Anil, T. Yesildere, and A. Silva-Fletcher. "False Aneurysms in Carotid Arteries Of Cattle and Water Buffalo during Shechita and Halal Slaughter." *Meat Science* 79, no. 2 (June 2008): 285–288.

Nichol, Katie. "First International Conference on Halal Cosmetics and Toiletries." *Cosmetics Design*, March 10, 2010. http://www.cosmeticsdesign-europe.com/Market-Trends/First-international-conference-on-Halal-cosmetics-and-toiletries.

———. "Opportunity Knocks for Natural and Organic Halal Cosmetics." *Cosmetics Design*, November 8, 2012. http://www.cosmeticsdesign.com/Market-Trends/Opportunity-knocks-for-natural-and-organic-halal-cosmetics.

Nguyen, Phong Tuan. "A Comparative Study of the Intention to Buy Organic Food between Consumers in Northern and Southern Vietnam." *AU-GSB E-Journal* 4, no. 2 (December 2011): 100–111. http://www.graduate.au.edu/Academic/AU-GSB%20e-Journal/Current%20Issue/Publication3/Phong.pdf.

Nilan, Pamela. "Muslim Media and Youth in Globalizing Southeast Asia." In *Media Consumption and Everyday Life in Asia*. Edited by Youna Kim. New York: Routledge, 2008.

———. "The Reflexive Youth Culture of Devout Muslim Youth in Indonesia." In *Global Youth? Hybrid Identities, Plural Worlds*. Edited by Pam Nilan and Carles Fiexa. New York: Routledge, 2006.

Nisa, Eva F. "The Internet Subculture of Indonesian Face-Veiled Women." *International Journal of Cultural Studies* 16, no. 3 (May 2013): 241–255.

Nkomo, Sibusiso. "MJC Denies 'Ducking and Diving.'" IoL News, January 19, 2012. http://www.iol.co.za/news/south-africa/western-cape/.

Norman, Azah Anir, Mohd Hairul Nizam Md Nasir, Shukor Sanim Mohd Fauzi, and Masilyana Azmi. "Consumer Acceptance of RFID-Enabled Services in Validating Halal Status." Paper presented at ISCIT 9th International Symposium on Communications and Information Technology, Incheon, South Korea, September 28–30, 2009: 911–914.

NNorom, I. C., J. C. Igwe, and C. G. Oji-Nnorom. "Trace Metal Contents of Facial (Make-Up) Cosmetics Commonly Used in Nigeria." *African Journal of Biotechnology* 4, no. 10 (October 2005): 1133–1138.

Nooshin, Laudan. "Underground: Rock Music and Youth Discourses in Iran." *Iranian Studies* 38, no. 3 (2005): 463–494.

Nurjuliana, M., Y. B. Che Man, D. Mat Hashim, and A. K. S. Mohamed. "Rapid Identification of Pork for Halal Authentication Using the Electronic Nose and Gas Chromatography Mass Spectrometer with Headspace Analyzer." *Meat Science* 88 (2011): 638–644.

Nuthall, Keith. "The Netherlands Pushes for Labels on Non-Stun Meat." *Global Meat News*, July 17, 2013. http://www.globalmeatnews.com/Industry-Markets/.

Ormond, Meghann. "Strategic Cosmopolitan Appeal: The Expediency of National Cultural Diversity in the Scripting of Malaysia as a Medical Tourism Destination." Paper presented at the conference Transnational Motilities for Care: State Market and Family Dynamics in Asia, Malaysia, September 9–11, 2009.

Osella, Caroline, and Filippo Osella. "Muslim Style in South India." *Fashion Theory* 11, no. 2/3 (2007): 1–20.

Pandey, Manisha, Rohit K. Verma, and Shubhini A. Saraf. "Nutraceuticals: New Era of Medicine and Health." *Asian Journal of Pharmaceutical and Clinical Research* 3, no. 1 (January–March): 11–15.

Paraszczuk, Joanna. "Saudi and Iranian Women Fight for Right to Compete." *Jerusalem Post*, August 3, 2012. http://www.jpost.com/middle-east/saudi-and-iranian-women-fight-for-right-to-compete.

Parry, C., and J. Eaton. "Kohl: A Lead-Hazardous Eye Makeup from the Third World to the First World." *Environmental Health Perspectives* 94 (August 1991): 121–123.

Parvez, Z. Fareen. "Debating the Burqa in France: The Antipolitics of Islamic Revival." *Qualitative Sociology* 34, no. 2 (June 2011): 287–312.

Pereira, Jared. "'Halal' Elevators at Four-Star Hotel." *FMT News*, January 9, 2013. http://www.freemalaysiatoday.com/category/nation/2013/01/09/halal-elevators-at-four-star-hotel.

Pew Forum on Religion and Public Life. "The Future of the Global Muslim Population Projections for 2010–2030." Analysis, January 27, 2011. http://www.pewforum.org/the-future-of-the-global-muslim-population.aspx.

Pfetten, Verena von. "Naked Mannequin Causes Decency Debate in Nebraska." *Styleite*, July 13, 2010, http://www.styleite.com/retail/naked-mannequin-nebraska.

Phadnis, Shilpa. "Indian Brands Get 'Halal' Stamp, Set to Woo Muslims in Global Markets." *Times of India*, May 21, 2012. http://timesofindia.indiatimes.com/business/india-business/.

Pillow, Andrew. "Muslim Women Participation in 2012 London Olympics Is the Start, Not the Goal." *Bleacher Report*, July 27, 2012, http://bleacherreport.com/articles/1275194-muslim-women-participation-in-2012-london-olympics-is-the-start-not-the-goal.

Pink, Johanna. Introduction to *Muslim Societies in the Age of Mass Consumption: Politics, Culture, and Identity between the Local and the Global*. Edited by Johanna Pink. Newcastle-upon-Tyne, England: Cambridge Scholars, 2009.

Pitman, Simon. "California Cosmetics Bill Becomes Law." *Cosmetics Design*, October 12, 2005. http://www.cosmeticsdesign.com/market-trends/california-cosmetics-bill-becomes-law.

———. "Industry Hits Back at EWG Product Safety Review," *Cosmetics Design*, October 26, 2005. http://www.cosmeticsdesign.com/market-trends/industry-hits-back-at-ewg-product-safety-review.

———. "Study Points to Cancer-Risk from Petroleum-Based Cosmetics." *Cosmetics Design*, February 12, 2007. http://www.cosmeticsdesign.com/formulation-science/study-points-to-cancer-risk-from-petroleum-based-cosmetics.

Podivinsky, Ellen, and John Mackay. "High Resolution Melting Analysis as a Novel

DNA Assay for Meat Speciation." Presented at Queenstown Molecular Biology meeting, Queenstown, New Zealand, August 29–31, 2011.

Pointing, John, and Yunes Teinaz. "Halal Meat and Food Crime in UK." Paper presented at the International Halal Food Seminar, Islamic University College of Malaysia, September 2004.

Poynting, Scott, and Victoria Mason. "The Resistible Rise of Islamophobia: Anti-Muslim Racism in the UK and Australia before 11 September 2001." *Journal of Sociology* 43, no. 1 (2007): 61–86. http://jos.sagepub.com/cgi/content/abstract /43/1/61.

Qasimi, Noor al-. "Shampoo: Editing, Advertising, and Codes of Modesty on Saudi Arabian Television." *Camera Obscura* 26, no. 2 (2011): 91–121.

Rabasat, Angel, and F. Stephen Larrabee. *The Rise of Political Islam in Turkey.* National Defense Research Institute. Published by RAND Corporation, 2008. http://www.rand.org/.

Ramadan, Tariq. "My Compatriots' Vote to Ban Minarets Is Fuelled by Fear." *The Guardian*, November 29, 2009. http://www.theguardian.com/commentisfree /belief/2009/nov/29/swiss-vote-ban-minarets-fear.

Rao, Vidya. "Halal Beauty Products' Appeal Goes beyond the Muslim Market." *Today Show*, MSNBC. Posted in *Muslim Village*, August 19, 2010. http://muslim village.com/2010/08/19/5478/halal-beauty-products-appeal-goes-beyond -the-muslim-market.

Rarick, Charles, Gideon Falk, Casimir Barczyk, and Lori Feldman. "Is It Kosher? No, It's Halal: A New Frontier in Niche Marketing." *Proceedings of the International Academy for Case Studies* 18, no. 1 (2011): 51–56.

———. "Marketing to Muslims: The Growing Importance of Halal Products." *Journal of the International Academy for Case Studies* 18, no. 1 (January 2012): 81–86.

Riaz, Mian N. "Fundamentals of Halal Foods and Certification." *Prepared Foods* 179, no. 1 (January 2010): 171–176. http://www.preparedfoods.com/articles /article-fundamentals-of-halal-foods-and-certification-january-2010.

Riaz, Mian N., and Muhammad M. Chaudry. *Halal Food Production.* New York: CRC Press, 2010.

Richardson, Robin. "Islamophobia or Anti-Muslim Racism—or What? Concepts and Terms Revisited." Lecture, University of Birmingham, England, December 9, 2009.

Richardson, Valerie. "Aborted Fetus Cells Used in Beauty Creams." *Washington Times*, November 3, 2009. http://www.washingtontimes.com/news/2009/nov /3/aborted-fetus-cells-used-in-anti-aging-products/?page=all.

Rivas, Jorge. "Young Muslim Designer Puts Her Fashions on New York Runways." *Colorlines*, November 4, 2011. http://colorlines.com/archives/2011/11/ muslim_designer_puts_her_fashions_on_the_runway.html.

Roach-Higgins, Mary Ellen, and Joanne B. Eicher. "Dress and Identity." *Textiles Research Journal* 10, no. 4 (Summer 1992): 1–8.

Robbins, Richard. *Global Problem and the Culture of Capitalism.* Boston: Allyn and Bacon, 2005.

Rohman, Abdul, and Yaakob B. Che Man. "Analysis of Cod Liver Oil Adulteration

Using Fourier Transform Infrared (FTIR) Spectroscopy." *Journal of the American Oil Chemists' Society* 86, no. 12 (2009): 1149–1153.

———. "Analysis of Lard in Cream Cosmetics Formulations Using FT-IR Spectroscopy and Chemometrics." *Middle-East Journal of Scientific Research* 7, no. 5 (2011): 726–732.

———. "Analysis of Pig Derivatives for Halal Authentication Studies." *Food Reviews International* 28, no. 1 (2012): 97–112.

Rudnyckyj, Daromir. "Spiritual Economies: Islam and Neoliberalism in Contemporary Indonesia." *Cultural Anthropology* 24, no. 1 (February 2009): 104–141.

Saeed, Mohammad, Zafar U. Ahmed, and Syeda-Masppda Mukhtar. "International Marketing Ethics from an Islamic Perspective: A Value Maximization Approach." *Journal of Business Ethics* 32, no. 2 (July 2001): 127–142.

Sagita, Dessy. "BPOM Discovers More Pork in 3 'Halal' Beef Jerky Brands." *Jakarta Globe*, June 2, 2009. http://www.thejakartaglobe.com/news/bpom -discovers-more-pork-in-3-halal-beef-jerky-brands/278644.

Salehudin, Imam. "Halal Literacy and Intention of Muslim Consumers to Switch from Products without Halal Label: A Measurement and Validation Study in Indonesia." Department of Management, Faculty of Economics, University of Indonesia. Posted at Social Science Research Network, June 13, 2010. http://ssrn .com/abstract=2004762.

Salzman, Marian. "Marketing to Muslims." *Ad Week*, April 30, 2007. http://www .adweek.com/news/advertising-branding/marketing-muslims-94650.

Samuel, Henry. "French Ban Muslim Woman from Pool for Wearing 'Burkini' Swimsuit." *The Telegraph*, August 12, 2009. http://www.telegraph.co.uk /news/worldnews/europe/france/6017524/French-ban-Muslim-woman -from-pool-for-wearing-burkini-swimsuit.html.

Sandikci, Özlem. "Researching Islamic Marketing: Past and Future Perspectives." *Journal of Islamic Marketing* 2, no. 3 (2011): 246–258.

Sandikci, Özlem, and Güliz Ger. "Constructing and Representing the Islamic Consumer in Turkey." *Fashion Theory* 11, no. 2/3 (2007): 189–210.

Sapsted, David. "Halal Dispute over Kentucky Fried Chicken." *The National*, March 15, 2010. http://www.thenational.ae/news/world/europe/halal -dispute-over-kentucky-fried-chicken.

Sarkar, Monica. "H&M's Latest Look: Hijab-Wearing Muslim Model Stirs Debate." CNN, October 4, 2015. http://www.cnn.com/2015/09/29/europe/ hm-hijab-model/.

Sawer, Patrick. "Swimmers Are Told to Wear Burkinis." *The Telegraph*, August 15, 2009. http://www.telegraph.co.uk/news/politics/6034706/Swimmers -are-told-to-wear-burkinis.html.

Sayed, Antar al-. "Islamic Bathing Suits Make Huge Sales in Egypt." *Al Arabiya*, July 15, 2010. http://www.alarabiya.net/articles/2010/07/15/113943.html.

Schuiz, Dorothea E. "Competing Sartorial Assertions of Femininity and Muslim Identity in Mali." *Fashion Theory* 11, no. 2/3 (2007): 253–280.

Schulze, W., H. Schultze-Petzold, A. S. Hazem, and R. Gross. "Experiments for the Objectification of Pain and Consciousness during Conventional (Captive Bolt Stunning) and Religiously Mandated ('Ritual Cutting')." Translation by Sahib M. Bleher. *Deutsche Tieraerztliche Wochenschrift* (German Veterinary

Weekly) 85 (1978): 62–66. Posted at Mustaquim Art and Literature. http://www.mustaqim.co.uk/halalstudy.htm.

Selwa, A., F. Al-Hazzaa, and Peter M. Krahn. "Kohl: A Hazardous Eyeliner." *International Ophthalmology* 19, no. 2. (1995): 83–88.

Sen, Gautam. "Neo-Imperialism, the West and Islam." *Economic and Political Weekly* 36, no. 43 (October 27, 2001). http://www.epw.in/commentary/neo-imperialism-west-and-islam.html.

Serkal, Mariam M. al-. "Sharjah Shops Told to 'Behead' Mannequins." *Free Republic*, February 20, 2008. http://www.freerepublic.com/focus/f-news/1973596/posts.

Sewell, Anne. "Pork Found in Halal Food in Norway and UK." *Digital Journal*, March 15, 2013. http://digitaljournal.com/article/345771#ixzz2RY3XT8A2.

Shah, Anup. "Children as Consumers." *Global Issues*, November 21, 2010. http://www.globalissues.org/article/237/children-as-consumers.

Shingler, Benjamin. "FIFA Panel Officially Allows Turbans, Hijabs In Soccer after Quebec Controversy." Canadian Press. Posted at CTV News Montreal, March 1, 2014. http://montreal.ctvnews.ca/fifa-panel-officially-allows-turbans-hijabs-in-soccer-after-quebec-controversy-1.1709704.

Shirazi, Faegheh. "Islam and Barbie: The Commodification of Hijabi Dolls." *Islamic Perspective*, no. 3 (2010): 10–23. http://iranianstudies.org/wp-content/uploads/2010/04/Islamic-perspective-Journal-number-3-2010.pdf.

———. "The Islamic Veil in Civil Societies." In *Governance in the Middle East and North Africa: A Handbook*. Edited by Abbas Kadhim, 155–172. London: Routledge, 2012.

———. *The Veil Unveiled: The Hijab in Modern Culture*. Gainesville: University Press of Florida, 2003.

———. *Velvet Jihad: Muslim Women's Quiet Resistance to Islamic Fundamentalism.* Gainesville: University Press of Florida, 2009.

Shirazi, Faegheh, and Smeeta Mishra. "Young Muslim Women on the Face Veil (Niqab): A Tool of Resistance in Europe but Rejected in the United States." *International Journal of Cultural Studies* 13, no. 1 (2010): 43–62.

Shoundial, Shreya. "Meet Salma, the 'Muslim' Barbie Doll." IBN Live, October 10, 2007. http://ibnlive.in.com/news/meet-salma-the-muslim-barbie-doll/50287-3-1.html.

Shubert, Atika. "Website Sells Shariah-Approved Sex Aids to Muslims," CNN, September 7, 2010. http://www.cnn.com/2010/WORLD/europe/09/07/muslim.sexual.health/index.html.

Slack, Daniel. "Another Good Reason to Keep Men Around: Everyday Commercial Uses Of Semen." *Newsvine*, April 29, 2009. http://daniel-slack.newsvine.com/news/.

Smith, Aaron. "Starbucks to Phase Out Bug Extract as Food Dye." *CNN Money*, April 19, 2012. http://money.cnn.com/2012/04/19/news/companies/starbucks-bugs/index.htm.

Smith, Sebastian. "Islam and Sensuality: Muslim Fashion Designer Covers Up." *Islam.ru*, September 5, 2012. http://islam.ru/en/content/story/islam-and-sensuality-muslim-fashion-designer-covers.

Smith-Spark, Laura. "Instead of Spiderman or Bratz Dolls, Children in the US

Could Soon Be Clutching a Talking Jesus Toy, a Bearded Moses or A Muscle-Bound Figure of Goliath." BBC News, July 30, 2007. http://news.bbc.co.uk/2/hi/americas/6916287.stm.

Sobecki, Nichole. "She Shoots, She Scores." *Global Post*, May 30, 2010. http://www.globalpost.com/dispatch/turkey/090429/turkey-football-womens.

Sparks, Paul, and Richard Shepherd. "Self-Identity and the Theory of Planned Behavior: Assessing the Role of Identification with 'Green Consumerism.'" *Social Psychology Quarterly* 55, no. 4 (1992): 388–399.

Sperling, Valerie. "Women's Organizations: Institutionalized Interest Groups or Vulnerable Dissidents?" In *Russian Civil Society: A Critical Assessment*. Edited by Alfred B. Evans, Laura A. Henry, and Lisa McIntosh Sundstrom. New York: M. E. Sharpe, 2006.

Starek, Roscoe B. "The ABCs at the FTC: Marketing and Advertising to Children." Speech, Federal Trade Commission, Washington, DC, July 25, 1997. https://www.ftc.gov/public-statements/1997/07/abcs-ftc-marketing-and-advertising-children.

Starrett, Gregory. "The Political Economy of Religious Commodities in Cairo." *American Anthropologist* 97, no. 10. (March 1995): 51–68.

Stone, G. P. "Appearance and the Self." In *Human Behavior and the Social Process: An Interactionist Approach*. Edited by A. M. Rose. New York: Houghton Mifflin, 1962.

Stryker, S. *Symbolic Interactionism: A Social Structural Version*. Menlo Park, CA: Benjamin Cummings, 1980.

Subir, Bhaumik. "Protection for Indian Tennis Star." BBC News, September 17, 2005. http://news.bbc.co.uk/2/hi/south_asia/4256052.

Suddin, Lada, Geoffrey Harvey Tanakinjal, and Hanudin Amin. "Predicting Intention to Choose Halal Products Using Theory of Reasoned Action." *International Journal of Islamic and Middle Eastern Finance and Management* 2, no. 1 (2009): 66–76.

Sydee, Jasmin, and Sharon Beder, "Ecofeminism and Globalisation: A Critical Appraisal." *Democracy and Nature: The International Journal of Inclusive Democracy* 7, no. 2 (July 2001). http://www.democracynature.org/vol7/beder_sydee_globalisation.htm.

Tajzadeh-Namin, A. A. "Islam and Tourism: A Review on Iran and Malaysia." *International Research Journal of Applied and Basic Sciences* 3 (2012): 2809–2814.

Talhami, Ghada. *Historical Dictionary of Women in the Middle East and North Africa*. Plymouth, England: Scarecrow, 2013.

Tan, Lincoln. "Halal Certification Group under Fire." *New Zealand Herald*, January 11, 2010. http://www.nzherald.co.nz/lincoln-tan/news/article.cfm?a_id=308&objectid=10619444.

Tarlo, Emma. "Hijab in London: Metamorphosis, Resonance, and Effects." *Journal of Material Culture* 12, no. 2 (2007): 131–156.

Tchoudinova, Elena. *La Mosquée Notre-Dame de Paris: Année 2048*. Paris: Tatamis, 2009.

Tengku, Noor, and Abdullah Shamsiah Tengku. "HDC to Issue Country's Halal Certificate and Logo." *Halal Focus*, April 4, 2008. http://halalfocus.net/2008/04/04/hdc-to-issue-country-s-halal-certificate-and-logo.

Teo, Angie. "Muslim Washing Rite Goes Hi-Tech with Wudu Machine." Reuters, January 31, 2010. http://www.reuters.com/article/2010/02/01/us-religion -muslims-wudu-idUSTRE6100FM20100201.

Thomas, Pradip. "Selling God/Saving Souls." *Global Media and Communication* 5, no. 1 (2009): 57–76.

Tiwary, Chandra. "Premature Sexual Development in Children Following the Use of Estrogen- or Placenta-Containing Hair Products." *Clinical Pediatrics* 37, no. 12 (1998): 733–739.

Tristam, Pierre. "Does the Quran Require Women to Wear the Veil?" About News, n.d. http://middleeast.about.com/od/religionsectarianism/f/me080209.htm.

Turvill, William. "Denmark Accused of Anti-Semitism as It Bans Religious Slaughter of Animals for Kosher and Halal Meat." *Daily Mail*, February 18, 2014. http://www.dailymail.co.uk/news/article-2562350/Denmark-accused-anti -Semitism-bans-religious-slaughter-animals-kosher-halal-meat.html.

Tyler, Richard. "Britain: Thousands of Tons of Condemned 'Meat Laundered' for Human Consumption." World Socialist Web Site, May 5, 2001. http://www .wsws.org/articles/2001/may2001/meat-m05.shtml.

US Holocaust Memorial Museum. "Kristallnacht: A Nationwide Pogrom." Washington, DC. http://www.ushmm.org/wlc/en/article.php?ModuleId=10005201.

Verbeke, Wim, Pieter Rutsaert, Karijn Bonne, and Iris Vermeir. "Credence Quality Coordination and Consumers' Willingness-to-Pay for Certified Halal Labelled Meat." *Meat Science* 95, no. 4 (December 2013): 790–797. At BioMedSearch, http://www.biomedsearch.com/nih/.

Vincent, Isabel, and Melissa Klein. "No Community Programs at 'Ground Zero' Mosque a Year after the Controversy." *New York Post*, December 9, 2012. http://www.nypost.com/p/news/local/manhattan/.

Vincent, Norah. "Veiled Intentions." *Salon*, February 1, 2002. http://www.salon .com/2002/02/01/burqa.

Walseth, Kristin, and Kari Fasting. "Islam's View on Physical Activity and Sport: Egyptian Women Interpreting Islam." *International Review of the Sociology of Sport* 138, no. 1 (2003): 45–60.

Waterfield, Bruno. "Dutch Parliament Votes to Ban Ritual Slaughter of Animals." *The Telegraph*, June 28, 2011. http://www.telegraph.co.uk/news/religion /8603969/Dutch-parliament-votes-to-ban-ritual-slaughter-of-animals.html.

Wilcox, R. Turner. *Dictionary of Costume.* New York: Charles Scribner's Sons, 1969.

Wilkinson, Doris Y. "The Doll Exhibit: A Psycho-Cultural Analysis of Black Female Role Stereotypes." *Journal of Popular Culture* 21, no. 2 (1987): 19–29.

Willsher, Kim. "France's Muslims Hit Back at Nicolas Sarkozy's Policy on Halal Meat." *The Guardian*, March 10, 2012. http://www.theguardian.com/world /2012/mar/10/nicolas-sarkozy-halal-meat-france-election.

Wilson, Jonathan. "Brand Islam Is Fast Becoming the New Black in Marketing Terms." *Media and Tech Network* (blog), *The Guardian*, February 18, 2014. http://www.theguardian.com/media-network/media-network-blog/2014/feb /18/islamic-economy-marketing-branding.

Wilson, Jonathan A. J., and Jonathan Liu. "Shaping the Halal into a Brand?" *Journal of Islamic Marketing* 1, no. 2, (2010): 107–123.

Withnall, Adam. "Denmark Bans Kosher and Halal Slaughter as Minister Says 'Animal Rights Come before Religion.'" *The Independent*, July 27, 2015. http://www.independent.co.uk/news/world/europe/.

Wren, Karen. "Cultural Racism: Something Rotten in the State of Denmark?" *Social and Cultural Geography* 2, no. 2 (2001): 141–162.

Yaghmaie, Ehsan. "Culture of Iran: How Women Applied Makeup 3000 Years Ago." Iran Chamber Society. http://www.iranchamber.com/culture/articles/how_women_applied_makeup_3000.php.

Yahmid, Hadi. "Mixed Swimming Worries Swiss Muslims." Swimwear for Muslim Women, January 14, 2009. http://swimwearformuslimwomen.wordpress.com/2009/01/14/mixed-swimming-worries-swiss-muslims/#more-25.

Yang, Yongsheng, and Wenxing Bao. "The Design and Implementation of Halal Beef Wholly Quality Traceability System." *IFIP Advances in Information and Communication Technology* 346, (2011): 464–472.

Yanover, Yori. "Swiss Politician Wants 'Kristallnacht for Mosques.'" *Jewish Press*, June 28, 2012. http://www.jewishpress.com/news/breaking-news/swiss-politician-wants-kristallnacht-for-mosques/2012/06/28.

Yeomans, Michelle. "Halal Cosmetics Proves to Be a Market Trend in the US." *Cosmetics Design*, February 16, 2012. http://www.cosmeticsdesign.com/Market-Trends/Halal-cosmetics-proves-to-be-a-market-trend-in-the-US.

Yurdadon, Ergun. "History of Sport in Islamic-Period Turkey." *Sports Journal* 6, no. 4 (Fall 2003).

Zahir, Sanam. *The Music of the Children of Revolution: The State of Music and Emergence of the Underground Music in the Islamic Republic of Iran with an Analysis of Its Lyrical Content*. Saarbrücken, Germany: Lembert Academic, 2008.

Index